SADOMASOCHISM, POPULAR CULTURE AND REVOLT

Sadomasochism, Popular Culture and Revolt: A Pornography of Violence explores powerful connections between violent pornography and current gender wars, generational conflicts, political struggles, and racial and ethnic unrest. Long before these conflicts dominated headlines worldwide, they become embedded and contextualized in popular culture.

Tracing the history of today's popular porn genres, including torture porn, revenge porn, war porn, and fascist porn, Tom Pollard reveals a "sadomasochistic trope" of fictional and real sexual violence and sexual justice that had largely remained hidden and suppressed. Today it has exploded into public awareness by mass movements like #MeToo demanding justice for sexual assault victims. This movement joins other recent social movements, including Black Lives Matter and advocates of safety from gun violence, which, along with #MeToo, constitute a "revolt of submissives" no longer willing to endure unwanted violence.

This thoughtful examination of the history and content of violent pornography reveals portentous patterns and developing trends. By examining pornography's violent content, Pollard forces us to confront wider social and cultural violence. *Sadomasochism, Popular Culture and Revolt* will be of great interest to scholars of gay and lesbian studies and queer studies, while being a vital text for undergraduate and graduate instructors of social movement studies in sociology, political science, American Studies, and history.

Tom Pollard is Professor of Social Sciences at National University in San Jose and a documentary filmmaker whose work has appeared on the BBC, the Discovery Channel, the Life Network, Canadian Broadcasting System, and various PBS channels. Tom has authored several books and articles about popular culture.

SADOMASOCHISM, POPULAR CULTURE AND REVOLT

A Pornography of Violence

Tom Pollard

NEW YORK AND LONDON

First published 2020
by Routledge
52 Vanderbilt Avenue, New York, NY 10017

and by Routledge
2 Park Square, Milton Park, Abingdon, Oxon, OX14 4RN

Routledge is an imprint of the Taylor & Francis Group, an informa business

© 2020 Taylor & Francis

The right of Tom Pollard to be identified as author of this work has been asserted by him in accordance with sections 77 and 78 of the Copyright, Designs and Patents Act 1988.

All rights reserved. No part of this book may be reprinted or reproduced or utilized in any form or by any electronic, mechanical, or other means, now known or hereafter invented, including photocopying and recording, or in any information storage or retrieval system, without permission in writing from the publishers.

Trademark notice: Product or corporate names may be trademarks or registered trademarks, and are used only for identification and explanation without intent to infringe.

Library of Congress Cataloging-in-Publication Data
A catalog record for this book has been requested

ISBN: 978-0-367-21179-0 (hbk)
ISBN: 978-0-367-21757-0 (pbk)
ISBN: 978-0-367-21759-4 (ebk)

Typeset in Bembo
by Apex CoVantage, LLC

CONTENTS

Sadomasochism, Popular Culture and Revolt: A Pornography of Violence explores powerful connections between violent pornography and current gender wars, generational conflicts, political struggles, and racial and ethnic unrest. Long before these conflicts dominated headlines worldwide, they became embedded and contextualized in popular culture.

List of Figures		*vi*
Preface		*vii*
1	Sex and Violence	1
2	Pornography Defined	18
3	Revenge	32
4	Torture	55
5	War	79
6	Fascism	99
7	Sadomasochism and Revolt	122
Index		*138*

FIGURES

1.1	Pasolini, *Salò: The 120 Days of Sodom*, 1975	6
1.2	Pasolini, *Salò: The 120 Days of Sodom*, 1975	7
2.1	Alfred Hitchcock, *Psycho*, 1960	25
3.1	Ingmar Bergman, *The Virgin Spring*, 1960	35
3.2	Quentin Tarantino, *Kill Bill vol. 2*, 2004	41
4.1	Stanley Kubrick, *A Clockwork Orange*, 1971	57
4.2	Stanley Kubrick, *A Clockwork Orange*, 1971	58
4.3	David Cronenberg, *Crash*, 1996	63
5.1	Alfred Hitchcock, *Psycho*, 1960	84
7.1	Quentin Tarantino, *Kill Bill vol 2*, 2004	126

PREFACE

Sadomasochism, Popular Culture and Revolt: A Pornography of Violence examines the socio/political roles played by pornography and popular culture. I became fascinated by this topic after reading about young American and Canadian women attracted to ISIS fighters who posted violent videos, including decapitations and crucifixions. For many, these depictions repulse and disgust, but others became eroticized. What factors contribute to these diverse reactions?

Sexuality and violence, when combined, become potent and play commanding roles in pornography and in real-world aggression. This book correlates recent transformations in violent pornography with an upwelling of authoritarianism, paternalism, nativism, and racism, as well as a concomitant upwelling of revolt against dominant groups and individuals. It chronicles socio/political reactions and mass movements against sexual abuse, Paternalism, and Authoritarianism in the burgeoning #MeToo, Black Lives Matter, and the March for Our Lives.

The 2016 election of Donald Trump energized and empowered mass resistance and revolt of previously subjugated groups. A fierce culture war now rages between aggressive, paternalistic "dominant" groups (fathers, husbands, bosses, teachers, law enforcement, military, political leaders, pastors, entertainers, medical doctors, judges) previously "submissive" groups (African Americans, Asians, Hispanics, wives, girlfriends, adolescents, youth, BDSMQ (bondage/dominance/sado/masochism/queer). The elections of 2016 and 2018, among the most contentious in American history, resulted in an awakened and electrified population of formerly submissive groups who abandoned subservience and began outing, shaming, and punishing their tormentors.

A thoughtful examination of the history and content of violent pornography reveals portentous patterns and developing trends. Unlike most pornography studies that focus exclusively on salacious sexual content, this study probes pornography's violent aspects for insights into real-world sadomasochism. It examines the role of popular culture in empowering ordinary individuals to create and post their own unique content.

I am greatly indebted to Ms Sue Dickey for reviewing and commenting on my manuscript, and to my friends Drs Carl Boggs and Michael Parenti for providing valuable insights and feedback at various junctures in the book's development. Jason Sanders of UC Berkeley Art Museum and Pacific Film Archive provided valuable assistance in researching the Archive's extensive collection of film images. I am also grateful to National University's College of Letters and Science for supporting presentations at academic conferences that yielded germane and insightful feedback on critical aspects of my project.

1

SEX AND VIOLENCE

Violent pornography today deserves at least partial blame for a spate of recent mass school shootings in the US, including at Parkland, Florida in 2018, according to US Representative Diane Black (R-TN), in her 2018 campaign for governor. Representative Black blames America's recent plague of school shootings on, ". . . deterioration of family", violent movies, mental illness and pornography. Black claims that pornography is readily available in grocery stores, beyond parental control, "It's available on the shelf when you walk into a grocery store. Yeah, you have to reach to get it, but there's pornography there".[1] Although I find no "violent pornography" in my local (California) grocery stores and wonder if it is sold in Tennessee grocery stories, violent sexual pornography is available free or at low cost in great abundance on the internet.

In February 2018 Google searches of "violent pornography" spiked to an all-time high, nearly double the rate of such searches over the past five years.[2] By 2019 internet searches for "violent porn" continued to climb and regularly spike,[3] *Pornhub*, one of the largest pornography providers, urges viewers to "Discover the growing collection of most relevant XXX movies and clips". "Although the internet teams with pornography, no other sex site attracts as many visitors and features more extreme brutal rough violent scenes than *Pornhub!*"[4] *Heavy-R*, another purveyor of violent porn, advertises viewers to, "Watch free **violent** sex videos at ***Heavy-R***, a completely free **porn** tube offering the world's most hardcore **porn** videos. New videos about **violent** sex added today!" *Porndig*, another popular website, advertises "Hardcore **Porn** and **violent** scripted scenes with actresses who love to be fucked with a pinch of violence! Absolutely free and exciting **porn** for you!"[5]

While violent pornography offends many, it appeals to a rapidly growing audience from a variety of socio/political backgrounds, ages, ethnicities, and genders. Violent pornography depicts previously forbidden sadomasochistic fantasies,

2 Sex and Violence

reflecting society's deepest, rawest, and most hidden drives despite practices that remain socially taboo and possibly illegal.

What role does violent pornography play in popular culture? Most pornography studies adopt either a pro-pornography or an anti-pornography perspective, and both sides debate alleged harms or benefits of porn. Some researchers deride porn as "deviant", "harmful", "addictive", "criminal", while others emphasize porn's "educational", "therapeutic", or "pleasurable" effects.[6]

For Baby Boomers, memories of violent pornography might include X-rated movie theaters, topless bars, or "stag films". Russell Sheaffer notes that scholars generally define stag films as early (i.e. twentieth century) and primitive pornographic films.[7] Peter Lehman adds that stag films often follow the plot lines of America's bawdy songs, which express venerable "dirty jokes" and "white trash" sensibilities. Popular stag films express ribald joke plot lines, including "the farmer's daughter", and "a priest and a rabbi walk into a bar . . .", and they often evoke violence. In one renowned instance, John Wayne Bobbitt, a 24-year-old Ecuadorian immigrant, infamously raped his wife Lorena after arriving home drunk. Outrages and angered by her husband's drunken (and unsatisfying) rape, Ms. Bobbitt slashed off his penis as he lay in a drunken stupor. The resulting tumult introduced graphic violence on John's and Lorena's part and inaugurated a spirited debate about male and female sexual violence. Lehman describes *John Wayne Bobbitt: Uncut* (1995), a stag film with a feminist twist: "if you don't learn better sexual technique and start being more sensitive to your partner's needs, you're going to get yours cut off too, and what's more, you'll deserve it".[8] Bobbitt's case evokes both rape-revenge as well as male castration fears and became an ideal narrative to express feminist issues of the era.

The word "pornography" derives from the Greek *porni* ("prostitute") and *graphein* ("to write") and originally signified a work of art or literature depicting prostitutes.[9] Today, pornography often carries pejorative connotations evoking extreme and presumably exploitative acts of communication, as in "that's pornographic!"

Culture of Violence

Violent pornography, of course, exists within a culture often described as violent. H. Rap Brown, 1960s' activist, famously observed that, "Violence is necessary. It is as American as cherry pie".[10] Author Chris Hedges argues that Americans inhabit a "culture of violence" enforced and perpetrated by vigilante groups, slave patrols, gunslingers, Pinkerton and Baldwin-Felts detectives, gangs of strikebreakers, gun thugs, company militias, White Citizens' Councils, the Knights of the White Camellia, and the Ku Klux Klan. Hedges notes that heavily armed mercenary paramilitaries, armed militias such as the Oath Keepers, and the anti-immigration extremist group Ranch Rescue, along with omnipotent and militarized police forces, form a portion of a seamless continuation of America's gun culture and

Sex and Violence **3**

vigilante tradition. He labels justifications for our current pro-gun culture "the rhetoric of violence".[11] Henry A. Giroux reminds readers of US history of violence, "Mind-numbing violence, war crimes, and indiscriminate military attacks on civilians on the part of the U.S. government are far from new and date back to infamous acts such as the air attacks on civilians in Dresden along with the atomic bombings of Hiroshima and Nagasaki during the Second World War".[12]

US military forces serve on continuous active duty worldwide and have fought wars annually since the founding of the nation in 1776. At present, the US fights overt hot wars on "terrorism" on many fronts, from Iraq, Afghanistan, Yemen, Syria, Somalia, Pakistan, Libya, and the Philippines to covert operations worldwide. It relies on bombers, missiles, military drones, special forces, and cyber-warfare to defeat its enemies. In August 2016 the US released guidelines for dealing with foreign and domestic terrorists. At first suppressed, the American Civil Liberties Union (ACLU) forced the US government to release these guidelines for the use of lethal American military force outside areas of active combat. It revealed that decisions ultimately reside with the President.[13]

The US's obsession with violence translates into overwhelming dominance in the sale of lethal weapon production worldwide. Presently, America supplies 75% of the global trade in arms. In addition, the US bears the burden of having the highest per capita rates of murder, the highest percent of its population possessing firearms, and the world's most violent popular culture.[14] In the US, twice as many women are murdered by males than American warriors fallen in battle. American women suffer not only physical abuse but also emotional and financial abuse.[15]

Shockingly high levels of domestic violence and highly visible instances of societal violence reinforce the idea that the US finds itself mired in a "culture of violence". This culture creates and nurtures violent pornography, which perpetuates stereotyped gender roles and valorizes violence toward women, divisive racial relations, and child exploitation.

Saturated in media violence, Americans overwhelmingly perceive violent crime as rising.[16] However, violent crime rates precipitously and continuously declined in the last two decades. Violent crimes reported by victims rose during the 1960s and 1970s, peaking in 1981 at 4,770 per 100,000 people. From that point until today violent crimes plummeted to 1,690 per 100,000 by 2009, a decrease of 65%. By comparison, the rate of violent crimes reported to law enforcement peaked in 1991 at 758.2 out of 100,000 before steadily plunging to 431.9 in 2009, a decline of 56%.[17] Crime rates plummeted even during the Great Recession, defying dire predictions of crime rate spikes.[18]

In the face of precipitously plunging crime rates, media ramped up depictions of violent events. Journalist Carolyn Gregoire already observed back in 2015, ". . . it's nearly impossible to turn on the TV, open up a web browser, or scroll through Twitter without being assaulted with notifications of a new world disaster (or two, or three . . .)". Because of the intense drama surrounding real-world violence, the news media focuses on violent events. Gregoire believes media's fascination

4 Sex and Violence

with real-world violence arises from humanity's "natural negativity bias", which attracts attention to the most threatening, depressing, and anxiety-causing events, i.e., media's sadomasochism. She further observes that media-depicted violence finds widespread acceptance because it initially appears less threatening than actual violence since, ". . . we don't process the input as threatening stimuli". We cannot avoid, she argues, internalizing negative stimuli from pop culture and the media, ". . . which can affect mood and cause one to feel more negatively towards today's cultural environment . . . ".[19] The pessimistic public climate regarding the alleged acceleration of criminal violence may induce some observers, like US Representative Diane Black, to blame high-profile school shootings on media violence and the prevalence of violent pornography.

Today's popular culture is perpetually saturated with violent and abusive language as well as actions. While many perceive violence as physical, Andrea Borghini explains that verbal abuse also qualifies as violence even in the absence of physical attack. She reminds us that verbal abuse includes accusing, undermining, verbal threatening, ordering, trivializing, constantly forgetting, silencing, blaming, name calling, and overtly criticizing. It relies on marginalizing and disrespecting victims, willing or otherwise. Bullying, which includes both physical and psychological violence, is often preceded by verbal threats and other violent verbal attacks.[20] Psychological/emotional abuse constitutes another expression of violence and plays a pivotal role in violent pornography. Psychological abuse exists when individuals or institutions subjugate or expose others to behaviors that may result in psychological trauma, chronic depression, or post-traumatic stress disorder. Psychological violence may affect intimate relationships, family relationships, or professional relationships.[21] Three general patterns of psychological abusive behavior include aggressing, denying, and minimizing. It results in deep, lasting effects on victims. The abuse may consist of intimidation, manipulation, and/or refusal to bestow praise.[22]

In his definition of violence, Martin Luther King included "violence of the spirit". King noted, "Nonviolence means avoiding not only external physical violence but also internal violence of spirit. You not only refuse to shoot a man, but you refuse to hate him".[23] King's statement might apply to contemporary debates about law enforcement, military action, and social policy. Other categories include economic, political, and social attacks. In 2017, Upstate Antifada, an antifascist organization at Clemson University, posted a manifesto that drew widespread media attention with the following claims, "Hunger is violence, homelessness is violence, war is violence, dropping bombs on people is violence, racism is violence, white supremacy is violence, no healthcare is violence, poverty is violence, contaminating water sources for profit is violence".[24] Most would agree that war and dropping bombs on people constitute violence but might disagree with their claims that racism, white supremacy, no healthcare, poverty, and contaminating water sources for profit constitute violence, each referencing hot-button political issues in the US.

Male physical aggression, an aspect of authoritarianism and paternalism that finds expression in domestic abuse, constitutes the largest category of societal violence. Domestic violence includes intimate partner physical and/or sexual violence, whether perpetrated by spouses/partners, relatives, acquaintances, or strangers. It exists worldwide and disproportionately affects women.[25] Statistics are staggering. Women endure 85% of intimate violence in the US, while men suffer just 15%. Male intimate partners murder an average of three females every day in the US, and over 38 million women are exposed to intimate partner abuse in their lifetimes. Nearly half of women in abusive relationships suffer rape, and every nine seconds a woman in the US suffers physical beatings by males.[26]

Violence and aggression often become linked in speech and writing, as in the definition of "aggression":

> a form of physical or verbal behavior leading to self-assertion; it is often angry and destructive and intended to be injurious, physically or emotionally, and aimed at domination of one person by another. It may arise from innate drives and/or be a response to frustration and may be manifested by overt attacking and destructive behavior, by covert attitudes of hostility and obstructionism, or by a healthy self-expressive drive to mastery.[27]

Like violence, aggression assumes many forms, including physical aggression. A study of childhood aggression reveals three dimensions of aggression: Instrumental, Hostile, and Relational. Instrumental aggression includes, ". . . aggression aimed at obtaining an object, privilege or space with no deliberate intent to harm another person". This category qualifies as non-violent aggression. Hostile aggression, on the other hand, constitutes, ". . . aggression intended to harm another person, such as hitting, kicking, or threatening to beat up . . . ". Finally, Relational aggression "focuses on a form of hostile aggression that does damage to another's peer relationships, as in social exclusion or rumor spreading".[28] This definition, however, like standard definitions of violence, omits consensual aggression for the pleasure of the "victim", who often begs or entices the "aggressor" to inflict pleasurable "pain".

In humans, and in other animals, aggression and violence often become sexualized. Sexual encounters take the form of fights, sometimes accompanied by thrashing, loud noises, biting, and scratching, then a final act of pushing away that looks distinctly unfriendly. In male and female felines, for example, such as lions and tigers, even after such displays, males and females remain in each other's proximity for multiple mountings.[29]

Sadomasochism

Despite possessing ancient roots, today's violent pornography harkens back no further than the eighteenth century. Donatien Alphonse François, Marquis de Sade (2 June 1740–2 December 1814), was one of the most influential voices of the

6 Sex and Violence

libertine movement. De Sade is best known today for his erotic novels, including *Justine, or the Misfortunes of Virtue*; *Juliette*; *The 120 Days of Sodom*; and *Philosophy in the Bedroom*. These combine philosophical discourse with pornography, depicting sexual fantasies with an emphasis on violence, criminality, and blasphemy against the Catholic Church.[30] De Sade was imprisoned during a third of his lifetime, and his books were suppressed until the beginning of the twentieth century. Today de Sade holds a reputation as a libertine, socialist, epicurean, and French revolutionary. His works savagely satirize clergy, the aristocracy, and the French king. He condemned conventional social and political values of the time, believing, ". . . the habit of judging others must inevitably make us hard and cruel". De Sade's writings anger and challenge feminists with his views that man's sexuality inevitably dominates female's. He held that, "The only way to a woman's heart is along the path of torment . . . and . . . a man's ejaculation", not her own orgasm, "hurls the woman into the most intense rapture". Marquis de Sade Philosophy in the Bedroom (1795) Translated by Richard Seaver and Austryn Wainhouse, *The New York Times*, 2002.

Four wealthy libertines take eighteen young people captive for four months during Fascist Italy's waning days. The captives endure bondage, humiliation, and other forms of sexual assaults, perversions, and eventually murder.

FIGURE 1.1 Pasolini, *Salò: The 120 Days of Sodom*, 1975
Source: Pacific Film Archive

Unlike de Sade's advocacy of male sexual domination, Austrian novelist Leopold von Sacher-Masoch approached sexuality from a submissive perspective. His most famous novel, *Venus in Furs* (1870), depicts a nobleman who eagerly volunteers to become the slave of a beautiful but cruel noblewoman.[31] The female in the novel enacts a sadistic sexual role by cruelly torturing her admirer, ultimately through encouraging him to witness the object of his desire being ravished by other men (cuckolds). Sacher-Masoch advocated what became known as masochism. He signed a contract with Baroness Fanny Pistor to be her slave for six months provided she wear furs as often as possible and even convinced his first wife, Aurora von Rümelin, to live out the experiences of his book.[32]

De Sade's and Masoch's vivid, deviant, violent characters became etched in popular culture, and in 1890, German psychiatrist Richard von Kraft-Ebing coined "sadism" and "masochism" in medical terminology in his work *Neue Forschungen auf dem Gebiet der Psychopathia sexualis* ("New research in the area of Psychopathology of Sex"). Sadism from de Sade and masochism from Sacher-Masoch inspired the term sadomasochism. De Sade explains the emotions felt by sadists upon inflicting pain, "In those delectable moments, the whole world is ours; not a single creature resists us, we devastate the world, we repopulate it with new objects which,

FIGURE 1.2 Pasolini, *Salò: The 120 Days of Sodom*, 1975

Source: Pacific Film Archive

8 Sex and Violence

in turn, we immolate. The means to every crime is ours, and we employ them all, we multiply the horror a hundredfold".[33] Sacher-Masoch wrote, "A slap in the face is more effective than ten lectures. It makes you understand very quickly".[34]

The libertines amuse themselves by increasingly abusing captives, eventually pushing them beyond endurance.

Sigmund Freud postulated the existence of two forms of masochism, primary and secondary. He identified "primary masochism" as when an individual experiences a complete rejection by the object of their desire, such as when the loved one rejects an admirer and finds another lover. Freud related it to the death drive (*Todestrieb*). In secondary masochism, however, masochists experience a more playful, less serious, less final rejection and punishment by the loved one.[35]

Behavioral scientists recently learned that both sexual and violent impulses arise from deep within the brain's hypothalamus region. A study of sex and violence using mice found that most male mice experienced anger and aggression when confronted by hungry competitors, and they only experienced sexual stimulation when confronted with females in heat. Approximately 20% of the males, however, possessed "crossed wires" and experienced sexual stimulation, anger, and aggression simultaneously, and when the animals fought with opponents, they often experienced sexual arousal as well as the expected "fight or flight syndrome". The boundary between sex and violence blurred in the 20% that experienced "crossed wires" and became "confused".[36] A similar process may occur in humans.

Pop Culture Violence

Whether or not it is the result of confused boundaries between sex and aggression, sexualized violence currently constitutes a potent and popular theme or trope in popular culture. Today's most popular genres are "torture porn", "Nazi porn", "war porn", "rape-revenge porn", and even "cuckold porn". Although these obviously violent porn genres currently inspire the most interest, all pornography genres rely on violence for dramatic intensity. Audiences experience shock, disgust, and often attraction to depictions of physical, psychological, verbal, and emotionally abused people. In 2010, A.J. Bridges, *et al* published the results of their groundbreaking research into the powerful, often misunderstood roles violence plays in pop culture. They analyzed 50 of the most popular porn movies, focusing on scenes of sexualized violence. Out of hundreds of scenes analyzed, 88% depicted physical violence, while 49% contained verbal violence. Over 90% of all scenes depicted either verbal or physical violence. Over 90% of victims were women, and 95% of the female victims were either neutral about the abuse they suffered or responded with pleasure. When men were victims of violence they were four times more likely to become upset at their attackers.[37]

Porn Consumption and Aggression

In 2016 Paul Wright, Robert S. Tokunaga, and Ashley Kraus reported the results of their meta-analysis of several recent quantitative studies investigating the connection between consumption of pornography, including violent porn and attitudes towards sexual aggression, both verbal and physical. They discovered, ". . . individuals who consume pornography more frequently are more likely to hold attitudes conducive to sexual aggression and engage in actual acts of sexual aggression than individuals who do not consume pornography or who consume pornography less frequently". However, Wright et al cautioned, ". . . nonsexual aggression in the laboratory cannot be directly equated to real-life acts of sexual aggression and attitudes do not always predict behavior".[38] In fact, I find no credible data strongly linking porn consumption with sexually aggressive actions.

Patriarchy

Patriarchy lies at the heart of the current wave of violence, both actual and fictional. Economic and political data reveal that the US remains a patriarchal nation. Currently, female workers earn 77 cents for every $1.00 earned by males. They occupy just 15% of upper management positions and less than 4% of CEOs of Fortune 500 companies.[39] Former President Jimmy Carter observed in 2014 that women, far more than men, endure many forms of violence, including intimate physical and sexual partner violence, female genital mutilation, child and forced marriage, sex trafficking, and rape.[40] Attacks of all kinds against women by men, especially physical attacks, perpetuate and enforce a patriarchal ethos that underlies not only American culture but also much of world culture. Gender violence of any form evokes bondage, domination, rape, and other forms of sadomasochism.

Feminist Simone Lieban Levin calls attention to a dramatic disconnect among many feminists regarding pornography's effects on women. She observed in *MS Magazine* that although the pornography industry favors patriarchal depictions of female subordination, including sexual subservience to males, it also increasingly features female-centric erotica and females as enjoyers rather than sufferers of pornography. Even so, Levin believes, ". . . to reform the pornography industry, we must first work to destigmatize it, starting with accepting it as a legitimate method of employment and sexual enjoyment for women".[41]

Racist Porn

Websites labeled racist include Racist videos-XVIDEOS.com, Racist Porn Videos Pornhub.com, Racist white girl porn videos, racist cop porn, Racist tube search, racist videos, Page 1, Black Girl Fucked by Two Racist Rednecks, to name a few. In 2013, porn star Aurora Snow surprised many with her candid critique of the underlying racism in the porn industry's casting, hiring, and compensation

10 Sex and Violence

policies. Snow specifically charged the porn industry with actively discouraging white female performers from engaging or simulating sexual relations with black males, echoing fierce, historic, and persistent white fears of black male sexuality. Journalist Keli Goff summarized what she learned from Snow. "It seems that the historical taboo of black men sleeping with white women is one sexual hang-up that even the porn industry is unwilling to get over".[42]

African American male "dom" (dominant) performers, along with white male performers engaging in real or simulated sex with African American female performers, currently enjoy wide popularity. According to celebrated African American porn performer Lexington Steele, racism in its various forms is, ". . . just an element of American culture that still exists, and that is the feeling that a white female will be deflowered or soiled, if you will, by doing a scene with a black male". However, ". . . that does speak to the continued existence of bigotry and racism, and I don't think porno is unaffected by certain elements of American culture". Steele added "And quite honestly, adult media is the only major business that allows for the practice of exclusion based on race". It turns out that the porn industry is controlled by white males and often reflects their perspectives. Steele states,

> "Ironically, if a black female performer takes the option to not perform with a white male performer, she's almost blacklisted—pardon the pun—by the majority of adult directors and producers, who in most cases are white and would take personal offense and spread the word that the girl should not be booked".[43]

Interest in racist pornography rose rapidly and substantially over the past four years. Comparing this with interest in violent porn over the same period indicates interest in violent pornography growing at roughly the same rate as racist porn, as gauged by *Google Trends*. Violent porn searches roughly paralleled the rate of racist porn searches.[44]

Racism has long been associated with violence, including the now-banned institution of slavery. Some charge the porn industry, especially the segment producing violent porn, with persistent and blatant racism. Mirelle Miller-Young and Cezary Jan Stusiewicz, in their seminal article, "5 Ways Porn is Bizarrely Racist Behind the Scenes", explain that white porn actors often charge more for simulating sex with people of color over what they charge for performing the same acts with whites, charging an "interracial rate" to counter any possible diminution of their worth resulting from the erotic depiction with an African American actor. "Black women [in porn]", according to Stusiewicz and Miller-Young, "are at the very bottom of the totem pole". In fact, Miller-Young charges that "African-American actresses are paid one half to three quarters of what white actresses earn for the same work. This is the sorest issue for black actresses in the adult business". Furthermore, white actors may refuse intimate scenes with African American actors, while the opposite is not the case. If African American actors refuse intimate scenes with white actors, they may find their ability to receive bookings severely curtailed. The entire porn business is so pro-white that performers from mixed backgrounds often promote themselves as white.[45] Whites usually land

Sex and Violence   **11**

dominant roles, while African Americans, especially females, play subservient or "sub" roles, another manifestation of the sadomasochism trope.

Censorship

Pornography is often conflated with erotica. Scholars define erotica as, ". . . literary or artistic works having an erotic theme; especially, books treating of sexual love in a sensuous or voluptuous manner". Erotic arts include those in which, ". . . the sexual element is regarded as part of the larger aesthetic aspect".[46] Some of the world's best known erotic literature includes such well-known classics as the Hindu *Kama Sutra*, Persian lyrical poems (ghazals), Ovid's *Ars Amatoria*, William Shakespeare's *Venus and Adonis*, the novels and letters of the Marquis de Sade, and D.H. Lawrence's *Lady Chatterley's Lover*.[47] Erotic material designed for less exalted sensibilities often receives an "obscenity" definition. Slade observed that, "In a legal sense, obscenity denotes criminality" and connotes "lower-class vulgarity".[48]

Today courts employ the "Miller Test" derived from Miller v. California (1973) which ruled that three factors determined obscenity: (1) whether "the average person, applying contemporary community standards" would find that the work, "taken as a whole", appeals to "prurient interest" (2) whether the work depicts or describes, in a patently offensive way, sexual conduct specifically defined by the applicable state law, and (3) whether the work, "taken as a whole", lacks serious literary, artistic, political, or scientific value.[49] Human diversity provides abundant examples of culture-specific sexual practices and beliefs that confuse the definition of obscenity.

Hollywood Violence

The motion picture rating code provides a mechanism for censoring in popular culture based not only on sexual content, but also on levels of violence. Currently, the Motion Picture Producers Association of America (MPAA) rates movies in the following categories: G or General Audiences, all ages admitted; PG or Parental Guidance Suggested, some material may not be suitable for children; PG-13, or Parents Strongly Cautioned. Some material may be inappropriate for children under 13; R, or Restricted. Under 17 requires accompanying parent or adult guardian; NC-17, No One 17 and Under Admitted. Both sex and violence attract audiences, and while movie ratings are based on both, the MPAA tolerates graphic violence far more readily than graphic sex. Therefore, producers pack movies and other pop culture products with increasingly high levels of violent images and narratives. A recent *Forbes* study found that Hollywood producers have succeeded in inserting violent scenes and images into movies rated PG-13 with the same amount of violence that had previously earned R for Violence ratings.[50]

The MPAA's relative laxness regarding violence stems from landmark decisions by the US Supreme Court. In 2011 the Court ruled, in *Brown v. Entertainment*

12 Sex and Violence

Merchants Association, that violence enjoys legal protection under the First Amendment. Justice Antonin Scalia, writing for the five-member majority, explained that violence, unlike sex, has never suffered from official censorship because of its ubiquity in pop culture. "*Grimm's Fairy Tales*", he explained, "are grim indeed". He also called attention to the "gory" plots of *Snow White, Cinderella, Hansel and Gretel*, and other children's classics in his oft-quoted opinion.[51]

Scalia's point about ubiquitous violence in pop culture, even in children's stories and fables, at first glance appears irrefutable, until one compares media violence in the past with today's hyperviolent entertainment productions. A 2014 study by the Annenberg Public Policy Center and the University of Pennsylvania discovered that 89.7% of all recent popular movies contain major characters engaging in violent acts, often involving firearms, knives, and other weapons. Seventy-seven percent of Hollywood's violent episodes also depict characters engaging in alcohol and/or sex, including sexual violence. By contrast, movies depicting smoking tobacco declined from 68% in 1985 to just 21.4% by 2010.[52] One comprehensive study concluded, ". . . violence is widely accepted as a central component of American lifestyle and culture. . . . Violence figures prominently in American public life and pleasure seeking".[52]

The linkage of sex with violent coercion uses The World Health Organization's definition of sexual coercion as:

> any sexual act, attempt to obtain a sexual act, unwanted sexual comments or advances, or acts to traffic, or otherwise directed, against a person's sexuality using coercion, by any person regardless of their relationship to the victim, in any setting, including but not limited to home and work.[54]

This definition presupposes the existence of perpetrators and victims and assumes a caustic dynamic between sadistic abusers and criminals on the one hand with innocent victims on the other. However, these two groups may depend on each other and, under the right circumstances may enjoy playing roles that appear abusive to outsiders. To the BDSMQ community, abusers (doms) need willing victims (subs), thereby establishing a psychosexual dynamic.

Violence as Terror

French social theorist Jean Baudrillard maintained in the late twentieth century that violence had become transformed into terror. "The violence of old was both more enthusiastic and more sacrificial", than it had recently become. "Today's violence, the violence produced by our hypermodernity, is terror. A simulacrum of violence, emerging less from passion than from the [television] screen: a violence in the nature of the image". To Baudrillard, violence transformed from actual physical attacks to mediated acts of domestic and foreign terrorism. Violence became "the hyperreal" through media, which is "more real than real". Artificiality has become more definitive of the real than reality itself.[55]

2016 Election

Observers from a variety of political and social perspectives note that the 2016 elections, which featured the successful candidacy of Donald Trump, focused on sexuality and violence to a greater degree than any other recent election. Donald Trump became the Republican Party's Presidential candidate. During the campaign, the future President Trump unleashed verbal violence against Hispanics by claiming that most undocumented Mexicans entering the US were "rapists" and "criminals". He extended these sentiments toward Muslims and vowed that, if elected, he would institute a "temporary ban" on their entry into the US. In addition, Trump vowed to resume the use of government torture against suspected terrorists, promising to reinstate "waterboarding" and even more extreme torture techniques, explaining, ". . . we're going to have to get much tougher as a country. We're going to have to be a lot sharper, and we're going to have to do things that are unthinkable almost".[56] In terms of unthinkable responses, Trump further vowed to, ". . . take out their families, when you get these terrorists, you have to take out their families. They care about their lives, don't kid yourself. When they say they don't care about their lives, you have to take out their families . . . ". He vowed to, "Knock the hell . . . ". out of terrorists as he condemned the Obama government for fighting a very 'politically correct' war.[57]

While Trump daily articulated a sadomasochistic worldview, the Republican National Convention approved a plank specifically targeting pornography. The plank warns,

> The internet must not become a safe haven for predators. It further states that Pornography, with its harmful effects, especially on children, has become a public health crisis that is destroying the life of millions. We encourage states to continue to fight this public menace and pledge our commitment to children's safety and well-being. We applaud the social networking sites that bar sex offenders from participation. We urge energetic prosecution of child pornography which is closely linked to human trafficking.[58]

Ironically, banning pornography, tends to create intense interest in the "forbidden fruit". Much of the controversy surrounding pornography focuses on access. Which groups have access to internet porn? Except for children whose parents enact restrictions against porn sites on computers, smart phones, and other smart devices, today virtually everyone has access to porn.

Violent pornography reveals pop culture's sadomasochistic underpinnings. Simulated prisoner abuse, a common porn trope, symbolizes society's hidden power dynamics in which potential sexual abusers inflict violence and sex upon unwilling victims. Violent rape graphically symbolizes paternalism and racism. Violent porn exemplifies society's sadomasochistic dimensions and predicts today's explosive social movements like the #MeToo movement, #Time's Up movement, and a variety of others.

Notes

1. Kaitlyn Shallhorn, "Tennessee Lawmaker Says Porn, Violent Movies among 'Root Causes' of School Shootings: A 'Big Part'," *Fox News*, May 30, 2018.
2. https://trends.google.com/trends/explore?date=today%205-y&q=violent%20 pornography retrieved August 6, 2018.
3. https://trends.google.com/trends/explore?q=violent%20pornography&geo=US retrieved August 6, 2019.
4. www.pornhub.com/.../search?search=extreme+brutal+rough+violent retrieved August 6, 2018.
5. www.porndig.com/channels/1042 retrieved August 6, 2019.
6. Clarissa Smith and Feona Attwood, "Anti/Pro/Porn Studies," *Porn Studies*, vol. 1, no. 1–2, 2014, pp. 7–23.
7. Russell Sheaffer, "Smut, Novelty, Indecency: Reworking a History of the Early-Twentieth Century American 'Stag Film'," *Porn Studies*, vol. 1, no. 4, 2014.
8. Peter Lehman, *Pornography: Film and Culture*. New Brunswick, NJ: Rutgers University Press, 2006.
9. John Philip Jenkins, "Pornography Sociology," https://www.britannica.com/topic/pornography retrieved April 20, 2019.
10. www.brainyquote.com/quotes/authors/h/h_rap_brown.html retrieved April 20, 2019.
11. Chris Hedges, "The Rhetoric of Violence," *Truthdig*, April 20, 2014.
12. Henry A. Giroux, "Violence USA: The Warfare State and the Hardening of Everyday Life," *Monthly Review*, May 1, 2013.
13. Karen De Young, "Newly Declassified Document Sheds Light on How President Approves Drone Strikes," *The Washington Post*, August 6, 2016.
14. Nicholas Thompson, "America's Culture of Violence," *The New Yorker*, December 15, 2012.
15. Alanna Vagianos, "30 Shocking Domestic Violence Statistics That Remind Us It's an Epidemic," *The Huffington Post*, February 13, 2015.
16. Lydia Saad, "Most Americans Believe Crime in U.S. Is Worsening," *Gallup Well-Being*, October 31, 2011.
17. FBI, "FBI Press Release 2009 Hate Crime Statistics," The FBI: Federal Bureau of Investigation, September 13, 2010.
18. James Q. Wilson. "Crime and the Great Recession," *CJ Magazine*, summer 2011.
19. Carolyn Gregoire, "What Constant Exposure to Negative News Is Doing to Our Mental Health," *The Huffington Post*, February 19, 2015.
20. Andrea Borghini, "What Is Verbal Violence," *ThoughtCo*, December 30, 2012.
21. Mary Ann Dutton, Lisa A. Goodman, and Lauren Bennett, "Court-Involved Battered Women's Responses to Violence: The Role of Psychological, Physical, and Sexual Abuse," in Roland D. Maiuro and K. Daniel O'Leary, eds., *Psychological Abuse in Violent Domestic Relations*. New York: Springer Publishing Company, 2000, p. 197.
22. Roland D. Maiuro, ed. *Perspectives on Verbal and Psychological Abuse*, New York: Springer Publishing Co. 2015.
23. Martin Luther King, Jr., "A Testament of Hope: The Essential Writings and Speeches of Martin Luther King," www.brainyquote.com/quotes/keywords/violence.html
24. Brandon Morse, "University 'Anti-Fascist' Group Justifies Violence and Vandalism against Peers," *TheBlaze*, February 28, 2017.
25. Claudia García-Moreno and Heidi Stöckl, "Protection of Sexual and Reproductive Health Rights: Addressing Violence against Women," in Michael A. Grodin, Daniel Tarantola, George J. Annas, et al., eds., *Health and Human Rights in a Changing World*. Abingdon, UK: Routledge, 2013, pp. 780–781, ISBN 9781136688638.
26. Alanna Vagianos, "30 Shocking Domestic Violence Statistics That Remind Us It's an Epidemic," *The Huffington Post*, February 13, 2015.
27. medical-dictionary.thefreedictionary.com/Aggression...

Sex and Violence **15**

28. L. Berk, *Infants, Children, and Adolescents* (3rd ed.). Boston: Allyn and Bacon, 1999.
29. www.intropsych.com/ch16_sfl/sex_and_aggression.html.
30. Tony Perrottet, "Who Was the Marquis de Sade?" *Smithsonian Magazine*, February 2015 accessed January 25, 2015.
31. Leopold von Sacher-Masoch, *Venus in Furs* at Project Gutenberg. New York: Penguin Classics, 2000 first published 1870. Read more at: www.brainyquote.com/quotes/authors/m/marquis_de_sade.html.
32. Stephen A. Bechen, "Sexual Masochism, a Perplexing Paradox," *Psychology Today*, March 16, 2014.
33. "Marquis de Sade," *Les prospérités du vice*. Union Generale D'Editions, 1070.
34. Leopold Von Sacher-Masoch and Emil Marriot, *Venus in Furs: A Novel: Letters f Leopold Von Sacher-Masoch and Emilie Mataja*. New York: Blast Books, 1989.
35. Sigmund Freud and James Strachey, *Three Essays on the Theory of Sexuality*. New York: Basic, 2007.
36. Ewen Calloway, "Sex and Violence Linked in the Brain," *Nature*, February 9, 2011.
37. Ana J. Bridges, Robert Wosnitzer, E. Scharrer, S. Chyng, and R. Liberman, "Aggression and Sexual Behavior in Best Selling Pornography Videos: A Content Analysis Update," *Violence Against Women*, vol. 16, no. 10, 2010, pp. 1065–1085.
38. Paul Wright, Robert S. Tokunaga, and Ashley Kraus, "A Meta-Analysis of Pornography Consumption and Actual Acts of Sexual Aggression in General Population Studies," *Journal of Communication*, vol. 66, 2016.
39. Shannon Ridgeway, "Patriarchy and How It Shows up for Everyone," *Everyday Feminism*, May 5, 2013.
40. Jimmy Carter, "Violence against Women and Girls," *The Lancet*, November 21, 2014.
41. Simone Lieban Levin, "Feminist Debates: Pornography," *Ms Magazine*, June 10, 2014.
42. Keli Goff, "Is the Porn Industry Racist?" *The Root*, April 3, 2013, www.theroot.com/is-the-porn-industry-racist-1790895844 accessed January 30, 2017.
43. *Ibid.*
44. Google Trends accessed January 30, 2017 comparing racist porn with violent porn.
45. Cezary Jan Strusiewicz and Mireille Miller-Jones, "5 Ways Porn Is Bizarrely Racist Behind the Scenes," *Cracked*, March 20, 2016.
46. www.britannica.com/art/erotica
47. Ovid's *Ars Amatoria*, William Shakespeare's *Venus and Adonis*, the novels and letters of the Marquis de Sade, and D.H. Lawrence's *Lady Chatterley's Lover*.
48. Joseph W. Slade, *Obscenity in America: A Reference Handbook* (abc, clio 2000).
49. "Zachary B YLT 2012 "The Miller Test and the Value of Obscene Speech," *Yale Law Tech*, October 15, 2012.
50. Scott Mendelson, "Blame Washington, Not Hollywood, for R-Rated Violence in PG-13 Films," *Forbes*, November 14, 2013.
51. Adam Liptak, "Justices Reject Ban on Violent Video Games for Children," *The New York Times*, June 27, 2011.
52. "Parents Become Less Sensitive to Violence and Sex in Movies," *Annenberg Public Policy Center*, October 20, 2014, www.annenbergpublicpolicycenter.org/movie-violence-associated-with...
53. "Violence in American Pop Culture," *123HelpMe.com*, June 23, 2014.
54 John Wihbey, "World Health Report on Sexual Violence Worldwide," May 19, 2011 https://journalistsresource.org/studies/international/human-rights/
55. Jean Baudrillard, *The Transparency of Evil: Essays on Extreme Phenomena*. London: Verso, 1990, 74.
56. Nick Visser, "Trump Ramps up His Call for Torture," *The Huffington Post*, June 30, 2016.
57. Tom LoBianco, "Donald Trump on Terrorists: 'Take Out Their Families'", *CNN Politics*, December 3, 2015.
58. Tal Kopan, "GOP Platform Draft Declares Pornography 'Public Health Crisis'", *CNN Politics*, July 11, 2016.

16 Sex and Violence

Bibliography

Baudrillard, Jean, *The Transparency of Evil: Essays on Extreme Phenomena*. London: Verso, 1990, p. 75.

Bechen, Stephen A., "Sexual Masochism, a Perplexing Paradox," *Psychology Today*, March 16, 2014.

Berk, Laura E., *Infants, Children, and Adolescents* (3rd ed.). Boston: Allyn and Bacon, 1999.

Borghini, Andrea, "What Is Verbal Violence," *ThoughtCo*, December 30, 2012.

Bridges, Ana J., Robert Wosnitzer, Erica Scharrer, Sun Chyung, and Rachel Liberman, "Aggression and Sexual Behavior in Best Selling Pornography Videos: A Content Analysis Update," *Violence Against Women*, vol. 16, no. 10, 2010, pp. 1065–1085.

Carter, Jimmy, "Violence against Women and Girls," *The Lancet*, November 21, 2014.

De Young, Karen, "Newly Declassified Document Sheds Light on How President Approves Drone Strikes," *The Washington Post*, August 6, 2016.

Dutton, Mary Ann, Lisa A. Goodman, and Lauren Bennett, "Court-Involved Battered Women's Responses to Violence: The Role of Psychological, Physical, and Sexual Abuse," in *Psychological Abuse in Violent Domestic Relations*, edited by Roland D. Maiuro and K. Daniel O'Leary. New York: Springer Publishing Company, 2000, p. 19.

"Emotional Abuse," *Counseling Center*, University of Illinois Urbana-Champaign, 2007. Archived from the original on November 20, 2014 accessed November 8, 2013. https://counselingcenter.utk.edu/self-help-materials/emotional-abuse

Freud, Sigmund, and James Strachey, *Three Essays on the Theory of Sexuality*. New York: Basic, 2007.

García-Moreno, Claudia, and Heidi Stöckl, "Protection of Sexual and Reproductive Health Rights: Addressing Violence against Women," in *Health and Human Rights in a Changing World*, edited by Michael A. Grodin, Daniel Tarantola, George J. Annas, et al. Abingdon, UK: Routledge, 2013, pp. 780–781, ISBN 9781136688638.

Giroux, Henry A., "Violence USA: The Warfare State and the Hardening of Everyday Life," *Monthly Review*, May 1, 2013.

Goff, Keli, "Is the Porn Industry Racist?" *The Root*, April 3, 2013, www.theroot.com/is-the-porn-industry-racist-1790895844 accessed January 30, 2017.

Gregoire, Carolyn, "What Constant Exposure to Negative News Is Doing to Our Mental Health," *The Huffington Post*, February 19, 2015.

Hedges, Chris, "The Rhetoric of Violence," *Truthdig*, April 20, 2014.

King, Martin Luther, Jr, "A Testament of Hope: The Essential Writings and Speeches of Martin Luther King," www.brainyquote.com/quotes/keywords/violence.html

Kopan, Tal, "GOP Platform Draft Declares Pornography 'Public Health Crisis'," *CNN Politics*, July 11, 2016.

Levin, Simone Lieban, "Feminist Debates: Pornography," *Ms Magazine*, June 10, 2014.

Liptak, Adam, "Justices Reject Ban on Violent Video Games for Children," *The New York Times*, June 27, 2011.

LoBianco, Tom, "Donald Trump on Terrorists: 'Take Out Their Families'," *CNN Politics*, December 3, 2015.

Mendelson, Scott, "Blame Washington, Not Hollywood, for R-Rated Violence in PG-13 Films," *Forbes*, November 14, 2013.

Morse, Brandon, "University 'Anti-Fascist' Group Justifies Violence and Vandalism against Peers," *TheBlaze*, February 28, 2017.

Perrottet, Tony, "Who Was the Marquis de Sade?" *Smithsonian Magazine*, February 2015 accessed January 25, 2015.

Ridgeway, Shannon, "Patriarchy and How It Shows up for Everyone," *Everyday Feminism*, May 5, 2013.

Saad, Lydia, "Most Americans Believe Crime in U.S. Is Worsening," *Gallup Well-Being*, October 31, 2011.

Shallhorn, Kaitlyn, "Tennessee Lawmaker Says Porn, Violent Movies among 'Root Causes' of School Shootings: A 'Big Part'," *Fox News*, May 30, 2018.

Sheaffer, Russell, "Smut, Novelty, Indecency: Reworking a History of the Early-Twentieth Century American 'Stag Film'," *Porn Studies*, vol. 1, no. 4, 2014.

Slade, Joseph W., *Obscenity in America: A Reference Handbook* (abc, clio 2000).

Smith, Clarissa, and Feona Attwood, "Anti/Pro/Porn Studies," *Porn Studies*, vol. 1, no. 1–2, 2014, pp. 7–23.

Strusiewicz, Cezary Jan, and Mireille Miller-Jones, "5 Ways Porn Is Bizarrely Racist Behind the Scenes," *Cracked*, March 20, 2016.

Thompson, Nicholas, "America's Culture of Violence," *The New Yorker*, December 15, 2012.

Vagianos, Alaana, "30 Shocking Domestic Violence Statistics That Remind Us It's an Epidemic," *The Huffington Post*, February 13, 2015.

Visser, Nick, "Trump Ramps up His Call for Torture," *The Huffington Post*, June 30, 2016.

Von Sacher-Masoch, Leopold, and Emil Marriot, *Venus in Furs: A Novel: Letters of Leopold Von Sacher-Masoch and Emilie Mataja*. New York: Blast Books, 1989.

2

PORNOGRAPHY DEFINED

The following is a legal definition of pornography: "Pornography is the depiction of sexual behavior that is intended to arouse sexual excitement in its audience".[1] Depictions of sexual behavior run the gauntlet between graphic depictions of genitalia ("the money shots") and romantic seduction scenes that may merely suggest or hint about sex. Pornographers use the terms "soft core" and "hard core" to distinguish the extent of sexual explicitness in which "soft core" is defined as, ". . . showing or describing sex acts but not in an extremely open and shocking way", and "hard core" as, ". . . showing or describing sex acts very openly".[2]

The pornography industry describes hard core as, ". . . containing explicit descriptions of sex acts or scenes of actual sex acts".[3] In the visual arts, the differences between hard and soft porn involve the kinds of shots permitted. Soft-core porn shots and images are not as graphic as hard-core shots and images. Soft core must only suggest titillation, while hard core includes explicit shots of genitalia and/or the act of coitus. Director Dag Yngvesson, in his documentary *A Journey Through Pornography* (1999), refers to hardcore as "real pornography" that requires "good wood" (a sustained erection) and "the money shot" (real sex).[4]

Both soft core and hard core may be classified into subgenres, depending on the characters involved. This may include males with females, males with males, females with females, young people with elders, and elders with younger people. The ultimate limit of transgressive porn involves child pornography. Children having sex with other children may eroticize some audiences, and there is a ready audience for adults titillating, abusing, and ultimately raping children. Other sexual fetishes include incest, bondage, whipping, masturbating, group sex, nudity, "fisting" (sexual penetration with a fist) "cuckqueening", in which women are cuckolded, and even defecation and urination.[5] Popular internet searches now include "violent porn" and "brutal porn", subcategories of hard porn displaying videos of sexualized violence.

Pornography Defined **19**

The advent of internet porn witnessed the birth of "reality porn", real videos of unsuspecting victims, stolen and posted to popular internet sites, even possibly used in an advertisement or as an unwitting enticement. Unauthorized photos and videos of women bathing topless or performing a variety of *risqué* activities then released on the internet may result in the victims becoming unwitting soft-core porn stars. Industry experts report over two million sales of unauthorized nude videos annually. In 1998, television producer Joe Francis launched "Girls Gone Wild", broadcasting stolen nude shots and videos of women. Responding to criticism for failing to secure permissions before airing sexy materials, Francis maintains it is all fun for the victims, who experience, ". . . fifteen minutes of fame . . ." after their videos go viral.[6] Internet porn today has become virtually ubiquitous. By 2010 between one quarter and one third of all internet users visited porn websites, a number that will surely grow with more free porn sites online and easy accessibility using smart phones and other devices.

Porn Stars

Just as movie stars dominate Hollywood films, porn stars dominate pornographic movies. Each star develops a fan base, the growth of which means financial success or failure for the film. Diehard porn fans recognize names of "hot porn stars". According to "100 Hottest Porn Stars", the names of the "hottest" include Indigo Augustine, an alt-right actor with guns tattooed on her chest, the words "Ripped" and "Killah" on her left and right buttocks, and nose and nipple piercings. Another, Linn Karter, starred in over 300 films in her six-year career, including one in which she posed with a look of pain while an aggressive man painfully squeezes one of her nipples as he has real sex with her. Madison Ivy models a submissive prone position as a male actor with clenched fist beats her. Male porn stars with a penchant for violence include Billy Glide, who has a reputation for "kicking ass", and former police officer Jack Lawrence who performs in uniform.

In 2018, Stormy Daniels (alias Stephanie Clifford) guaranteed notoriety after filing a lawsuit against President Donald Trump regarding an alleged affair she had with then-private citizen Trump. She requested that non-disclosure contract be overturned, stating she felt pressured to sign an agreement to keep an affair with Trump secret in exchange for a $130,000 payment. Daniels, who claimed the relationship was technically consensual, received widespread sympathy for what many believed inappropriate pressure from billionaire Trump to engage in sex with him. Daniels' case made her an instant celebrity, and pornographers wasted little time in posting both her hard- and soft-core videos. Her plucky defiance of Trump and his agents led *The New York Times'* Matt Flegenheimer, Rebecca R. Ruiz, and Katie Van Syckle to predict, "It is she, some in Washington now joke, and not the special counsel, Robert S. Mueller III, who could topple Mr. Trump".[7]

To learn what goes on behind the scenes in the porn industry, journalist Madeline Haller of *Men's Health* interviewed porn star James Deen in 2013. Deen states that acting in porn movies is not the same thing as having sex. "People need to realize porn is not *real*. Porn is entertainment. It's a movie being made to arouse the viewer", he asserts. "Therefore, people should not be having sex the way people have sex in pornos". The sex differs in, ". . . the length of time that we have sex, the amount of positions we go through, the way we pose for the camera—stuff like that—it all happens a specific way for film. So porn shouldn't be the model that you mold your sex life after".[8] Agent Mark Spiegler, who represents some of the most highly paid female porn stars, notes that salaries have declined precipitously for female stars. "While a decade ago the average female performer would make about $100,000 a year", Spiegler told THR, ". . . she now might make as little as $50,000—all while juggling responsibilities such as social-media outreach and personal appearances".[9]

This may be the effect of the internet being awash in pornography, a testament to the intensity of demand for this multi-billion-dollar industry. Most porn internet sites are free, and the number of porn sites has exploded.[10] In 2014 *The Huffington Post* Announced that porn sites surpassed Netflix, Amazon, and Twitter combined as 30% of the Internet became devoted to pornography.[11] And modern technology increases its accessibility. By 2015, porn became available on Apple computer watches.[12]

Porn and Violence

Most pornography depicts acts of violence. Over 88% of "teen porn features spanking, gagging, and slapping, while nearly half contains verbal aggression. The aggressors were overwhelmingly male, while the victims were overwhelmingly female".[13] The popularity of violent pornography displaying violent attacks by men perpetrated against women becomes alarming when one considers outcomes. British anti-pornography advocate Gail Dines, in her 2010 *Pornland: How Porn Has Hijacked Our Sexuality*, claims, "We are now bringing up a generation of boys on cruel, violent porn". She warns, ". . . given what we know about how images affect people, this is going to have a profound influence on their sexuality, behavior, and attitudes towards women".[14]

Using a wide range of methodologies, researchers like Dines attempt to show that viewing pornography is often associated with damaging outcomes. However, journalist Natasha Vargas-Cooper asserts, "I have yet to see a credible study that links proliferation of pornography to an increase of abuse of women". She notes, however, a rapid rise in the percentage of young women who reported experiencing anal sex. In 1992, 20% of women aged 25–29 reported experiencing anal sex, a popular form of sadomasochism, but by 2010 46% of similarly aged women reported anal sex.[15] A separate study of men reveals, ". . . 83 percent reported seeing mainstream pornography, and that those who did were more likely to say they would commit rape or sexual assault (if they knew they wouldn't be caught) than men who hadn't seen porn in the past 12 months".[16] Australia, which experienced

Pornography Defined **21**

a steep decline in general violence, finds the rates of domestic and sexual violence soaring. Gendered violence has escalated to the point that now two women are killed each week—twice the historical average. In 2015 alone, thirty-five women were murdered, the majority by male partners.[17]

To feminists, and health care professionals, pornographic depictions of women's and children's sexuality distort the truth about their desires while subliminally or blatantly reinforcing men's sense of dominance over females, supporting the use of force, violence, and degrading acts against women.[18] Psychiatrist Mary Anne Layden reports that pornography depicting females as sexually subordinate to males damages all genders and negatively affects children. "The damage is seen in men, women, and children, and in both married and single adults. It involves pathological behaviors, illegal behaviors, and some behaviors that are both illegal and pathological. Pornography is an equal opportunity and very lethal toxin".[19] By contrast, researcher P.J. Wright discovered that pornography consumers display more positive views on a wide variety of sexual experiences than non-porn consumers.[20] Psychologists consider positive perspectives on sexuality to be healthier than negative perspectives, including fear.

Among a plethora of sexual choices, pop culture provides audiences with sexually attractive violent pornography. Author Susan Roth defines violent pornography as "dehumanizing constructions of male and female sexuality and a legitimation of the power imbalance between males and females that makes it look desirable and inevitable". However, porn consumers may gain valuable insights into sadomasochism that are not generally aired. Roth suggests, "Perhaps if pornography were viewed in the context of a true emotional awareness of violence as it occurs toward women, there would be more unanimity in what it has become— a popular form of entertainment". Roth recognizes that sadomasochism possesses a powerful, hidden dimension to human sexuality and gender roles. As she states, pornography is currently the most popular activity on the internet.[21] Sociologist Cassia Wosick estimates that the global pornography industry produces $97 billion worldwide, with between $10 and $12 billion produced annually in the US. While the global pornography industry experienced shrinkage due to technological challenges, more recently, ". . . things are looking up . . ." for the industry in the US.[22]

Gonzo (Extreme) Porn

Today professional pornography has been overtaken by amateur-produced "gonzo" or "extreme porn". One early example of gonzo porn is *On the Prowl* (1989), produced and directed by Jamie Gillis. In this pioneering film Gillis and another porn actor, Renee Morgan, prowl the streets of San Francisco searching for random men to seduce. Today "prowl" videos abound on the internet, including *Ava Divine Midnight Prowl*, and *Midnight Prowl: Britany Beth*. Hundreds of porn prowl videos are now available. In most of these women become objectified and often play the role of subs to male doms.

22 Pornography Defined

Tristan Taormino's *Chemistry* series presents other well-known examples of gonzo porn. Taormino places selected porn actors in a house together for 36 hours and follows them around as they have "spontaneous sex" with each other. Taormino's actors use a "perv cam" that empowers them to shoot whatever they want, from each other's sex scenes to fully clothed discussions about what they did and didn't like about the sex they had just had.

According to Gail Dines, gonzo porn, ". . . depicts hard-core, body-punishing sex in which women are demeaned and debased".[23] Psychologist Paul Joannides observes that gonzo porn ". . . has become particularly disrespectful and increasingly violent toward the female actors". He concludes that gonzo porn "has taken disrespect toward women to a new low, or should I say high".[24] He predicts, "You will see, with mind-numbing repetition, gagging, slapping, verbal abuse, hairpulling, pounding anal sex, women smeared in semen, sore anuses and vaginas, distended mouths, and more exhausted, depleted, and shell-shocked women than you can count". David Ronen observes that only radical social change will solve the problem of sexual violence: "Feminists don't see more sex or better orgasms as the answer to women's oppression. We need to overthrow the systems of patriarchy, capitalism, and racism and in their place put a world based on equality, justice, and dignity for all".[25]

Today's audio/video technology, with which porn videos may be created on individual smart phones, has revolutionized the porn industry. Presently, 95% of all porn is produced not in studios but in homes using smart phones and other micro cameras and editing systems. Critics now refer to amateur porn as "gonzo porn". Today over 58 million Google searches for "gonzo porn" appear. Amateur-produced and -directed porn often features sadomasochism. Producer John Stagliano, a popular gonzo porn proponent, asks rhetorically: "Pleasure and pain are the same thing, right?" Stagliano also finds vaginal sex "bullshit" and believes that anal is the new reality, and that fisting and double penetrations, both involving violence, are the new norm.[26]

By 2015 Americans reported spending an average of 5.6 hours daily online, up from 5.3 hours in 2014. Pornhub, a video-sharing gonzo porn website, is the largest porn site on the internet. Each year it analyzes its millions of visits for themes. In 2015 the most popular search on Pornhub in the US was "step mom". The second most popular porn search was "lesbian", while the third most popular search was for "teens".[27] "Step mom" websites have proliferated, with scores more added monthly. There are sites for "Japanese step mom" porn, "skinny step mom" porn, "hot and horny step mom" porn, "step mom gives head" porn, among many others. The popularity of this subject may tell us something about today's incest taboos and fantasies.

The increase in lesbian searches may be attributable in part to the growing numbers of female searchers. Women now comprise 25% of all porn viewers in the US, a substantial increase from previous years. Dr Meredith Chivers found that women are sexually aroused by a wide variety of stimuli, including lesbian images,

Pornography Defined **23**

whether they are gay or straight, whereas straight men are usually not aroused by gay porn, and gay men are generally not aroused by straight porn.[28]

Critic/filmmaker Jennifer Moorman examined the pornography created by numerous feminist "extreme" pornographers. Moorman interviewed Lizzy Borden, Julie Simone, Kimberly Kane, Jacky St. James, Tasha Rein, Diana DeVoe, Roberta Findlay, and Candida Royale and analyzed the content and tone of their pornography. Many of the films created by these pornographers, including the ultra-graphic *Forced Entry* (1973, 1974, 1975) resemble male-produced pornography complete with violent scenes of (mostly males) whipping and flogging female victims. Some of these feminist filmmakers feature rape victims turning on their attackers. Moorman admits that "Extreme porn presents unique challenges for the feminist media analysist". She points out that even the most violent, hard-core feminist filmmakers—are helping to broaden cultural perceptions of women's desires. She adds that "the women who make extreme porn contribute to changing perceptions about femininity, a woman's point of view, and the roles of women as cultural producers".[29]

Origins of Censorship

Soft porn and soft-porn stars began with the birth of motion pictures in the 1890s when filmmakers began producing erotic movies to appeal to men. In 1896, Thomas Edison released *Fatima's Coochie-Coochie Dance*, a *danse du ventre*, or belly dance, originally an Egyptian art form. The *danse du ventre* is performed by a single woman who walks rather than dances across a floor while gyrating and twisting her body sensuously, ideal action for movie cameras and projectors. The two art forms, one mechanical and one human, coalesced on the same stage during Chicago's Columbia Exhibition (world's fair) in 1893. Thomas Edison brought them together to demonstrate his newly invented kinetoscope, a peep-hole short movie viewer, which became the world's first commercial motion picture projector. A short time later, Thomas Edison produced *The May Irwin Kiss*, a twenty-second short of May Irwin and John Rice re-enacting their sumptuous kissing scene from *The Widow Jones* Broadway play. The film broke new bounds of affectionate realism, but some called it scandalous and called for censorship.[30] 1907 witnessed the first censorship law in the US by the city of Chicago. The National Censorship Board appeared in 1909 in response to a growing number of complaints of kinetoscope parlors showing "indecent" and "immoral" motion pictures. Ministers as well as journalists launched crusades to "clean up" movies through censorship. What enraged these critics were sensuous dancing, passionate kissing, female body parts, prostitution, and drug use.[31]

The late 1910s and throughout the 1920s saw the age of "vamps", seductive women including Theda Bara, Clara Bow, Pola Negri, Jean Harlow, Marlena Dietrich, Barbara Stanwyck, and Mae West. They played daring roles of "gold diggers" who preyed on males in exchange for sex and affection. Theda Bara bridges

24 Pornography Defined

the gap between 1890s' Arab and Middle-Eastern exotic stereotypes as the first self-identified "vamp". She claimed to be born in the Sahara Desert to a French artist and an Egyptian concubine but was born Theodosia Goodman in 1885 in Cincinnati, Ohio. Bara rose to stardom in *A Fool There Was* (1915), a dramatization of Rudyard Kipling's "The Vampire", (1897) poem about the sexual predation of a gold-digging young woman. Bara continued in roles of female seductresses, acquiring the nickname of "The Vamp" by her fans, a title that quickly spread to all seductive actresses of the time. The popularity of these erotic, sensuous, and highly popular actresses in films like *The Plastic Age* (1925), *Red Headed Woman* (1932), *Baby Face* (1933), and *She Done Him Wrong* (1933) fueled censorship efforts emanating from Protestants, Catholics, and Jews which eventually resulted in The Motion Picture Production Code of 1930, which became known as the Hays Code after its enforcer, Will H. Hays.[32]

The Hays Code prohibited pornography, licentiousness, "suggestive" nudity, sexual perversions (unspecified) and rape as well as any acknowledgment of males and females engaging in sexuality, even when married (to one another). It found, "Even within the limits of pure love, certain facts have been universally regarded by lawmakers as outside the limits of safe presentation". The Code subscribed to what some label the "theory of imitative behavior", or the belief that movie audiences tended to imitate behavior witnessed in movies. According to critic David Denby, Hays' strict on-screen behavioral standards regarding sexuality gradually and inexorably evolved toward greater realism. The "film noir" movement reprised the pre-Code femme fatale as tough, seductive, cynical "femme noir". The 1940s' gritty, urban "film noir" genre featured hard-hearted females seducing naïve and often doomed males. Titles include *The Maltese Falcon* (1941), *Double Indemnity* (1944), *The Postman Always Rings Twice* (1946), *The Big Sleep* (1946), *Gilda* (1946), and *Sunset Boulevard* (1950) in which sexually predacious females played by Mary Astor, Barbara Stanwyck, Lana Turner, Lauren Bacall, Rita Hayworth, and Gloria Swanson seduced and betrayed their male counterparts, similar to the gold diggers of the pre-Code age.

The Code's prohibition of nudity, particularly female nudity, became challenged during the 1940s. In 1940 United Artists filmmaker Howard Hughes submitted a script of his upcoming Western titled *The Outlaw*, starring Jack Buetel as outlaw Billy the Kid, Thomas Mitchell as Sheriff Pat Garrett, and Walter Huston as Doc Holliday. However, most of the film's energy emanates from Jane Russell as Rio McDonald. Hughes emphasized Russell's voluptuous figure (38/24/36), which angered Joseph Breen, Will Hays' chief Code enforcer. In December, 1940, Breen wrote to Hughes demanding, "Great care will be needed in this scene of the struggle between Billy and Rio in the hayloft to avoid any questionable angles or postures". Breen also warned Hughes "There must be no exposure of Rio's person in the scene when her dress gets torn". He also warned "Care will be needed in this scene of Billy pulling Rio down on the bed and kissing her, to avoid sex suggestiveness".[33]

Alfred Hitchcock perfected an effective method to avoid the MPAA censorship he found most objectionable. In his 1960 classic *Psycho* Hitchcock relied on a strategy that involved inserting shots into the rough cut that he knew were overly violent and sexual. When the Hays office objected he quickly cut them from the film, keeping shots he preferred. In another case Hitchcock agreed to reshoot a scene of Marion Crane (Janet Leigh) undressing to her underwear in preparation for the famous shower scene if Hays Code officials, notably Breen himself,

FIGURE 2.1 Alfred Hitchcock, *Psycho*, 1960
Source: Pacific Film Archive

26 Pornography Defined

appeared on set to ask questions and offer advice. The Hays office representative however did not appear, and Hitchcock kept the original scene.[34]

Hitchcock successfully eluded Hays Production Code censors. He promised to cut scenes deemed "too sexual" and "too violent" but delayed implementing cuts, finally abandoning them after Production Code officials failed to check the film's progress.

Critic David Denby famously observed that "Today, much of the sexual imagery that alarmed past censors seems trivial, the alarm itself near-hysterical".[35] Groundbreaking soft-core pornographic films appeared in the 1970s. In 1973 Gerard Damiano released *Deep Throat*, a sexually explicit movie starring Linda Lovelace, about a woman who possesses a clitoris deep within her throat. She can only experience sexual orgasms inside her throat. She discovers solace in fellatio and begins seeking oral gratification. This film, produced for only $25,000, became an immediate smash hit, playing in independent theaters, is estimated to have grossed over $45 million in the US alone, although no consensus exists as to the total gross.[36] Some speculate that the continuing attraction of audiences to this movie earned over $600 million by 1980. Critics now credit Damiano's low-budget sexual comedy as the first pornographic film to gain widespread audiences and a, ". . . cult porn film that brought blue movies to mainstream . . . ".[37]

In 1972 the English classic "golden age of porn" film *Behind the Green Door* appeared, directed and produced by the Mitchell brothers. It premiered at the Cannes Film Festival, where it became the first porn film to compete for the Palme D'Or. Even though this film includes lesbianism and interracial coupling, the basic message ultimately reinforces male sexual domination.

Bambi Woods plays Debbie Benton in *Debbie Does Dallas* (1978), another "golden age of porn" classic. Debbie lands a job on the Cowgirls, a squad of cheerleaders for the Dallas Cowboys. However, she lacks the funds to travel there. Her fellow high school cheerleaders help her raise some money, but her boss Mr Greenfield (Robert Kerman) launches her business career by offering to pay $10 to see her breasts, another $10 to touch them, another $10 to suckle them, and an undisclosed amount if he can "score a touchdown" with her. Several of Debbie's girlfriends also begin performing sexual favors for their boyfriends. The girls form a "Teen Services" company and inform potential clients that they will do anything they are asked to do. Debbie enjoys the new business and ultimately grants Greenfield his wish to "score a touchdown" by having sex with him in a variety of positions. This film is yet another example of male sexual domination of females and thus contributes toward violence toward women.[38]

Black Throat (1984), directed by Gregory Dark, stars Traci Lords as Debbie, Sahara as Madame Mambo, and Christy Canyon as Dominatrix. It also stars Kevin James as The Dude, Jack Baker as Jamal, and Peter North as Slave/Mambo's Client. The film's tagline reads "Deep Throating with an Ethnic Flavor!" The thin plot involves The Dude, Jamal, and Mambo's Client, among others, seeking sex at Madame Mambo's bordello. The cast also indulges in threesomes and other forms

Pornography Defined **27**

of group sex. The score consists of a monotonous light rock soundtrack. *Black Throat* became embroiled in controversy when it was revealed that Traci Lords, the major star, was only 15 years old at the time of filming. Her sex scenes were edited out, and her name stricken from the credits for a few years. Restored copies are now readily available featuring Lords. *Black Throat* received a nomination by the Adult Film Association of America for Best Adult Video and won the X-Rated Critics Award, USA for Best Video.

Soft Porn Goes Mainstream

By the 1990s violent soft porn had begun blending in with mainstream movies. Paul Verhoeven's *Basic Instinct* (1992) incorporates potentially pornographic plot elements including sadomasochism, lesbianism, voyeurism, and drug addiction into a stylish police thriller. Verhoeven's plot centers around San Francisco police detective Nick Curran's (Michael Douglas) investigation of former rock star Johnny Boz's (Bill Cable) murder the previous night by being tied up and then stabbed multiple times with an ice pick. Curran suspects wealthy novelist Catherine Tramell (Sharon Stone), Boz's girlfriend and the last one seen with Boz on the night of his death. When asked if she was dating Boz, Tramell responds by proclaiming "I wasn't dating him. I was fucking him!" Later, at police headquarters, she famously opens her legs under a white mini skirt, exposing her vagina during the interrogation at police headquarters, which critics found "titillating". She later tells him, "You know I don't like to wear underwear, don't you Nick". Curran eventually succumbs to Tramell, and in a later scene, Curran confronts Tramell's lesbian lover Roxy (Leilani Sarelle) with, "Let me ask you something, Roxy, man to man. I think she's the fuck of the century, what do you think?" Thomas Austin comments on the ". . . partial insertions of sex scenes within the thriller narrative". Austin notes that the public disapproval and controversies surrounding *Basic Instinct*'s "gratuitous" sex and violence, ". . . makes the film a guilty pleasure".[39] In fact, Verhoeven spent a great deal of time and effort emulating pornographic films of the past.[40]

Paul Thomas Anderson's *Boogie Nights* (1997) broke new ground in integrating pornography with mainstream movies by focusing on the porn industry itself. Anderson's film depicts the porn industry during the "Golden Age of Porn". Critics like Roger Ebert consider it a comedy classic. Anderson chose to set his film during the disco era (late 1970s). It stars Mark Wahlberg as Eddie Adams (whose stage name is Dirk Digler), a youthful porn actor who rises to critical acclaim among professional pornographers. Film director Jack Horner (Burt Reynolds) who specializes in "exotic films" and his girlfriend/assistant, cocaine-addicted Amber Waves (Julianne Moore). Ever searching for new talent for his films, Jack meets Eddie a busboy at a local LA restaurant who charges people to view his unusually large (13 inch) penis. Jack offers him an actor position in his "exotic" movies. On Dirk's first day on the movie set, Jack decides that Dirk should be photographed having unprotected sex with Amber. The film ultimately turns violent, including a murder and a suicide.

28 Pornography Defined

The MPAA ultimately awarded *Boogie Nights* an R rating, ". . . for strong sex scenes with explicit dialogue, nudity, drug use, language and violence". Film critics consider Anderson's film a groundbreaker for its sexuality and violence. Roger Ebert wrote that *Boogie Nights*, ". . . is an epic of the low road, a classic Hollywood story set in the shadows instead of the spotlights but containing the same ingredients: Fame, envy, greed, talent, sex, money".[41] Because of the dialogue, direction, and acting, Anderson's film still resonates, nearly 20 years after it first appeared.[42]

Mommy Porn is a subgenre of erotica that grew out of the mainstream success of E.L. James' erotic novel *Fifty Shades of Grey* (2011). Literary critic Alessandra Stanley pointed out in her review of the runaway bestseller, "Sex is a hard sell". Sexual entertainment media delivers free pornography 24/7, so why purchase a novel about a BDSMQ relationship? Because, as Stanley observes, "Sex has to be transgressive to cause a stir". She explains "This S-and-M story about a virginal college student and the handsome young billionaire who binds her, sounds racier than it is. Mostly it's an updated throwback to scandalous novels of the past, including *Jane Eyre* and the 1920s' desert rape fantasy *The Sheik*".[43] *50 Shades of Grey* racked up astounding sales of over 100 million copies, and James followed it up with two popular sequels and a blockbuster movie version in 2015 directed by Sam Taylor-Johnson and starring Dakota Johnson as Anastasia Steele and Jamie Dorman as Christian Grey. Critic Anthony Lane, on the film's release on Valentine's Day, 2015, exclaimed, "That's a bold move, since the film is not just unromantic but specifically anti-romantic; take your valentine along, by all means, but, be warned, it'll be like watching 'Rosemary's Baby' at Christmas. Try holding hands as the hero taunts the rituals of sentiment, such as going out for dinner and a movie, That's not really my thing".[44] The movie earned an amazing $571 million with a production budget of just $40 million.[45] The novel was removed from libraries in the US in Brevard County Public Libraries, Florida, and the film was banned in Malaysia, Indonesia, Nigeria, Kenya, United Arab Emirates, Papua New Guinea, Cambodia, and the Russian Caucasus region.[46]

50 Shades of Grey appeared during an upwelling of popular culture running contrary to the venerable dominant on subordinate narrative that forms the basis of most pornography, as well as much melodramas in popular culture. Heroes appeared challenging subordination, including *Kill Bill's* protagonist the Bride, *Black Panther*, and *Wonder Woman*. They symbolize today's mass movements, including #MeToo, #Time'sUp, and Black Lives Matter. They arrived during a period which saw a rapid increase in women as porn consumers and increasingly, as creators. Technology enabling today's exploding, amateur-porn revolution also assists sexual assault victims repel and dissuade attackers.

Notes

1. legal-dictionary.thefreedictionary.com/pornography
2. www.merriam-webster.com/dictionary/soft-core

Pornography Defined **29**

3. www.merriam-webster.com/dictionary/hard%20cor
4. Dag Yngvesson, A Journey Through Pornography, 1999 (quoted in documentary); www.youtube.com/watch?v=S0i8B0vmmHw
5. Herrman, Bert, Trust—the Hand Book: A Guide to the Sensual and Spiritual Art of Handballing. San Francisco: Alamo Square Press, 1991, pp. 46–47, 58. ISBN 978-0-9624751-5-3, https://filthy.media/weirdest-new-porn-genres
6. David Kohn, "Girls Gone Wild," *48 Hours*, April 16, 2002.
7. Matt Flegenheimer, Rebecca R. Ruiz, and Katie Van Syckle, "Stormy Daniels, Porn Star Suing Trump, Is Known for Her Ambition: 'She's the Boss'," *The New York Times*, March 24, 2018.
8. Madeline Haller, "Inside the Mind of a Porn Star," *Men's Health*, February 19, 2013.
9. Aly Wiseman, "Here's What Female Porn Stars Get Paid for Different Type of Scenes," *Business Insider*, November 15, 2012.
10. "Pornography: Naked Capitalism," *The Economist*, September 26, 2015.
11. 9to5 staff, "Porn Sites Get More Visitors Each Month Than Netflix, Amazon, and Twitter Combined," *The Huffington Post*, May 4, 2013.
12. Ana J. Bridges, Robert Wosnitzer, Erica Scharrer, Chyung Sun, and Rachael Liberman, "Aggression and Sexual Behavior in Best-Selling Pornography Videos: A Content Analysis Update," *Violence Against Women*, vol. 16, no. 10, 2010, pp. 1065–1085, 9to5mac.com/community/how-to-watch-porn-on-apple-watch-nsfw/
13. Stephan Deusner, Culture Caught Looking: Gail Dines, "Pornland: How Porn Has Hijacked Our Sexuality," at Politics & Prose, *The Washington Post*, July 14, 2010, www.internetsafety101.org › Dangers › Pornography 101.
14. Judy Bindel, "The Truth about the Porn Industry," *The Guardian*, July 2, 2010.
15. Natasha Vargas-Cooper, "Hard Core: The New World of Porn Is Revealing Eternal Truths about Men and Women," *The Atlantic*, 10727825, vol. 307, 2011, no. 1.
16. Gail Dines, "Is Porn Immoral? That Doesn't Matter: It's a Public Health Crisis," *The Washington Post*, April 8, 2016.
17. Laura McNally, "Pornography, Violence, and Sexual Entitlement: An Unspeakable Truth," *ABC Religion and Truth*, May 29, 2015.
18. William L. Marshall, "Revisiting the Use of Pornography by Sexual Offenders: Implications for Theory and Practice," *The Journal of Sexual Aggression*, vol. 6, 2000, pp. 67–77.
19. Mary Anne Layden, "Pornography and Violence: A Look at New Research," www.socialcostsofpornography.com/Layden_Pornography_and_Violence.pdf
20. Paul J. Wright, "U.S. Males and Pornography, 1973–2010: Consumption, Predictors, Correlates," *Journal of Sex Research*, vol. 50, no. 1, 2013, pp. 60–71.
21. Susan Roth, "Review of *Adult Users Only: The Dilemma of Violent Pornography*," in Susan Gubar and Joan Hoff, eds., *Signs: Journal of Women and Culture in Society*, vol. 16, no. 2, Winter 1991.
22. Chris Morris, "Things Are Looking up in America's Porn Industry," *NBC News*, January 20, 2015.
23. Gail Dines, *Pornland: How Porn Has Hijacked Our Sexuality*, Boston: Beacon Press, 2010.
24. Paul Joannidas, "Paul's Sex Term of the Day: Gonzo Porn," *Psychology Today*, January 15, 2008.
25. David Rosen, "Is the Rise of Filthy Gonzo Porn Actually Dangerous, or Are People Overreacting," *AlterNet*, July 7, 2013.
26. The Plaid Zebra, "The Violence of Gonzo Porn Makes 2 Girls 1 Cup Look Tame," *Plaid Zebra*, August 29, 2014 accessed July 20, 2017.
27. "Pornhub's 2015 Year in Review," *Pornhub Insights*, January 6, 2016, www.pornhub.com/insights/pornhub-2,015-year-in-revi... accessed April 22, 2019.
28. Daniel Bergner, "What Do Women Want?" The New York Times, January 22, 2009, www.pornhub.com/insights/pornhub-2015-year-in-revi...

30 Pornography Defined

29. Jennifer Moorman, "The Hardest of Hard Core: Locating Feminist Possibilities in Women's Extreme Pornography," *Signs: Journal of Women in Culture & Society*, April 1, 2017.
30. Tim Dirks, "The History of Film, the Pre-1920s and the Infancy of Film," *AMC Film Sight*, www.filmsite.org/pre20sintro.html
31. Tom Pollard, *Sex and Violence: The Hollywood Censorship Wars*. Boulder, CO: Paradigm Publishers, 2009, 24.
32. See Tom Pollard, *Sex and Violence: The Hollywood Censorship Wars*. Boulder, CO: Paradigm Publishers, 2009.
33. Gerald Gardner, *The Censorship Papers: Movie Censorship Letters from the Hays Office, 1934–1968*. New York: Dodd, Mead & Company, 1987, 27.
34. Evan Andrews, "8 Classic Films That Ran Afoul of Hollywood Censors," *History in the Headlines*, March 31, 2015.
35. David Denby, "Sex and Sexier, the Hays Code Wasn't All That Bad," *The New Yorker*, May 2, 2016.
36. Michael Hiltzik, (March 10, 2005). "Bad 'Deep Throat' Revenue Numbers Are Multiplying". Los Angeles Times. p. C-1. www.boxofficemojo.com/movies/?id=insidedeepthroat.htm retrieved April 22, 2019.
37. Hannah Osborne, "Linda Lovelace's *Deep Throat* Uncut Screened in SOHO for First Time," *IBT News*, August 22, 2013.
38. Jim Buckley (director) *Debbie Does Dallas* (1978), www.socialcostsofpornography.com/Layden_Pornography_and_Violence.pdf
39. Thomas Austin, *Hollywood Hype and Audiences: Selling and Watching Popular Film in the 1990s*. Manchester, England: Manchester University Press, p. 78.
40. Thomas Austin, "Gendered (dis)pleasures: 'Basic Instinct' and Female Viewers," *Journal of Popular British Cinema Flick Books*, 1999, pp. 4–22, www.imdb.com/title/tt0103772/
41. Roger Ebert, "Boogie Nights," *Roger Ebert.com*, October 17, 1997.
42. Alex French and Howie Kahn, "Livin' Thing: An Oral History of *Boogie Nights*," grantland.com/features/boogie-nights/
43. Alessandra Stanley, "Glass Slipper as Fetish," *The New York Times*, April 2, 2012.
44. Anthony Lane, "No Pain, No Gain: *50 Shades of Grey*," *The New Yorker*, February 23 and March 2, 2015.
45. www.boxofficemojo.com/movies/?id=fiftyshadesofgrey.htm
46. Kelly West, "Fifty Shades of Grey Is Banned in All of These Countries," Cinemablend-www.cinemablend.com/new/Fifty-Shades-Grey-Banned-All-Countries-69914.html

Bibliography

Andrews, Evan, "8 Classic Films That Ran Afoul of Hollywood Censors," *History in the Headlines*, March 31, 2015.

Austin, Thomas, *Hollywood Hype and Audiences: Selling and Watching Popular Film in the 1990s*. Manchester, England: Manchester University Press, 2002, p. 78.

Bindel, Judy, "The Truth about the Porn Industry," *The Guardian*, July 2, 2010.

Denby, David, "Sex and Sexier, the Hays Code Wasn't All That Bad," *The New Yorker*, May 2, 2016.

Dines, Gail, "Is Porn Immoral? That Doesn't Matter: It's a Public Health Crisis," *The Washington Post*, April 8, 2016.

Dines, Gail, *Pornland: How Porn Has Hijacted Our Sexuality*. Boston: Beacon Press, 2010.

Dirks, Tim, *The History of Film, the Pre-1920s and the Infancy of Film*, AMC Film Sight, www.filmsite.org/pre20sintro.html

Ebert, Roger, "Boogie Nights," *Roger Ebert.com*, October 17, 1997.

Flegenheimer, Matt, Rebecca R. Ruiz, and Katie Van Syckle, "Stormy Daniels, Porn Star Suing Trump, Is Known for Her Ambition: 'She's the Boss'," *The New York Times*, March 24, 2018.

French, Alex, and Howie Kahn, "'Livin' Thing: An Oral History of *Boogie Nights*," grantland.com/features/boogie-nights/

Gardner, Gerald, *The Censorship Papers: Movie Censorship Letters from the Hays Office, 1934–1968*. New York: Dodd, Mead & Company, 1987, p. 27.

Haller, Madeline, "Inside the Mind of a Porn Star," *Men's Health*, February 19, 2013. www.internetsafety101.org › Dangers › Pornography 101.

Joannidas, Paul, "Paul's Sex Term of the Day: Gonzo Porn," *Psychology Today*, January 15, 2008.

Lane, Anthony, "No Pain, No Gain: *50 Shades of Grey*," *The New Yorker*, February 23 and March 2, 2015.

Layden, Mary Anne, "Pornography and Violence: A Look at New Research," www.socialcostsofpornography.com/Layden_Pornography_and_Violence.pdf

Marshall, William L., "Revisiting the Use of Pornography by Sexual Offenders: Implications for Theory and Practice," *The Journal of Sexual Aggression*, vol. 6, 2000, pp. 67–77.

McNally, Laura, "Pornography, Violence, and Sexual Entitlement: An Unspeakable Truth," *ABC Religion and Truth*, May 29, 2015.

Moorman, Jennifer, "The Hardest of Hard Core: Locating Feminist Possibilities in Women's Extreme Pornography," *Signs: Journal of Women in Culture & Society*, April 1, 2017.

Morris, Chris, "Things Are Looking up in America's Porn Industry," *NBC News*, January 20, 2015.

"Naked Capitalism," *The Economist*, September 26, 2015, 9to5mac.com/community/how-to-watch-porn-on-apple-watch-nsfw/

Osborne, Hannah, "Linda Lovelace's *Deep Throat* Uncut Screened in SOHO for First Time," *IBT News*, August 22, 2013.

The Plaid Zebra, "The Violence of Gonzo Porn Makes 2 Girls 1 Cup Look Tame," *Plaid Zebra*, August 29, 2014 accessed July 20, 2017.

Pollard, Tom, *Sex and Violence: The Hollywood Censorship Wars*. Boulder, CO: Paradigm Publishers, 2009, p. 24.

Alexis Kleinman, "Porn Sites Get More Visitors Each Month Than Netflix, Amazon, and Twitter Combined," *Huffington Post*, May 4, 2013.

Rosen, David, "Is the Rise of Filthy Gonzo Porn Actually Dangerous, or Are People Over-reacting," *AlterNet*, July 7, 2013.

Roth, Susan, "Review of Adult Users Only: The Dilemma of Violent Pornography," in *Signs: Journal of Women and Culture*, edited by Susan Gubar and Joan Hoff, vol. 16, no. 2, Winter 1991.

Stanley, Alessandra, "Glass Slipper as Fetish," *The New York Times*, April 2, 2012.

Vargas-Cooper, Natasha, "Hard Core: The New World of Porn Is Revealing Eternal Truths about Men and Women," *The Atlantic*, 10727825, vol. 307, no. 1, 2011.

West, Kelly, "Fifty Shades of Grey Is Banned in All of These Countries," *Cinemablend*, www.cinemablend.com/new/Fifty-Shades-Grey-Banned-All-Countries-69914.html

Wiseman, Aly, "Here's What Female Porn Stars Get Paid for Different Type of Scenes," *Business Insider*, November 15, 2012.

Wright, Paul J., "U.S. Males and Pornography, 1973–2010: Consumption, Predictors, Correlates," *Journal of Sex Research*, vol. 50, no. 1, 2013, pp. 60–71.

3

REVENGE

Revenge constitutes an essential element of violent pornography and, of course, it is not a new phenomenon. It harkens back to psychologists Ian McKee and N.T. Feather who studied revenge as behavior and discovered that vengeful people tend to be motivated by power, authority, and the desire for status. "They don't want to lose face".[1] In comparison with the general population, revenge seekers, "tend to be less forgiving, less benevolent, and less focused on universal consecutiveness-type values".[2]

Violent revenge dates to ancient mythology. The ancient Greek goddess Hera burned with jealousy after Zeus, her husband, fathered Heracles with a mortal woman. Hera sent deadly poisonous snakes to infant Heracles' cradle, but the demigod and future hero strangled them all. Philosopher Friedrich Nietzsche wryly observed, "It is impossible to suffer without making someone pay for it; every complaint already contains revenge".[3]

Revenge includes the possibility of a boomerang effect on the vengeance seeker. Whether a person experiences or imagines physical, sexual, social, political, or economic harm, a vengeance quest often harms perpetrators more than the intended victims. Douglas Horton, the late Protestant leader and academic, offered these words, "When seeking revenge, dig two graves—one for yourself".[4] Filmmaker Jane Goldman cautions, "Vengeance is the act of turning anger in on yourself. On the surface, it may be directed at someone else, but it is a surefire recipe for arresting emotional recovery".[5]

Psychiatrist Sandra L. Bloom, co-director of the Center for Nonviolence and Social Justice, School of Public Health of Drexel University observes, ". . . hurt people hurt people. The motivation is revenge, not because human beings are fundamentally evil, but because vengeance is part of the innate survival mechanics of a complex social species". To Bloom, vengeance is a normal function of human behavior. She found that normally, ". . . children learn how to modulate and manage the desire to 'get even' for hurts to their bodies, their sense of identity, and their cherished beliefs". However, Bloom learned that this desire does not end with childhood, but rather, ". . . the urge to retaliate for wrongs lingers through adulthood". With maturation, children usually learn to manage and suppress their vengeful impulses as they learn the social rules of fair play, apology, justice, and how to cooperate with others. However, children suffering from trauma and neglect tended to emphasize revenge more than those from normal childhoods. "If they come from violent and abusive homes, children learn to be violent, learn that violence is a viable and effective means of solving problems". She cautions, ". . . because abusive adults were often exposed to abuse and/or neglect as children, an important way of viewing the intergenerational cycle of abuse is through the lens of displaced revenge".[6]

Sexual abuse represents one of humanity's most violent and transgressive crimes, violating individual, family, and community values. Jane Caputi, author of *The Age of Sex Crime*, observes that "unfortunately, in this culture, sex is completely interfused with violence, with notions of domination and subordination". These notions, she believes, are inextricably intertwined with our ideas of gender, noting that, ". . . our gender roles are constructed so we have these two constructed genders, masculine and feminine, that are defined by one being powerful and one being powerless. And so therefore, powerlessness and power themselves become eroticized. And in that, violence becomes eroticized".[7]

Emanuel Tanay, MD, Professor of Psychiatry, observed that entertainment and news media in effect propagandize for violence. Tanay observes, "Anything that promotes something can be called propaganda. What we call entertainment constitutes propaganda for violence". Tanay notes "If you manufacture guns, you don't need to advertise, because it is done by our entertainment industry". As for the likelihood that average people face numerous existential dangers from strangers, a common Hollywood plot, he pointedly observes, "Most homicides are committed by people who know each other, and who have some momentary conflict and have a weapon handy. Usually only hit men, who are very rare, kill strangers". However, he acknowledges that mentally ill individuals may become susceptible to dramatized violence. "They are naturally more vulnerable, because they are in the community, they are sick, and they may misinterpret something".[8]

Pornography plays a vital role in "propaganda for violence" by sexualizing, energizing, and transforming violence into something much more powerful: sexualized violence. In the 1960s and 1970s a few filmmakers began crafting violent, sexual movies organized around graphic rapes, beatings, and killings committed by thuggish villains who seemed to beg to be stopped and savagely punished. The first half of these movies depicted violent sexual attacks on an innocent victim, but in the second half they became even more graphic as half-dead victims rose, rehabilitated themselves, and ruthlessly stalked, lured, and brutally maimed and murdered their assailants. The result was a violent-laden genre like no other.

34 Revenge

The Virgin Spring (1960)

Alexandra Heller-Nicholas's critical study of rape-revenge movies reveals not only the genre's history but, even more interesting, some sense of its metaphorical meanings.[9] Drawing from thirteenth-century folklore, Swedish director Ingmar Bergman's *The Virgin Spring* (1960) pioneered rape-revenge movies. Bergman set his film in medieval Sweden at the rural home of a prosperous Christian family. The father, played by Max von Sydow, and mother (Brigitta Valberg) send their young, virginal daughter Karin (Birgitta Petterssonn) and her pregnant foster sister Ingeri (Gunnel Lindblom) on an errand to deliver candles to the local church, which lies in a village on the other side of a dense wood. Ingeri, who secretly worships the pagan Norse god Odin, harbors violent feelings of jealously toward Karin. The two young women split up while in the woods, and Ingeri implores Odin to curse Karin. Karin soon meets two traveling goat herders accompanied by a boy. She invites them to share her lunch, and the two men brutally rape and murder her while Ingeri watches in secret from the woods. The original rape scene was cut by American censors, but what remains is sufficiently chilling and nauseating. The three then leave the crime scene with Karin's clothes and strike out in the woods. That night the travelers seek shelter from Karin's parents, Töre and Märeta, not knowing who they really are. Later the guests offer Karin's dress for sale to Karin's mother. She immediately recognizes it and realizes what the proffered sale must mean. She replies, masking her horror, "I must ask my husband what a fitting reward would be for such a valuable garment". After she informs him of the proffered sale he says, "Bring the slaughtering-knife!" He then locks the three travelers inside the house and brutally butchers them, then follows Ingeri to the crime scene to recover Karin's buried body. When they lift her out of her shallow grave a spring gushes gurglingly out of the hole. Töre, heart heavy with guilt, prays to God,

> You see it, God. You see it. The innocent child's death, and my revenge. You allowed it. I don't understand You. I don't understand You. Yet, I still ask your forgiveness. I know no other way to live". He continues addressing God, "I promise You, God . . . here on the dead body of my only child, I promise you that, to cleanse my sins, here I shall build a church. On this spot, of mortar and stone, and with these, my hands.

Alexandra Heller-Nicholas believes that the themes in this film transcend rape and murder in Bergman's masterful hands. She finds that Bergman uses Karin's brutal rape as a dramatic and emotional "trigger" that provokes a battle between Karin's father's need for vengeance and the murderous demons unleashed in him by the crimes against his daughter.[10] Bergman's film remains a cult classic, famous for its graphic scenes of violence.

Revenge **35**

FIGURE 3.1 Ingmar Bergman, *The Virgin Spring*, 1960
Source: Pacific Film Archive

In this pioneering rape-revenge film youthful virgin Karin (Birgitta Pettersson) innocently shares her lunch with two goatherds and a boy while walking through the woods. The goatherds rape and murder her, then ask her parents for a night's lodging, not knowing who they really are, and attempt to sell Karin's dress to her mother. Töre (Max von Sydow), her enraged father, savagely slays the goatherds with a large knife, then builds a shrine to his daughter on the site where she was murdered.

The Last House on the Left (1972)

Renowned horror director Wes Craven attributes the inspiration for his seminal rape-revenge film, *The Last House on the Left* (1972) to his efforts toward, ". . . a blatant reworking . . ." of *The Virgin Spring's* plot. Craven explains that he became enamored of Bergman's, ". . . stunning visual sense, restraint, depth, and dark vision . . ." and inspired to create an American version of this timeless medieval legend.[11] Craven's version features two young suburban girls, Mari Collingwood (Sandra Peabody) and Phyllis Stone (Lucy Granthan), who drive to a nearby city to attend an underground rock concert. While there, a gang of escaped convicts

36 Revenge

led by Krug Stillo (David Hess) and his criminally minded girlfriend Sadie (Jaramie Rain) kidnaps them. They gang rape the two girls, then force them to urinate on themselves and have sex with each other. Finally, they murder Mari and leave Phyllis for dead in the woods. As in *The Virgin Spring*, the Krug Stillo gang spend the night at the home of Mari's parents, Dr Collingwood and his wife Estelle, not knowing who they really are. Estelle notices that one gang member, Fred "Weasel" Podowski (Fred J. Lincoln), is wearing Phyllis's peace symbol locket, and she finds blood-stained clothing in their baggage. Secretly enraged, Estelle seduces Weasel and bites off his penis, while Dr Collingwood eventually kills all the others. Roger Ebert points out, ". . . the father takes on the gang single-handedly and murders them. Does any of this sound familiar? Think for a moment. Setting aside the modern details, this is roughly the plot of Ingmar Bergman's *The Virgin Spring*". Ebert concludes that Craven's film, ". . . is a powerful narrative, told so directly and strongly that the audience (mostly in the mood for just another good old exploitation film) was rocked back on its psychic heels".[12] Craven's film, which cost approximately $90,000 to produce, earned over $13 million.[13] The stunning financial success of *The Last House on the Left* ensured that other filmmakers would follow the formula first established by Ingmar Bergman.

I Spit on Your Grave (1978)

Meir Zarchi's *I Spit on Your Grave* (1978) stunned even horror audiences with its graphic depictions of repeated rapes, beatings, dismemberments, and vengeful, violence-saturated murders. It stars nubile Camille Keaton as Jennifer Hills, a budding New York short story writer who takes up summer residence in a remote cabin on a wooded bank of a river near a small town. Upon arrival, she attracts the attention of Johnny (Eron Tabor), the local gas station owner, and his two friends Stanley (Anthony Nichols) and Andy (Gunter Kleemann). Matthew (Richard Pace), a retarded, easily manipulated youth, encounters Jennifer when delivering her grocery order. She befriends him, but to curry favor with the other men, Matthew lies to them, bragging that he saw her breasts. Intrigued, Stanley and Andy case Jennifer's cabin from their speedboat and while prowling around on the river after dark. The next day, as she floats in still water in a canoe, the men begin harassing her by yelling and speeding in their power boat around the canoe. They then pull her to shore and drag her into the woods by her arms and legs. They order Matthew, a virgin, to rape her. When he refuses, Johnny rips off her bikini and does so himself. She punches him in the face and runs into the woods, but the men quickly catch her again. This time Andy brutally sodomizes her after which the four hastily depart in the boat. Bloody and covered in dirt, Jennifer manages to crawl back to the cabin, but soon the men return. This time Matthew rapes her as the others shred her manuscript and throw the pages around the property. Jennifer passes out on the floor, covered in mud from the woods and oozing blood. At that point, Johnny, Stanley, and Andy leave as Johnny hands Matthew a knife and

Revenge **37**

orders him to stay behind and stab her to death so she can't testify against them. Matthew loses his nerve, and instead of stabbing her, he wipes some of her previously spilled blood on the knife that he uses to convince the guys that he killed her.

After Jennifer regains consciousness she cleans herself, and slowly gathers strength. Over the next two weeks as she pieces together her manuscript, she starts secretly spying on Johnny and his family. Then she orders groceries from the store, knowing that Matthew will make the delivery. When Matthew arrives, she invites him to disrobe and mount her naked body, and as he does she slips a waiting noose around his neck and hangs him to death. The next day she drives to Johnny's gas station and seductively entices Johnny to take a ride with her to the cabin. There she lures Johnny into taking a bubble bath with her, then knifes him in the groin and locks him inside the bathroom, where he bleeds to death. Stanley and Andy, alarmed by their friends' disappearances, set out in their motorboat to investigate. At the cabin, Andy disembarks with an axe with which to murder Jennifer. However, Jennifer silently climbs aboard the boat and pushes Stanley into the water. Stanley, who can't swim, cries to Andy for help, and as Andy swims towards Stanley, Jennifer takes his axe and wields it on him. The murder scene is gruesomely and graphically depicted. She then circles the boat around Stanley, echoing what the men had done to her. When Stanley begs her to spare his life, she turns off the motor and pretends to allow him to climb aboard. As he does so and nears the prop, she suddenly restarts the motor, graphically slicing the last of the threesome to death.

I Spit on Your Grave, initially marketed under the title *Day of the Woman*, enjoyed a limited release in 1978 but was re-released in 1980 to a wider audience. At the time it received scathing reviews. Roger Ebert wholeheartedly condemned it as, ". . . a vile bag of garbage". Ebert stated that the film was, ". . . so sick, reprehensible and contemptible that I can hardly believe it's playing in respectable theaters . . . . But it is. Attending it was one of the most depressing experiences of my life".[14] Despite negative reviews, critics now credit Zarchi's film with revitalizing the rape-revenge cycle, which enjoys renewed popularity today. Alexandra Heller-Nicholas argues that the 25-minute rape scene helps explain why this film became such an influential cult hit. She explains that ". . . the power of *I Spit on Your Grave* stems from its steadfast depiction of rape as ugly and terrifyingly brutal" because it "leaves us powerless . . ." and ". . . moves the onus of trying to comprehend the brutal incomprehensibility of rape firmly onto the spectator".[15]

MS.45 (1981)

MS.45 (1981), directed by Abel Ferrara, carries on the tradition of *I Spit on Your Grave* and features a meek, mute young woman named Thana (Zoe Lund), who becomes a seamstress at a small New York City clothing company. One day a frightening stranger with a sad clown mask grabs her from behind, pulls her into an alley and brutally rapes her. When she finally drags herself back to her

38 Revenge

apartment she walks into a burglary and is raped a second time. This time, when it is over, she seizes an iron fireplace tool and bludgeons her rapist to death. The next day she cuts his body into small pieces and wraps each piece in plastic before discarding them around the city. Later, she gets out of a taxi so that she can throw away another plastic bag. A grubby man retrieves it and tries to return it as an excuse to approach her. She is alarmed and runs away but he runs after her. However, he has chosen the wrong victim. She pulls out the 45-caliber handgun she had retrieved from her home-invader-rapist and empties the clip on him. Thereafter, she dresses like a prostitute each night and trolls the streets, offering herself as bait for would-be rapists. When they make hostile moves against her, she shoots them dead. Even when an entire gang surrounds her, she pulls out the pistol and guns them all down. The final scene takes place at a costume Halloween party. She arrives dressed as a nun. Her boss takes her into a back room and tries to sexually molest her but when he lifts her dress he sees the pistol strapped to her leg. She pulls it out, kills him, then begins using the gun on other predatory males at the party. Finally, she is stopped by one of her girlfriends who plunges a knife into her back. Her expression turns to shock when she realizes that she, Thana, the bane of wolf whistlers and rapists, dies at the hands of a woman.

Thelma and Louise (1991)

Ridley Scott's *Thelma and Louise* (1991) became the most popular and celebrated rape-revenge movie of its era. Scott cast Geena Davis as Thelma Dickinson, an abused and neglected wife, who impulsively embarks on a Western road trip with her best friend Louise (Susan Sarandon) in Louise's 1966 Thunderbird convertible to stay at Louise's friend's cabin. Louise is afraid of her husband Darryl (Christopher McDonald) and decides not to tell him in person but to leave a note at their house. While he is at work, she leaves and slips a pistol into her purse.

They start their vacation in a happy mood. Thelma tells Louise, "You said you 'n' me was gonna get out of town and for once just really let our hair down. Well, darlin', look out, 'cause my hair is comin' down!" After an idyllic convertible drive, Louise convinces a reluctant Thelma to stop at a country roadhouse for drinks, where they meet Harlan Puckett (Timothy Carhart). Puckett strikes up a friendly conversation and buys them drinks while blatantly flirting with Thelma. Harlan orders another drink for Thelma and invites her to dance. Once she becomes intoxicated, Harlan ushers Thelma past Louise into a dark parking lot, where he throws her over a car trunk, pulls down her panties, and tries having sex with her. When Thelma resists, Harlan violently strikes her and begins to rape her. Suddenly, Louise appears with her pistol and shouts at Harlan, "Get away from her, you fuckin' asshole, or I'm gonna splatter your ugly face all over this nice car". As Harlan dismounts Louise he protests, "Easy, we're just having a little fun". Louise shouts, "Sounds like you got a real fucked up idea of fun". She orders him to turn and face her saying, "In the future, when a woman's crying like that, she isn't having any fun!" He snaps, "Bitch, I shoulda gone ahead and fucked her!" Louise's anger reaches boiling point as she demands, "What did you say?" Harlan replies, "I said suck my cock!" At that point Louise raises the pistol, points it at Harlan, and pulls the trigger.

Louise saves and avenges Thelma, revealing unknown strength and power. She intimates that by killing Harlan, she also avenged a similar event from her past. She is cynical about the patriarchal legal system meting out vengeance for rape victims and explains to Thelma, "Who's going to believe that he was raping you when you were dancing cheek to cheek all night? We don't live in that kind of world, Thelma!" Instead of a just society where women receive equal value and respect, Thelma and Louise inhabit a patriarchal world of cheating, abusive husbands and boyfriends. Ultimately, they learn they cannot survive in a patriarchal world, so the pair commit suicide by driving over the edge of the Grand Canyon.

Stir of Echoes (1999)

David Koepp's *Stir of Echoes* (1999) melded elements of supernatural horror with the familiar rape-revenge archetype. Based on a novel by cult horror author Richard Matheson (famed for *I am Legend*, 1954), protagonist Tom Witzky (Kevin Bacon) begins experiencing the ghostly apparition of a 17-year old young woman named Samantha Kozac (Jennifer Morrison). After learning that a young girl disappeared in his urban neighborhood, Tom uncovers the bricked-in grave of a woman. The discovery triggers a vivid vision of Samantha lured into the abandoned house, then brutally raped and murdered by the teenage sons of some of his neighborhood friends. When Tom confronts their fathers with these charges, they threaten to silence him and his wife Maggie (Kathryn Erbe). The men attempt to murder the couple as threatened, but one of them hesitates, filled with remorse, and turns on his accomplices, killing them and freeing Tom and Maggie. As they drive away, Tom's young son, who possesses psychic abilities, hears voices from the houses they pass, as if every house possesses macabre secrets. In the end, Tom spies a healthy, beautiful Samantha walking briskly along before disappearing into another dimension, presumably better than her hidden grave. Alexandra Heller-Nicholas observes, "Tom has brought Samantha justice and freed her spirit, but to do so Samantha found it necessary to show him rape through her own eyes and make him understand what it *felt* like".[16]

Kill Bill Vol. 1 and 2 (2003–2004)

Quentin Tarantino's iconic *Kill Bill Vol. 1 and 2* (2003–2004) chronicle the elaborate and violent revenge that The Bride (Uma Thurman) metes out against Bill (David Carradine), her former boss and lover. The title card reads, "Revenge is a dish best served cold. Old Klingon proverb". Bill heads a deadly assassination team called the Deadly Viper Assassination Squad which he has unleashed against

40 Revenge

The Bride, who dressed in a wedding dress expecting to marry Bill, is instead ambushed and violently attacked by his gang. Bill speaks the film's first lines by asking The Bride as he points a gun to her head,

> "Do you find me sadistic? You know, I bet I could fry an egg on your head right now, if I wanted to. You know, Kiddo, I'd like to believe that you're aware enough even now to know that there's nothing sadistic in my actions. Well, maybe towards those other . . . jokers, but not you. No Kiddo, at this moment, this is me at my most . . . "

[cocks pistol]

Bill: "masochistic"
The Bride: "Bill . . . it's your baby"

[BLAM! He shoots her in the head.]

She goes into a deep coma, awakening four years later in a hospital bed. She feigns sleep as two men enter her room. She hears Buck (Michael Bowen), an orderly, tell a large truck driver (Jonathan Loughran) if he pays Buck $75, he can do whatever he wants with her supposedly comatose body except make any marks on her body or. He pays Buck who leaves the room then eagerly mounts The Bride and begins to kiss her. She suddenly springs to life, biting him and severing his lower lip, leaving him unconscious and bleeding profusely. She attempts to climb out of bed but four years in a coma have left her legs powerless. She hears approaching footsteps and crawls behind the door as Buck enters. She slashes Buck's heel, causing him to fall. At that point she grabs his head, drags him toward the door, and begins slamming the door into his head while demanding he reveal Bill's whereabouts. Stunned by the blows and badly shaken, he replies that he does not know Bill. The Bride then recalls something he said four years earlier after she arrived unconscious at his hospital, "Well, ain't you the little slice of cutie pie they said you were. 'Jane Doe', huh? Well, we don't know shit about you, huh? Well, I'm from Huntsville, Texas. My name is Buck, and I'm here to fuck, ha-ha-ha". Back in the present she gently asks him, "Your name is Buck, right?" His eyes widen. She says, with rising anger, "And you came to fuck, right?" Frightened, he replies, "Wait a minute, WAIT a minute!" With that she smashes the door powerfully into his head, instantly killing him.

The Bride embarks on a mission to revenge herself against the members of the Viper Squad. She targets Vernita Green (Vivica A. Fox), otherwise known as Copperhead, who says, "I suppose it's a little late for an apology, huh?" The Bride replies, "You suppose correctly". Vernita admits, "Look. I know I fucked you over. I fucked you over bad. I wish to God I hadn't, but I did. You have every right to want to get even". The Bride replies,

> "No, no, no, no, no. No, to get even, even-Steven . . . I would have to kill you . . . go up to Nikki's [her little girl] room, kill her . . . then wait for

FIGURE 3.2 Quentin Tarantino, *Kill Bill vol. 2* (2004)
Source: Pacific Film Archive

your husband, the good Dr. Bell, to come home and kill him. That would be even, Vernita. That'd be about square".

The Bride (Uma Thurman), AKA The Black Mamba, sets out for vengeance against former Deadly Viper Assassination Squad colleagues who abused and attempted to kill her, including Bill (David Carradine), AKA Snake charmer, her traitorous mentor and former lover, Bill's brother Budd (Michael Masden), AKA Sidewinder, and Elle Driver (Daryl Hannah), AKA California Mountain Snake.

Feminist or Misogynist

Some classify classic rape-revenge thrillers like *I Spit on your Grave* and *Ms. 45* as "feminist". Critic Charles Bramesco believes that, "Grindhouse artifacts like *Ms. 45* and *I Spit on your Grave* behave like superhero movies . . .". The rapes and beatings inflicted upon Jennifer and Thana transform them into "the hyper-violent avenging angel[s] that the pervasive ubiquity of lecherous male sexuality demands".[17] By contrast, critic Hilary Neroni argues that the basic plot of female rape victims lashing out at misogynistic males ". . . does not mean, of course, that these films were feminist projects". More probably audiences (typically teenage boys) felt drawn to the "male fantasies of women being beaten and tortured, followed by the masochistic fantasy of the torturers being tortured in return".[18] These films were designed to elicit sympathy for the victims and anger toward the rapists, in other words, they focus on voyeurism and sadomasochistic rage.

42 Revenge

Critic Noah Berlatsky notes that although 1970s' and 1980s' critics like Roger Ebert, Mike Martin, and Marsha Porter hated the revenge porn films when they first appeared, contemporary critics validate these films as feminist-friendly. Berlatsky states,

> "The antipathy to *I Spit on Your Grave*, and to rape-revenge more generally, focuses on the gruesome depiction of rape, and graphic depictions of revenge, frequently involving castration and severed genitals. The genre revels not just in images of violence in general, but in images of sexualized violence, particularly against women".

However, ". . . there is terrifying violation, and then there is revenge you can feel good about. The films use women's trauma to justify stereotypically male pleasures of hyperbolic violence". Female heroines avenging thuggish male brutality may appeal to the same audiences who enjoyed the rape scenes. They might enjoy the revenge scenes even more because of righteous indignation against hyper-villainous males. Berlatsky concludes that ". . . rape-revenge fits feminism into male genre narratives that Hollywood can embrace".[19]

Melissa Hugel maintains that *Kill Bill* conforms to an unstated rule that a woman must fear a man before she can defeat him. Hugel asks if films like *Kill Bill* function as feminist, as many contend, or rather function as misogyny in disguise. Hugel believes that *Kill Bill* and the other rape-revenge thrillers, ". . . do not depict the reality of how these assaults can affect women". Instead of offering realistic depictions of rape-induced injury and trauma, ". . . they look to fetishize the act and use it as motivation for unabashed gore and violence". Hugel laments, " . . . what should be empowering films featuring women rising out of past trauma to exact justice are often instead turned into a form of torture porn".[20]

Hugel points out similarities (and differences) between rape-revenge and torture porn. Some hard-core porn sites, including *Heavy-R*, feature rape videos as well as torture porn. *Heavy-R* features "fisting, hardcore, bridal shower gang rape (like *Kill Bill*), humiliation, lesbian, old vs young, pissing, poop, shemale, and young".[21] Another popular site, *PornHub* even, includes a "tickling revenge porn" video section.[22]

Taken (2008)

Not all rape-revenge films feature females as avengers. *Taken* (2008), directed by Pierre Morel, begins with, "They took his daughter. He'll take their lives". Set in Paris, this rape-revenge film stars Liam Neesom as Bryan, a retired intelligence agent and highly trained commando, who finds himself under pressure from his ex-wife Lenore (Famke Janssen) to sign a Parental Consent Form to allow Kim (Maggie Grace), their 17-year-old daughter, to go to Paris with her 17-year-old girlfriend Amanda (Katie Cassidy) and stay with Amanda's cousins. Kim promises to use her time in the city to visit museums. Upon taking Kim to the airport, Bryan sees a European map with several cities in various countries circled. Angered, he confronts Lenore, who admits that the girls secretly plan to follow their favorite rock band, U2, on their European tour.

Revenge **43**

Learning Kim's true intensions, Bryan explodes and fears for both girls' safety. His fears prove well-founded as he telephones Kim in Paris just as two men enter the apartment and carry Amanda away, kicking and struggling. Bryan instructs Kim to hide under a bed and keep her phone turned on so he can hear everything. One of the thugs suddenly pulls Amanda out from under the bed, and she shouts, as per instructions, a physical description of her kidnapper,

> "Beard! Six feet! Tattoo! Right hand, Moon and Star". A silence follows, and Bryan hears heavy breathing on the phone and says "I don't know who you are. I don't know what you want. If you are looking for ransom, I can tell you I don't have money. But what I do have is a very particular set of skills; skills I have acquired over a very long career. Skills that make me a nightmare for people like you. If you let my daughter go now, that'll be the end of it. I will not look for you, I will not pursue you. But if you don't, I will look for you, I will find you, and I will kill you". The assailant replies, "Good luck".

Bryan immediately confronts Lenore and her billionaire husband Stuart (Xander Berkeley) and informs them of the girls' kidnapping demanding that Stuart provide him with a private jet to Paris that leaves, ". . . one hour ago". Stuart complies. Upon landing Bryan seeks out a former French Intelligence colleague who directs him to the Albanian community where Kim was probably taken. After many violent scenes in which he shoots, punches, and electrocutes Albanian thugs, Bryan eventually captures Marko (Arben Bajraktaraj), boss of the kidnapping/sex slavery gang. He demands to know Kim's whereabouts, but Marko refuses to cooperate. Bryan begins preparing Marko for torture by electrocution and threatening him:

You know, we used to outsource this kind of thing. But what we found was the countries we outsourced to had unreliable power grids. Very Third World. You'd turn on a switch—power wouldn't come on, and then tempers would get short. People would resort to pulling fingernails. Acid drips on bare skin. The whole exercise would become counterproductive. But here, the power's stable. Here, there's a nice even flow. Here, you can flip a switch and the power stays on all day. Where is she?' Bryan increases the voltage, and after Marko passes out, he punches him in the face and stabs metal rods into his legs, exclaiming, "Wake up! I need you to be focused! Are you focused yet?"

Even after Marko collapses and confesses to Bryan that he has sold Kim to a man named Saint Clair, Bryan turns the power back on, leaving Marko screaming in agony. He assumes an ultra-sadistic role, while Marko provides the masochistic counterpart. This sadomasochistic dichotomy reappears in other scenes. In one, Bryan shoots his corrupt friend Jean-Claude's wife Isabelle in the arm and warns Jean-Claude "It's just a flesh wound, but if you don't get me what I need the last thing you'll see before I make your children orphans is the bullet I put between her eyes!" At that point Jean-Claude frantically searches for and finds the information Bryan demands. Bryan will face a final adversary before discovering Kim on a yacht about to be raped by a man in Arab dress. The man does not immediately

44 Revenge

release Kim and asks Byron to negotiate. In reply, Byron shoots and kills him. *Taken* received a PG-13 rating for intense sequences of violence, disturbing thematic material, sexual content, some drug references and the use of bad language. Despite the slightly restrictive rating, *Taken* became a runaway blockbuster and airline/hotel room favorite, earning an impressive $226 million on a production budget of only $25 million.[23]

Taken provides a more paternalistic, mainstream version of the earlier rape-revenge trope. Instead of Kim serving as avenger, her father exacts graphically brutal vengeance on her thuggish attackers. In one scene Bryan brutally and efficiently dispatches an Arab sheik mounting his daughter. The act of rescuing her from a vast criminal underground transforms him into an ultra-violent killing machine, displaying his advanced commando-style training. This film inspired two sequels, *Taken 2* (2012) and *Taken 3* (2015), which also received PG-13 ratings. The sequels become even more violent than the original version, prompting *The Washington Post* movie critic Cecelia Kang to observe "The violent *Taken* movies are Rated PG-13. Do movie ratings make sense anymore?"[24]

Rape-Revenge on Television

On November 16, 2016, a new rape-revenge television series premiered titled *Sweet/Vicious*. This *MTV* series, created and scripted by Jennifer Kaytin Robinson, depicts two college students, Jules (Eliza Bennett) and Ophelia (Taylor Dearden), who transform into offbeat vigilantes wreaking revenge for rapes and other sexual assaults committed by a few of their classmates. Their joint mission begins after Ophelia discovers Jules, disguised in a hoodie, beating and kicking a rapist, she asks to join her in her mission to mete out justice for sex offenders, but Jules declares "I work alone". She explains to Ophelia "I know how to do things most people don't. There is stuff happening out there, and no one is doing anything about it. People are just getting away with awful things. I'm trying to make some of that right". Ophelia responds, "That's the plot of Batman".

Robinson wrote the original pilot in 2014, and later realized it only became more relevant recently. She admits: ". . . it's not that the cause is getting worse, it's always been bad. It's just that now we have people talking about it and fighting for it, which is great". She became interested in creating a series about sexual assault because of her own experiences in the male-dominated entertainment industry, explaining that,

> "I really hope that this show, and also just the amount of people—men and women alike—who are coming out and saying that this is not okay, shows and educates younger generations that none of it is okay, it should never be normalized, and you should always speak out against it".[25]

Critic Amanda Hess believes that Robinson's series ". . . may be television's first campus-rape buddy comedy". Hess observes, ". . . the show's more serious statements emerge at the margins of its violent plots". Robinson's show also takes some

Online Revenge Porn

A new form of revenge porn came into existence in recent years as intimate partners began exchanging nude selfies online. However, once intimate relationships end the temptation often arises for the injured or jilted partner to post those intimate photos and videos, taken in the heat of passion, to social media sites which allow the posting of unauthorized photos and videos. The definition of "revenge porn" is, ". . . the publication of explicit material portraying someone who has not consented for the image or video to be shared. The law now makes it illegal to disclose a 'private sexual photograph or film' without the consent of the person depicted in the content, and with the intent to cause them distress".[27] The practice of besmirching an ex-lover's reputation through revenge porn is now outlawed in 43 US states and the District of Columbia as the issue continues to receive global media exposure.

The first recorded instance of revenge porn occurred in 1980 when *Hustler* magazine featured a "Beaver Hunt", publishing nude photos of women including at least one unwilling and unknown victim. Those photos, taken by her husband during a camping trip, were later stolen. Alongside the images, *Hustler* claimed the unnamed woman loved collecting arrowheads (true) and craved being "screwed by two bikers" (false). In 2000, Italian researcher Sergio Messina identified and named *"real core pornography"*—photos and videos of ex-girlfriends initially shared in Usenet groups.[28] By 2016, revenge porn ranked among the most popular internet searches. That same year, Merriam Webster added "revenge porn" to its lexicon, defining it as, "Sexually explicit images of a person posted online without that person's consent especially as a form of revenge or harassment".[29]

In 2008, the porn site *XTube*, which compiles previously posted pornography, began receiving reports alleging pornographic content had been posted without the subjects' consent.[30] In 2010, Hunter Moore launched the website: *IsAnyoneUP* featuring user-submitted pornography. It became an early revenge porn site. Moore published compromising photos and videos mostly of women but also of men, posted by ex-boyfriends or, in some cases, ex-girlfriends, all aiming to humiliate and shame their ex-partners. Along with the unauthorized visuals, Moore also published victims' names, addresses, employers, and social media links. Moore soon earned the title of "Most Hated Man on the Internet" by a BBC reporter. Moore claimed his website was perfectly legal, and that he was merely publishing, ". . . user generated content". He boasted that he was a, ". . . professional life ruiner . . ." while comparing himself to Charles Manson. Followers of Moore's website often refer to themselves as "the family", presumably after the Manson family. Before the site was shut down, Moore fans routinely posted comments on it about the porn victims, often calling them "sluts" and "cunts", characterizing

46 Revenge

them as, ". . . sex-crazed hos who loved gang banging and were addicted to group sex". Countless victims lost their jobs and suffered damaged relationships. Some even committed suicide after suffering humiliation and shame due directly to internet revenge porn.[31]

After Moore posted topless photos of social activist/politician Charlotte Laws' daughter, Laws launched an investigation of the Sacramento porn king, collecting testimony from numerous victims. Laws condemned revenge porn as, ". . . pure misogyny. It's about hating women. It's about hurting them. That was the sole purpose of the site".[32] She turned over her evidence to prosecutors, who then launched their own investigation. In December 2015, Moore was convicted and sentenced to 30 months in prison and levied a $2,000 fine. More importantly, Moore was sentenced to three years' probation, during which time he was to submit every internet comment to his probation officer before posting.[33] Considering the harm done to victims of Moore's website, his sentence may appear to be light. It was, however, significantly longer than former Congressman Anthony Weiner's sentence of 21 months, received in 2017 for texting photos of himself wearing only underwear to a fifteen-year-old girl.

Anti-Revenge Porn Laws

California ranks among 43 US states and the District of Columbia which have anti-revenge porn laws. Currently many foreign countries enforce anti-revenge porn laws. In July 2016 US Representative Jackie Speier (D-California) introduced the Intimate Privacy Protection Act that would mandate prison terms of up to five years for persons convicted of maliciously posting or hacking intimate content without consent. Speier's legislation would add intimate privacy protection to those in states without such laws.[34]

New Jersey became the first state to pass a revenge porn law, legally called the "non-consensual-porn law" in 2004. Posting intimate photos or videos of someone else without their consent need not be an act of revenge. People have surreptitiously filmed consensual sex acts, and rapes, and then decided to make the footage available on the internet. The law makes it a crime for any person to post, ". . . any photograph, film, videotape, recording or any other reproduction of the image of another person whose intimate parts are exposed or who is engaged in an act of sexual penetration or sexual contact . . ." unless the other person, ". . . has consented to such a disclosure . . .". Sometimes people have obtained sensitive, personal material by hacking into an iCloud account, as happened in 2014 to actress Jennifer Lawrence when someone in Pennsylvania posted nude photos of her. In November 2016 a Pennsylvania judge sentenced one of Lawrence's hackers to 18 months in jail after she sued him under Pennsylvania's non-consensual pornography statute. Lawrence was represented in court by Carrie Goldberg, one of a new breed of lawyers specializing in representing victims of non-consensual porn.[35]

Revenge **47**

In response to recent outlawing of revenge porn, in 2015 Google began offering information to anyone who had had their intimate photos and/or videos posted on Google without consent. In an article titled, "Remove 'revenge porn' from Google", the popular search engine advised, "We only remove image or video that meets our requirements: You are nude or shown in a sexual act; the content was intended to be private; you never consented to the content being publicly available". Google further stated, "While we can prevent a page from appearing in our search results, we are not able to remove content from websites that host it, so we recommend reaching out to the webmaster for the site to request removal first". Google included a form for victims of revenge porn to use when requesting removal of a link to revenge porn.[36] Another organization called Cyber Civil Rights Initiative published an online guide to revenge porn removal.[37]

In May 2016 Minnesota Governor Mark Dayton signed the revenge porn bill, and Minnesota joined the other US states that had enacted revenge porn laws. The "intent to harass" clause does not appear in the final version after vigorous opposition to its inclusion grew, strengthened by the Cyber Civil Rights Initiative report assuring that, "This bill cannot plausibly be read as a threat to the distribution of constitutionally protected material of legitimate interest to the public".[38]

In March 2017 hundreds of unauthorized nude, semi-nude, and otherwise obscene photographs of more than two dozen female marines, along with their names, ranks, and contact information, appeared on a secret Facebook page with a Google Drive link. The unauthorized photos, along with obscene comments about several of the women, appeared to a special male only group on *Marines United*'s website, an organization of active and retired men from the Marine Corps, Navy Corpsman, and British Royal Marines, boasting over 30,000 members. The photos appeared with an appeal for more unauthorized, sexually explicit photos of Marine Corps females and often calling for sexually assaulting the victims. Following the protests flooding Facebook and Google Drive, officials promptly took down the photographs.

The Navy launched investigations as Marine Corps Commandant General Robert B. Neller condemned the postings as, "distasteful . . ." and revealing, "lack of respect".[39] However, during a Senate hearing in March 2017, General Neller came under fire by female Senators due to the Marine Corps' inaction on gender issues. New Hampshire Senator Jeanne Shaheen (D) challenged Neller, stating, "It's hard to believe something is really going to be done". Because of recent Marine Corps' effort to exempt female arines from combat roles, "Why should we believe it's going to be different this time than it has in the past?" New York Senator Kirsten Gillibrand (D) rejoined when Neller promised that the Marine Corps will change, "When you say it's got to be different, that rings hollow".[40]

After the story broke, members of *Marines United* began forming other revenge porn sites and began posting photos directly to those sites. Marine Veteran Thomas Brennan, who helms a non-profit internet group called The War Horse, became the first to expose *Marines United* immediately after discovering the

48 Revenge

revenge porn site. In retaliation for exposing the site, Brennan and his immediate family received numerous death threats. Per one member of *Marines United*, "They can investigate all they want, it's not illegal to share nudes lol". The writer appears unaware of the 34 US states and the District of Columbia that enforce anti-revenge porn laws.[41]

In July 2017, actor Rob Kardashian allegedly posted nude photos of his former fiancée Blanc Chyna online without her consent. Lawyer Lisa Bloom, who recently won a revenge porn case involving actress Mischa Barton, believes that Kardashian's actions violated California's 2013 revenge porn law criminalizing individuals that post "intimate body parts of another identifiable person, or an image of that person engaged in sexual intercourse, sodomy, oral copulation or masturbation" without the victim's consent.[42]

Revenge porn internet sites function as part of the "manosphere", an informal assemblage of often disparate men's rights websites. The men's rights movement is often attributed to Warren Ferrell (*The Myth of Male Power*), who takes a sharply divergent approach to men's issues than earlier, more supportive approaches during the 1990s by poet Robert Bly ("mythopoetic men's movement"). Instead of mythopoetry, Farrell exhorts males to rise in rebellion against female hegemony fostered by the various feminist movements. Males desperately need to organize against feminist power because, "In America and in most of the industrialized world, men are coming to be thought of by feminists in very much the same way that Jews were thought of by early Nazis. The comparison is overwhelmingly scary".[43] The manosphere also includes *Register-Her.com*, a self-described, ". . . offender registry that punishes females falsely reporting rape by listing them, attaching photos, and sometimes, their contact information". Paul Elam, founder of *Register-Her.com*, explains that he created the service to assist males falsely accused of rape. According to him, males falsely accused of rape over 40% of the time are, ". . . immediately presumed guilty by society. They are publicly vilified while their accuser's identity is protected. When allegations are proven false, it's far too late: the damage has already been done. For the accuser there is rarely any downside risk".[44]

Copyright Infringement

Revenge porn began to dominate the media in January 2018, after a sitting governor was indicted for the crime. Missouri Governor Eric Greitens, married with children, had recently won an election as a "family values" Republican. However, an extramarital affair with his former hair stylist emerged in which Greitens allegedly photographed his former stylist, a woman, blindfolded and hands bound, without her knowledge on March 21, 2015. He then threatened her with release of the explicit photograph if she leaked any details of their relationship to the press. Per the victim's ex-husband, his ex-wife told him Greitens, ". . . used some sort of tape, I don't know what it was, and taped my hands to these rings and then put a blindfold on me . . . I didn't even know. I feel like I don't even know. I was just numb". Although Greitens denied the revenge porn charge, he admitted the couple engaged in a "consensual relationship". Circuit Attorney Kim Gardner announced that "The Grand Jury has found probable cause to believe that Governor Greitens violated Missouri State Statute 565.252, which was in place at the time of the violation". As Gardner explained of the indictment, "this statute has a provision for both a felony and misdemeanor". Because the photo was taken, "in a place where a person would have a reasonable expectation of privacy, and the defendant subsequently transmitted the image contained in the photograph in a manner that allowed access to that image via a computer", Greitens was charged with a felony.[45] Greitens' revenge porn case threatened to upend Missouri's political makeup, possibly assisting US Senator Claire McCaskill's (D) reelection campaign in normally Republican-dominated Missouri. She remarked that Greitens boasted at one point that he, ". . . was going to do things that literally no other governor had ever done . . . Little did we know it was sex in the basement".[46] Greitens resigned May 2018 after a legislative investigation found him guilty of being implicated in a scandal involving a sexual relationship with his former hair stylist for over four months and claims that he had taken an explicit photograph of her without her permission. He was also accused by prosecutors of misusing his charity's donor list for political purposes.[47]

Kaitlan Lynn Folderaur observes that copyright law provides "a more lucrative and reliable avenue for revenge porn victims to seek redress against their perpetrators and can also provide a substantial deterrent against those who would otherwise face little or no repercussions for their act of revenge and bullying". She added that victims seeking redress and restitution still face daunting challenges because the must prove monetary losses from copyright infringement on what are usually unregistered photos and videos.[48]

Most ethical, moral, and legal problems concerning revenge porn involve the granting of consent. Julia Chan reminds us that consent is critical to the issue of revenge porn. Chan applies the issue of consent to "upskirt" photography, in which males voyeuristically photograph a woman's crotch from inside her skirt using hidden cameras in their shoes. In 2018 a clothes designer employed a professionally taken upskirt shot to emphasize the manufacturer's undergarments. The advertisement evoked controversy from those who believed the provocative photo promoted surreptitious upskirting, which has been perceived as sexual violence.[49]

The first women to stand up against revenge porn (Charlette Laws, Jackie Spier) were quickly joined by many others, as well as by sympathetic men. Their successful efforts to enact legislation criminalizing unauthorized posting of intimate photos and other materials foreshadowed the previously unimaginable popularity of the #Metoo movement. Confronting and opposing male sexual violence has become the latest, and perhaps the most powerful, form of feminism.

50 Revenge

Sexting—Sending Sexually Explicit Images

The "smart phone revolution" places high quality cameras in everyone's hands and has enabled sexting and revenge porn. Researcher Holly Jacobs discovered that over half (53%) of heterosexual respondents admitted to having shared a nude or otherwise sexually explicit photo with someone else, and 75% of LGBT respondents had done so. A 2012 study of males and females active on *Match.com* revealed that 57% of males and 45% of females had received an intimate image on their mobile phones Moreover, 22% of heterosexual respondents and over 23% of LGBTQ respondents reported having been victimized by non-consensual "revenge porn".[50]

Currently, twenty US states have legal limitations on sexting in place. Perhaps the most transgressive issue involving sending and receiving sexually intimate photos and videos involves forwarding without consent. Non-consensual sharing of sexts occurs at alarming rates. A recent study by Kinsey Institute professor/researcher Justin Garcia, revealed that 20% of social media users send sexts. Even though 73% of senders expected their sexts to remain private, nearly 25% of those receiving sexts report they have been forwarded to at least one and often multiple respondents. Garcia observed that "As sexting becomes more common and normative, we're seeing a contemporary struggle as men and women attempt to reconcile digital eroticism with real-world consequences".[51]

With smart phones available to large segments of the public, issues surrounding sexting proliferate. One problem involved teenagers sexting each other. Police in Mountain View, California, opened an investigation in 2016 into an alleged scheme in which high school students exchanged nude photos of female students using a shared Dropbox account that apparently spanned several schools in the San Francisco Bay Area. A "handful of students", all minors, became the subject of the police investigation. The police froze the Dropbox account to prevent students from sharing existing nude photos or uploading new ones. None of the students in the nude-sharing case were in romantic relationships with each other, and authorities were not certain how the nude photos were obtained. It seems certain, however, that they were not obtained with the consent of the subjects involved.[52]

Criminal sexual violence results or may result from revenge porn. The intended victims are usually ex-girlfriends, and occasionally ex-boyfriends. Those posting revenge porn hope to elicit mental anguish in their victims, but probably underestimate the extent of the damage. Females constitute over 90% of revenge porn victims, and many of these victims commit suicide. A recent study found that 51% of revenge porn victims contemplate suicide.[53] Sexting, like revenge porn, may wreak havoc with one's reputation, family, and career.

Displaced Revenge

In 2014 psychologists Arne Sjöström and Mario Gollwitzer published surprising results of their clinical study of displaced revenge showing transgressors who suffered real or imagined abuse from an individual or a group enjoy satisfying "sweetness" feelings after exacting vengeance on a member or members of that group, even those deemed innocent of offenses. These are acts of "displaced revenge" or "vicarious retribution". The authors define displaced revenge ". . . retributive reactions toward prior transgressions that are not directed against the original transgressor(s), but rather against uninvolved targets". Displaced revenge represents an aspect of "group-based retribution", which refers to, ". . . cycles of vengeful acts committed by members of two (or more) opposing groups".[54] Displaced revenge seems ubiquitous in the current digital culture, but some scholars have pushed back against this tendency. Edward Said, in *Orientalism*, his seminal study of anti-Asian stereotyping, warns "You cannot continue to victimize someone else just because you yourself were a victim once—there has to be a limit".[55] Said was referring to the Israel-Palestinian at the time, although his remarks can apply to any majority/minority conflict.

Displaced revenge helps explain the widespread appeal of rape-revenge thrillers. Classics like *I Spit on your Grave*, *MS. 45*, *The Last House on the Left*, and *Kill Bill* provide attractive heroes who recover, train, and enact devastating revenge on male rapists and female accomplices, vengeance that many feminists and feminist supporters, both male and female, apparently enjoyed watching. Audiences identifying with the victims of sexual violence experience "sweetness" emotions upon viewing the adversaries receiving their just rewards.

Revenge porn's ultimate attraction lies in its promise of redressing real or imagined grievances, of righting ancient gender injustices. Revenge porn victims transform into vengeance-wielding superheroes, symbolic substitutes for disliked or disadvantaged groups. Like all violent pornography, revenge porn revolves around a struggle between villains and victims, dominants and submissives, advocates and skeptics. It helps enable formerly submissive groups to unite in powerful social movements like #MeToo and other anti-sexual violence movements currently in ascendency.

Notes

1. In Michael Price, "Revenge and the People Who Seek It," *Monitor*, vol. 40 no. 6, June 2009, p. 34.
2. I.R. McKee and Norman T. Feather, "Revenge, Retribution, and Values: Social Values and Punitive Sentencing," *Soc Just Res*, vol. 21, 2008, p. 138. doi: 10.1007/s11211-008-0066-z.
3. Friedrich Nietzsche, *Human, All Too Human: A Book for Free Spirits*. Cambridge: Cambridge University Press, 1996.
4. Douglas Horton, "While Seeking Revenge, Dig Two Graves," https://www.brainyquote. com/quotes/dougla_horton_
5. https://www.brainyquote.com/quotes/jane_goldman_
6. S.L. Bloom, "Commentary: Reflections on the Desire for Revenge," *Journal of Emotional Abuse*, vol. 2, no. 4, 2001, pp. 61–94.
7. Interview: Jane Caputi, "No Safe Place: Violence Against Women," *PBS*, www.pbs. org/kued/nosafeplace/interv/caputi.html.
8. Arline Kapline, "Violence in the Media: What Effects on Behavior," *Psychiatric Times*, October 5, 2012.
9. Alexandra Heller-Nicholas, *Rape-Revenge Films: A Critical Study*. Jefferson, NC: McFarland & Company, 2011, pp. 2–3.
10. *Ibid.*

52 Revenge

11. Wes Craven, "10 Movies That Shook Me up," *Entertainment*, October 26, 2009, www.ew.com/ew/gallery/0,,20310838_20314742_20694520,00.html accessed December 15, 2016.
12. Roger Ebert, "The Last House on the Left," *Roger Ebert.com*, January 1, 1972.
13. The Last House on the Left (1972)-Box office / business.
14. Roger Ebert, "I Spit on Your Grave," *Roger Ebert.com*, July 15, 1980.
15. Alexandra Heller-Nicholas, *Rape-Revenge Films: A Critical Study*. Jefferson, NC: McFarland & Company, 2011, p. 16.
16. *Ibid.*, p. 77.
17. Charles Bramesco, "Bound to Vengeance," *The Dissolve*, June 24, 2015.
18. Hilary Neroni, *The Violent Woman: Femininity, Narrative, and Violence in Contemporary American Cinema*. Albany, NY: State University of New York Press, 2005, p. 171.
19. Noah Berlatsky, "The Rape-Revenge Genre's Gender Revelations," *The Establishment*, December 29, 2015.
20. Melissa Hugel, "*Kill Bill* and Our Troubled Relationship with Rape-Revenge Movies," *Arts.Mic*, October 15, 2013, mic.com/articles/67263 accessed December 9, 2016.
21. Melissa Hugel, "Kill Bill and Our Troubled Relationship With Rape Revenge Movies", *MC* October 15, 2013, www.heavy-r.com/free_porn/rape-forced-punish-reven accessed December 9, 2016.
22. www.pornhub.com/video/search?search=tickling+reven accessed April 24, 2019.
23. Taken, "Box Office Mojo," 2009, https://www.boxofficemojo.com/movies/?id=taken.htm accessed April 24, 2019.
24. *The Washington Post*, October 20, 2014.
25. Christina Radish, "'*Sweet/Vicious*' Creator Jennifer Kaytin Robinson on How the Sexual Assault Series Landed on MTV," *Collider*, December 6, 2016.
26. Amanda Hess, "Rape, Revenge and How We Watch," *The New York Times*, January 15, 2017.
27. David Barrett, "What Is the Law on Revenge Porn," *The Telegraph*, April 13, 2015.
28. Alexa Tsoulis-Reay, "A Brief History of Revenge Porn," *New York Magazine,* July 21, 2013.
29. Revenge porn, https://www.merriam-webster.com/dictionary/revenge porn accessed April 24, 2019.
30. Alexa Tsoulis-Reay, "A Brief History of Revenge Porn," *New York Magazine*, July 21, 2013.
31. Carol Cadwalladr, "Charlotte Law's Fight with Hunter Moore, the Internet's Revenge Porn King," *The Guardian*, March 30, 2014.
32. *Ibid.*
33. Lizzie Plaugic, "Revenge Porn Website Operator Hunter Moore Sentenced to 30 Years in Prison," *The Verge*, December 3, 2015.
34. Steve Nelson, "Lawmakers Unveil Proposal to Take Nip Out of Revenge Porn," *US News and World Report*, July 14, 2016.
35. Margaret Talbot, "Taking Trolls to Court," *The New Yorker*, December 5, 2016.
36. https://support.google.com/websearch/answer/6302812?hl=en accessed April 24, 2019.
37. www.cybercivilrights.org/online-removal/ accessed April 24, 2019.
38. Kevin Collier, "Why Hollywood Wants Revenge Porn to Stay Legal," *Vocativ*, March 29, 2016.
39. Jesse J. Holland, "NCIS Investigating Posting of Nude Photographs of Female Marines," *Associated Press*, March 6, 2017.
40. Lolita C. Baldor, "Marine Leaders Vow to Combat Online Nude Photo Sharing," *Daily Herald*, March 14, 2017.
41. Lydia O'Conner, "Marines' Nude Photo Scandal Goes Beyond That One Group," *The Huffington Post*, March 9, 2017.

42. Nancy Dillon and Peter Sblendorio, "Rob Kardashian Could Face Jail Time for Blanc Chyna Revenge Porn Pics Under California Law," *Daily News Entertainment*, July 5, 2017.
43. Steven Svoboda, "An Interview With Warren Farrell," http://www.menweb.org/svofarre.htm accessed April 24, 2019, www.brainyquote.com/quotes/authors/w/warren_farrell.html.
44. Paul Elam, "Register-Her.com Goes Worldwide," *M: A Voice for Men*, September 13, 2011.
45. Sophia Tesvaye, "Missouri's GOP Governor Indicted in Revenge Porn Blackmail Scheme," *Salon*, February 22, 2018.
46. Max Londberg and Laura Bauer, "It Was Sex in the Basement, McCaskill Lampoons Greitens at Democratic Event," *The Kansas City Star*, January 27, 2018.
47. Mitch Smith and Julie Boseman, "Republican Governor: A Rising GOP Star, Resigns Amidst Scandal," *The New York Times*, May 29, 2018.
48. Kaitlan M. Folderaurer, "Not All Is Fair (Use) in Love and War: Copyright Law and Revenge Porn," *University of Baltimore Law Review*, vol. 44, no. 2, 2015, Article 5, https://scholarworks.law.ubalt.edu/ublr/vol44/iss2/5
49. Julia Chan, "Violence or Pleasure? Surveillance and the (Non-) Consensual Upskirt," *Porn Studies*, October 2017.
50. Derek E. Baumbauer, "Exposed," *Minnesota Law Review*, June 2014.
51. "Despite Expectations of Privacy, One in Four Share Sexts, Study Finds," *Science-Daily*, August 4, 2016, www.sciencedaily.com/releases/2016/08/160804141036.htm accessed April 24, 2019.
52. Robert D. Salonga and Sharon Noguchi, "Police Investigating Nude Picture-Sharing Scheme," *The Bay Area News Group*, December 13, 2016.
53. "51% Have Suicidal Thoughts as a Result of Being a Victim of Porn Revenge," *Sachtimes*, March 8, 2016.
54. Arne Sjöström and Mario Gollwitzer, "Displaced Revenge: Can Revenge Taste 'Sweet' If It Aims at a Different Target?" *Journal of Experimental Social Psychology*, vol. 56, 2015, pp. 191–202.
55. Edward W. Said, *Orientalism*, New York: Pantheon Books, 1978.

Bibliography

Baldor, Lolita C., "Marine Leaders Vow to Combat Online Nude Photo Sharing," *Daily Herald*, March 14, 2017.
Barrett, David, "What Is the Law on Revenge Porn," *The Telegraph*, April 13, 2015.
Baumbauer, Derek E., "Exposed," *Minnesota Law Review*, June 2014.
Berlatsky, Noah, "The Rape-Revenge Genre's Gender Revelations," *The Establishment*, December 29, 2015.
Bloom, Sandra. L., "Commentary: Reflections on the Desire for Revenge," *Journal of Emotional Abuse*, vol. 2, no. 4, 2001, pp. 61–94.
Bramesco, Charles, "Bound to Vengeance," *The Dissolve*, June 24, 2015.
Cadwalladr, Carol, "Charlotte Law's Fight with Hunter Moore, the Internet's Revenge Porn King," *The Guardian*, March 30, 2014.
Chan, Julia, "Violence or Pleasure? Surveillance and the (Non-)Consensual Upskirt," *Porn Studies*, October 2017.
Collier, Kevin, "Why Hollywood Wants Revenge Porn to Stay Legal," *Vocativ*, March 29, 2016.
Craven, Wes, "10 Movies That Shook Me up," *Entertainment*, October 26, 2009.
Dillon, Nancy, and Peter Sblendorio, "Rob Kardashian Could Face Jail Time for Blanc Chyna Revenge Porn Pics under California Law," *Daily News Entertainment*, July 5, 2017.

54 Revenge

Ebert, Roger, "I Spit on Your Grave," *Roger Ebert.com,* July 15, 1980.

Ebert, Roger, "The Last House on the Left," *Roger Ebert.com,* January 1, 1972.

Elam, Paul, "Register-Her.com Goes Worldwide," *M: A Voice for Men,* September 13, 2011.

Folderauer, Kaitlan Lynn, "Not All Is Fair (Use) in Love and War: Copyright Law and Revenge Porn," *University of Baltimore Law Review,* vol. 44, 2015.

Heller-Nicholas, Alexandra, *Rape-Revenge Films: A Critical Study,* Jefferson, NC: McFarland & Company, 2011, pp. 2–3.

Hess, Amanda, "Rape, Revenge and How We Watch," *The New York Times,* January 15, 2017.

Holland, Jesse J., "NCIS Investigating Posting of Nude Photographs of Female Marines," *Associated Press,* March 6, 2017.

Hugel, Melissa, *"Kill Bill* and Our Troubled Relationship with Rape Revenge Movies," *Arts. Mic,* October 15, 2013, mic.com/articles/67263 accessed December 9, 2016.

Ian Robert to McKee. "Revenge, Retribution, and Values: Social Attitudes and Punitive Sentencing," *Social Justice Research,* vol. 21, 2008, p. 138. doi: 10.1007/s11211-008-0066-z

Interview: Jane Caputi, "No Safe Place: Violence against Women," *PBS,* www.pbs.org/kued/nosafeplace/interv/caputi.html

Kang, Cecelia, "Taken," *The Washington Post,* October 20, 2014.

Kapline, Arline, "Violence in the Media: What Effects on Behavior," *Psychiatric Times,* October 5, 2012.

Londberg, Max, and Laura Bauer, "It Was Sex in the Basement, McCaskill Lampoons Greitens at Democratic Event," *The Kansas City Star,* January 27, 2018.

Nelson, Steve, "Lawmakers Unveil Proposal to Take Nip Out of Revenge Porn," *US News and World Report,* July 14, 2016.

Neroni, Hilary, *The Violent Woman: Femininity, Narrative, and Violence in Contemporary American Cinema,* Albany, NY: State University of New York Press, 2005, p. 171.

Nietzsche, Friedrich, *Human, All Too Human: A Book for Free Spirits.* Cambridge: Cambridge University Press, 1996.

O'Conner, Lydia, "Marines' Nude Photo Scandal Goes Beyond That One Group," *The Huffington Post,* March 9, 2017.

Plaugic, Lissie, "Revenge Porn Website Operator Hunter Moore Sentenced to 30 Years in Prison," *The Verge,* December 3, 2015.

Radish, Christina, "'*Sweet/Vicious*' Creator Jennifer Kaytin Robinson on How the Sexual Assault Series Landed on MTV," *Collider,* December 6, 2016.

Salonga, D. Robert, and Sharon Noguchi, "Police Investigating Nude Picture-Sharing Scheme," *The Bay Area News Group,* December 13, 2016.

Sjostrom, Arne, and Mario Gollwitzer, "Displaced Revenge: Can Revenge Taste 'Sweet' If It Aims at a Different Target?" *Journal of Experimental Social Psychology,* vol. 56, 2015, pp. 191–202.

Smith, Mitch, and Julie Boseman, "Republican Governor, a Rising GOP Star, Resigns Amidst Scandal," *The New York Times,* May 29, 2018.

Talbot, Margaret, "Taking Trolls to Court," *The New Yorker,* December 5, 2016.

Tesvaye, Sophia, "Missouri's GOP Governor Indicted in Revenge Porn Blackmail Scheme," *Salon,* February 22, 2018.

Tsoulis-Reay, Alexa, "A Brief History of Revenge Porn," *New York Magazine,* July 21, 2013.

Turner, Karen, "Why the Studios Are Taking a Stand against an Anti-Revenge Porn Bill," *The Wall Street Journal,* April 11, 2016.

4

TORTURE

After the terrorist attacks of September 11, 2001, a disturbing trend in pornography developed in film, social media, the internet, and video games. It became known as "torture porn". By 2005 torture was well established in pop culture, and in 2005 *The New York Times* critic Adam Green observed that Fox TV series *24* had transformed the occasional use of torture as a plot device to, ". . . a potent mix of diverse elements". During the 2005 season alone, Green observed, Fox ramped up its torture scenarios to include, ". . . a two-stage nuclear conspiracy plot; the formation of an unsympathetic confederation of sleeper cells, defense contractors and rogue scientists; and even a subplot about Sino-American conflict . . . ". Green speculated, ". . . it's possible that this year's *24* will be most remembered not for its experiments with television formulas, but for its portrayal of torture in prime time".[1]

On January 28, 2006, movie critic David Edelstein published "Now Playing at Your Local Multiplex: Torture Porn" in *New York* magazine. Edelstein posed two interesting questions, "Why has America gone nuts for blood, guts, and sadism?" And, "Seen any good surgery on unanesthetized people lately? Millions have, in *Hostel*, which spent a week as America's top moneymaker". He also reviewed *Saw*, *The Devil's Rejects*, and *Wolf Creek*, which he collectively dubbed "torture porn". These films represent a violence-laden genre that appeared in response to, "The 9/11 attacks and the scrapping of former U.S. policies forbidding torture. . . ".[2]

Western torture porn began at the end of the nineteenth century in Paris's Pigalle (Montmartre) district. In 1896, playwright Oscar Méténier purchased the smallest theater in Paris to stage his plays and named it *Le Théâtre du Grand-Guignol*, which means "big puppet show". Méténier named it after a popular French puppet character, Guignol, famous for outspoken social commentary. Although Méténier's theater qualified as Paris's smallest, its *décor* instantly captivated theatergoing audiences. Agnès Peirron describes, "Two large angels hung above the

56 Torture

orchestra and the theater's neo-Gothic wood paneling; and the boxes, with their iron railings, looked like confessionals (the building had, in fact, once been a chapel)". The theater became an instant success, depicting vagrants, prostitutes, and con artists for the first time speaking in their own language, groups that seldom appeared in mainstream theater of that era. The theater developed a reputation as a venue for short, transgressive one-act plays. A nightly program featured "la douche ecossaise" or "hot and cold shower" with between five and six one-act plays alternating between "cold" horror and gore plays and "hot" comedic ones, saving the goriest for the final play.[3]

Méténier based his play *Mademoiselle Fifi* on a novel by Guy de Maupassant, the renowned short story author, and brought a prostitute to the stage for the first time. Prostitution had existed for centuries in Paris, and in the 1880s painter Henri Toulouse-Lautrec began painting portraits of prostitutes frequenting the area's cabarets. Polite society refused to accept the popularity of "the oldest profession". Police censors shut down *Mademoiselle Fifi*, only later to be brought back by popular demand. Méténier's subsequent play, *Luil*, featured a prostitute and a criminal in a hotel room.

In 1898, Max Maurey assumed directorship and transformed the theater into a "house of horror", injecting graphic scenes of gore and violence. Partially for publicity, Maurey hired a house doctor to treat patrons who fainted or suffered other ill effects during performances. Maurey featured novelist and playwright André de Lorde, known as the "Prince of Terror". De Lorde collaborated with his therapist, experimental psychologist Alfred Binet, on several plays depicting insanity, a subject rarely staged or even discussed at that time. De Lorde's and Léo Marchès's *L'Homme de la Nuit* (*The Man of the Night*) introduced audiences to Sergeant Bertrand, a necrophiliac convicted of violating tombs and abusing corpses. De Lorde's and Henri Bauche's *L'Horrible Passion* (*The Horrible Passion*) depicted a youthful nanny who strangled children in her care. Subsequent plays depicted the suffering of people who contracted rabies, leprosy, and syphilis, also taboo subjects for theatrical depiction. Later productions depicted maiming, scalping, and killing by guns and the guillotine as well as altered states of awareness caused by drugs and hypnosis. Audiences were thrilled by depictions of decapitation in which severed heads remained conscious for a few moments.[4]

During the 1920s rising objections from the clergy and other concerned citizens about scenes of graphic violence and salacious sexual content of motion pictures crystalized in the Motion Picture Producers and Distributors of America's Production Code (MPPDA), which discouraged depictions of "sexuality and vulgarity" in movies. The Production Code at first received lax enforcement, but by 1934 the MPPDA periodically reviewed Hollywood's shooting scripts and rough cuts, refusing to award seals of approval to transgressive films, especially those depicting sexuality. [5] Violence remains Hollywood's chief stand-in for sex. This inspired the horror genre in the 1950s and 1960s. Audiences flocked to films depicting stabbing, bludgeoning, shooting, maiming, and killing. In Britain, blood-saturated films like Hammond Film Production's *The Curse of Frankenstein* (1957) and *The Horror of Dracula* (1958) enjoyed widespread popularity. And, the Japanese film *Jigoku* (1960) directed by Nobuo Nakagawa, and the Hollywood film *Psycho* (1960), directed by Alfred Hitchcock, both contain significant scenes of blood and gore.

Hitchcock's *Psycho* proved especially noteworthy in its violence, especially the infamous "shower scene", a shocking 45-second shower murder. Hitchcock chose to shoot *Psycho* in black and white because he knew that color shots of red blood would never be allowed under the Production Code. Even in black and white, the British Film Institute's Michael Brooke observed, "They [audiences] had never seen anything quite like it before—the total shock of killing off a lead character a third of the way in, and just the complete feeling of disorientation".[6]

Hitchcock apparently intended *Psycho* as black comedy and expressed shock that audiences took it seriously. In a 1964 *BBC* interview, the iconic director disclosed that, "The content was, I felt, rather amusing and it was a big joke". Hitchcock explained that *Psycho*, which critics often credit as his best work, ". . . was intended to make people scream and yell and so forth". However, he added, he intended for the screams to be of pleasure, not of horror, ". . . no more than screaming and yelling on a switchback railway . . . so you mustn't go too far because you want them to get off the railway giggling with pleasure".[7]

Alex Delarge (Malcolm McDowell) leads his sadistic gang of "droogs" in gang-raping an innocent housewife (Adrienne Corri), leaving her husband Frank Alexander (Patrick Magee) for dead.

FIGURE 4.1 Stanley Kubrick, *A Clockwork Orange*, 1971

Source: Pacific Film Archive

Extreme violence in popular culture often takes the form of "black comedy", a translation from the French *humour noir* coined by the surrealist theorist André Breton in 1935 while interpreting the writings of Jonathan Swift.[8] Black comedies feature violence considered to be "over the top", especially in the hands of capable filmmakers like Hal Ashby, Stanley Kubrick, the Coen brothers, and Quentin Tarantino. Films like Kubrick's *Dr. Strangelove* (1964) and *A Clockwork Orange* (1971), Ashby's *Harold and Maude* (1971), the Coen brothers' *Barton Fink* (1991) and *Fargo* (1996), and Tarantino's *Pulp Fiction* (1994) and *Inglorious Basterds* (2009) owe a debt to Hitchcock's film. *A Clockwork Orange* pioneered a psychopath as protagonist (Alex) who eventually becomes deprogramed to violence through behavior modification techniques.

Alex DeLarge (Malcolm McDowell) and his gang of "droogs" including Georgie (James Markey), Dim (Warren Clarke), and Pete (Michael Tarn) sit at the Korova Milk Bar stoned on milk laced with narcotics.

Critic Paul Johnson credits *Psycho* as an early precursor to "black comedy" and the first horror film and precursor to the slasher genre. Hitchcock's pioneering use of "first person" cinematography in *Psycho*, in which the camera appears to assume a life of its own instead of the traditional "third person" detached camera, also became a feature in the horror genre. Critic Roger Clarke concludes that *Psycho*, ". . . changed cinema forever". Critic David Thomas argues, "It's one of the most influential films ever made". He credits *Psycho* as, ". . . the beginnings of a flood of violence. Violence becomes more acceptable in film. It's a whole new attitude to the criminal personality".[9] *Psycho* became a huge financial success, earning an

FIGURE 4.2 Stanley Kubrick, *A Clockwork Orange*, 1971
Source: Pacific Film Archive

astonishing $32 million on a production budget of just $800,000. Paramount was so pessimistic about the film's box office potential that it required Hitchcock to make a substantial contribution to the budget out of his own pocket, and in turn, allowed him to receive most of the profit, making the director very wealthy.[10]

In 1963, US director Hirshell Gordon Lewis released *Blood Feast* that included many scenes of explicit bloodletting and gore. Lewis, who had formerly directed soft porn "nudie cutie" films, realized after Hitchcock's success that a new market existed for bloody horror films in the old style of the Grand Guignol. Lewis dictated a skimpy 14-paged script to his secretary. He hired some inexpensive actors, including Mal Arnold, to play Fuad Ramses, an Egyptian caterer working in Miami. Ramses hatches a plan to resurrect the goddess Isis by cooking a mixture of body parts hacked from young virgin women in a reanimation ceremony. He proceeds to attack several young, attractive women and cuts off an arm from one, a leg from another, and a scalp, a tongue, a brain, and a heart from other victims. He chooses an engagement party for a young debutante for the reanimation ceremony. To ward off censors, Lewis has Ramses tracked down and forced to hide inside a garbage truck, where he is violently killed by the truck's trash compacting blades. Like many horror films that followed, *Blood Feast* capitalized on graphic violence in every conceivable way, placating censors by including bloody retribution scenes in which the villain dies a horrific death.

Lewis shot his entire film in just four days on a budget of just $24,500 but guessed correctly about the potential demand for a gore-soaked soft-porn movie and ended up grossing as much as $70 million, more than twice the amount Alfred Hitchcock earned for *Psycho*. Like *Psycho, Blood Feast* helped inspire a genre of low-budget "slasher" horror films that featured young women being stabbed, sliced, and tortured.[11] Slasher films rely on the time-honored plot featuring violence-saturated action torturers (usually white males) and helpless but not necessarily unwilling victims, mostly female, conforming to the standard sadomasochistic trope.

Tobe Hopper's *The Texas Chainsaw Massacre* (1974) depicts an epic journey to hell in a remote Texas home. Sally Hardesty (Marilyn Burns) and her invalid brother Franklin (Paul A. Partain) set out in their Volkswagen van along with Sally's boyfriend Jerry (Allen Danziger), her best friend Pam (Teri McMinn), and Pam's boyfriend Kirk (William Vail) to visit their grandfather's grave in rural Texas after hearing disturbing reports that some person or persons had been digging up graves, and robbing and molesting corpses at the local cemetery. When they discover the grave unmolested, they head to the site of their grandparents' remote home, a two-story rock house called the Old Franklin Home, then abandoned. On the way they pick up a strange hitchhiker (Edwin Neal), who frightens them with his looks and speech. Franklin even comments, "I think we just picked up Dracula". As they pass an abandoned slaughterhouse the hitchhiker explains, "My family's always been in meat". Franklin whispers to Sally, "A whole family of Draculas!" Sally and her boyfriend Jerry enter the rundown, apparently abandoned

60 Torture

house, exclaiming, "Oh I wish they hadn't let it fall apart!" Jerry responds ominously, "Now it looks like the birthplace of Bela Lugosi!"

They find the house, which is not, after all, abandoned when they later encounter Grandfather (John Dugan), an emaciated old man who appears to be almost dead until he sucks some blood from Sally's hand which has been sliced by Old Man (Jim Siedow). They also encounter Old Man's monstrous son Leatherface (Gunnar Hansen), who dispatches unsuspecting humans by hitting them on the head with a sledgehammer or slicing them with a chain saw. The family operates a smoker oven that transforms human corpses into smoked meats. Sally, the last remaining Hardesty, escapes with the assistance of a cattle truck driver (Ed Guinn). The Hardesty family had entered a forbidden, deadly world despite all the ominous signs they had passed. In that netherworld, they faced fierce, demonic beings hungering and thirsting for their meat and blood or hungering to rape their bodies. They became ensnared in a frightening world in which only the strongest and most determined survived. The terrors faced by the Hardesty family may have evoked 1970s' issues like the terrorist attacks on Israeli athletes at the Munich Olympics, the US bombing of North Vietnam, the Yom Kippur War, the Manson Family killings, urban riots, or the rising crime rate. Artistically, however, the film failed to impress most critics, including Roger Ebert. Ebert complained that the film, ". . . is as violent and gruesome and blood-soaked as the title promises—a real Grand Guignol of a movie. It's also without any apparent purpose, unless the creation of disgust and fright is a purpose".[12]

In 1977, Wes Craven directed *The Hills Have Eyes*, a torture thriller featuring the Carter family, headed by recently retired policeman Bob (Russ Grieve), his wife Ethyl (Virginia Vincent), their children Bobby (Robert Houston), Brenda (Susan Lanier), and eldest daughter Lynne (Dee Wallace), along with Lynne's husband Doug (Martin Speer), their baby daughter Katy (Brenda Marinoff), and two German Shepherd dogs. In celebration of their silver wedding anniversary, Bob, Ethyl and their children decide to hitch up an airstream trailer to the family car and drive through a desolate southwestern landscape. They stop for fuel at a rundown gas station named Fred's Oasis, where Fred (John Steadman) cautions them to remain on the main road. Later the road they select becomes a dirt road, where they hit a booby trap and slide into a ditch, breaking an axel. At that point their descent into hell begins. Bob decides to hike back to Fred's Oasis for help while the others scout around in the vicinity.

Bob finally reaches the station but is suddenly and inexplicitly confronted by Fred, who emphatically warns Bob about "the Hill people", a group of cannibals that inhabit the neighboring hills. Bob sets off with Fred to warn the others but Fred's deranged son Jupiter (James Whitworth), assisted by Pluto (Michael Berryman), captures Fred and Bob. Jupiter beats Fred to death with a crowbar, then ties Bob up and sets him on fire, where he suffers a slow, torturous death. Meanwhile Pluto, appearing savage and hideous, breaks into the trailer and begins frantically searching for food, defended by Bobby and Doug. Deformed by years of US nuclear tests, the Hill people rely on capturing and devouring hapless passersby. Mars (Lance Gordon), one of the Hill people, enters the trailer and rapes Brenda. Ruby (Janis Blythe), another member of the Hill people, decides to help Doug and his baby, the two remaining Carter family members. Together they kill Mars. The Hill people, living beyond the constraints of normal civilization, represent the evils of nuclear weapons testing gone awry. Hill people, like zombies, Leatherface, and other torture porn villains, challenge civilization and all human values.

American director George G. Romero coined the next violent horror phase "splatter porn" after he released *Dawn of the Dead* in 1978. *Dawn of the Dead* features reanimated corpses feasting on living humans, who wallow in blood and gore even more graphically than the zombies in Romero's 1968 feature *Night of the Living Dead*.[13] Zombies, or reanimated dead humans, represent humanity's dark, aggressive nature. Zombies behave like extreme psychopaths who would never be allowed to coexist with humans. They represent humanity's most aggressive and violent nature, the dominant side of sadomasochism, while their victims represent the submissive side.

Movie-Inspired Torture

The overwhelming success of early "splatter films" opened the door to violent mainstream thrillers. Martin Scorsese's classic neo-noir *Taxi* (1976) stars Robert De Niro as Travis Bickle, a slightly psychotic Vietnam veteran who applies to be a New York City taxi driver. During his interview the dispatcher asks Bickle, "Waddya wanna hack for, Bickle?" Bickle replies, "I can't sleep nights". The dispatcher says, "There's porno theaters for that". Bickle replies, "Yeah, I know. I tried that". Bickle becomes attracted to Betsy (Cyblle Shepherd) but offends her when he takes her to see a Swedish porn film on their first date. Later Bickle encounters Iris (Jody Foster), a twelve-year-old prostitute struggling with her pimp, Sport (Harvey Keitel). Bickle attempts to rescue Iris but is overpowered by Sport. Bickle then attempts to assassinate a Presidential candidate, and when that fails returns to "rescue" Iris, killing Sport and a bodyguard while doing so.

John Hinckley viewed *Taxi* over fifteen times. He purchased a copy of the film's score and obsessed about forging a romantic relationship with Jodie Foster. Hoping to impress Foster, on March 30, 1981, Hinckley shot and wounded President Ronald Reagan, Press Secretary James Brady, and two security officers. During his trial Hinckley said, "Guns are neat little things, aren't they? They can kill extraordinary people with very little effort". Dejected after Foster ignored Hinckley and his crime, Hinckley lamented, "Jodie Foster may continue to outwardly ignore me for the rest of my life, but I have made her one of the most famous actresses in the world".[14]

Oliver Stone's campy black comedy, *Natural Born Killers* (1994), further ramps up torture and violence. Stone's film features rampage killers Mickey Knox (Woody Harrelson) and Malory Knox (Juliette Lewis), who kill Malory's paedophilic father Ed Wilson (Rodney Dangerfield) then embark on a killing spree in New Mexico.

62 Torture

After terrorizing and killing all the patrons of a roadside café, they swear undying love for each other as they spare the life of a cook to relate their murderous deeds to the media. They embark on a murderous, mayhem-filled journey along "Route 666" in New Mexico, Colorado, and Utah, torturing and murdering 48 people along the way, pursued by a television host Wayne Gayle (Robert Downey, Jr.), who is looking for stories to ensure high ratings for a forthcoming documentary about mass murderers.

After viewing *Natural Born Killers*, 18-year-old Benjamin James Darrus and his 18-year-old girlfriend Sarah Edmondson left their rented cabin in Oklahoma on the morning of March 6, 1995 and embarked on a spree of torture and murder that resulted in one death and another victim paralyzed from the neck down. Stone's film also inspired Nathan Martinez to shoot and kill his stepmother and half-sister after he viewed the movie six times. The film initially spurned numerous acts of torture culminating in eight murders.[15] *Natural Born Killer's* fans included Eric Harris and Dylan Klebold, perpetrators of the Columbine High School Massacre in 1999 in which 12 students died and 24 others were injured. Harris and Klebold became fascinated with the movie during the months preceding their rampage. Klebold wrote in his journal "God I can't wait till they die. I can taste the blood now—NBK ['NBK' stands for *Natural Born Killers*]".[16]

Self-Torture

Self-torture is one of humanity's oldest (and kinkiest) pleasures. A group of Shia Muslims whip themselves vigorously with *zangirs* with whips made of knife blades until their backs are bloody. Devout Hindus celebrate the ritual of *kavadi* in which believers use meat hooks and skewers to pierce their legs, faces, and tongues. Christianity's venerable tradition of "mortification of the flesh" dates to the origins of the Catholic church. Self-inflicted pain and discomfort range from wearing abrasive hair shirts and heavy chains to various forms of self-flagellation, even self-castration.[17]

Behavioral and social scientists examine a closely related phenomenon: non-suicidal self-injury (NSSI), in which a percentage of the general population enjoys wounding themselves, often by cutting or burning themselves. Healthcare professionals have reached no consensus about the causes of or cures for this affliction, although as many as 20% of the population may experience pleasure from painful experiences, such as cutting themselves with knives. Those with high incidences of NSSI found that the pain they inflicted on themselves led to decreased activity in the areas of the brain associated with negative emotion. In other words, they experienced an absence of pain replaced by pleasurable sensations.[18]

Self-inflicted pain/pleasure becomes expressed in popular culture as masochism. One of the most blatantly masochistic movies is David Cronenberg's iconic *Crash* (1997). It features James Ballard (James Spader), Catherine Ballard (Deborah Kara Unger), Helen Remington (Holly Hunter), among, others who inhabit an underground community comprised of those who take pleasure from sex after car crashes. The final scene shows James and Catherine Ballard comforting each other sexually after deliberately staging a dramatic crash:

James Ballard: Catherine, are you all right?
Catherine Ballard: James. I don't know.
James Ballard: Are you hurt?
Catherine Ballard: I think I'm all right . . .
 [*James starts groping and kissing her*]
Catherine Ballard: . . . I think I'm all right.
James Ballard: Maybe the next time, darling. Maybe the next time.

Roger Ebert observed, "Take out the cars, the scars, the crutches and scabs and wounds, and substitute the usual props of sex films, and you'd have a porno movie". However, Ebert ultimately decides Cronenberg's film is not porn because, "It's about the human mind, about the way we grow enslaved by the particular things that turn us on, and forgive ourselves our trespasses".[19]

FIGURE 4.3 David Cronenberg, *Crash*, 1996
Source: Pacific Film Archive

64 Torture

James Ballard (James Spader) fondles his wife Catherine (Deborah Unger) after both survive deliberately staged car crashes which they find sexually stimulating. David Cronenberg directs actor James Spader about his sexualized reaction to a staged car crash on the set of *Crash*.

Pop culture may provide some vulnerable fans with negative narratives that prove too compelling. On July 20, 2012 James Holmes entered an Aurora, Colorado movie theater showing *Dark Knight Rising* sporting orange hair and dressed like the infamous character, the Joker. He then opened fire with a small arsenal of weapons, killing 12 and injuring 58. On August 7, Westlake, Ohio, police arrested a man sitting in an empty theater armed with a loaded 9 mm Glock pistol and several knives waiting for the audience to arrive for a screening of *Dark Knight Rising*.[20] Other copycat attempts reportedly came from Maryland, Oregon, and New York City. James Holmes himself might have copied an attack that occurred on January 23, 2009 at a Belgian day-care center by Kim de Gelder, who became known as the Dendermonde Joker, who, dressed like the Joker, stabbed two children and a teacher to death and wounded 12 others at a nursery in the Flemish village of Dendermonde.[21]

The Dark Knight relies on popular "master narratives", including a crime-fighting superhero (Batman) pitted against the Joker, a sardonic supervillain who had been bullied in early life and strikes back at the world becoming Batman's nemesis. The Joker's back story begins one tragic night when as an aspiring comedian, he joins a gang of low-level thieves attempting to rob a playing card company to which they gained access through an adjacent chemical plant. On the day of the robbery, he learns that his wife has suffered a fatal accident at home. Shocked and distraught, he tries to leave but fellow gang members force him to play his role in the crime. When the robbery attempt fails, police kill most gang members and continue firing at him. Batman takes over and pursues him through the chemical plant where he eventually escapes by diving into a vat of discarded chemicals. The acids in the vat disfigure his face, skin, and hair color, transforming him into a badly scarred, shocking-looking Joker. His disfigurement and his wife's death twist his personality. He later complains to Batman, "When I saw what a black, awful joke the world was, I went crazy as a coot! You have to keep pretending that there's some point to all this suffering".[22]

The Joker was one of the original Batman characters in the debut issue of *Batman* comics appearing on April 25, 1940. His creators depicted him as a criminal psychopath and mastermind with a warped, sadistic personality. One of his creators, Bob Finger, drew an image of the German actor Conrad Veidt as a disfigured man with his face carved into a perpetual grin in German Expressionist filmmaker Paul Leni's 1928 horror film *The Man Who Laughs*. This horrific image later transformed into Batman's iconic antagonist in numerous comic books, movies, and graphic novels.[23]

Sadomasochistic Clowns

The Joker evokes an ancient folk fear of "scary clowns", dating back to the sixteenth century Italian commedia dell'arte character Harlequin. Nineteenth-century pantomime player Joseph Grimaldi added garish makeup and elements of slapstick comedy to his clown pantomime routines. Grimaldi experienced extreme calamity and pain in his personal life, leading him to exclaim, "I am grim all day, but I make you laugh at night". In 1981, children in Brookline, Massachusetts, reported clowns traveling in vans attempting to lure them inside with promises of candy. Sinister clown sightings recurred in 1985 and 1991. Scary clown stories were spread by children, and reappeared in 2016 in at least 20 US states, causing temporary school closings and police checkpoints. The entire scary clown episode may have been inadvertently started by a young man in gruesome black and white clown costume carrying black balloons in Green Bay, Wisconsin. All scary clowns reference a popular stereotype of clowns happy on the outside but sad on the inside. Journalist Bess Lovejoy observed, "with stories like these it's a wonder clowns were ever invited to birthday parties in the first place".[24]

The Joker scarifies his own face, evoking self-abuse, self-mutilation, blood-letting, and other forms of auto-torture. With his bloodlust and thirst for vengeance against Batman, as well as his general disdain for humanity, he is more than sad. He becomes diabolically violent and bloodthirsty. He comes far closer to vampires and other violent abusers than to circus clowns. Serial rapist and murderer John Wayne Gacy also worked as Pogo the Clown by day and serial rapist/murderer by night. At times Gacy committed his crimes while dressed in his clown costume. His attitude and behavior closely resemble The Joker's.[25] Both killer and character evoke sadomasochism, engaging in BDSM-like behavior.

The Aurora-inspired massacres illustrate the nearly hypnotic effect of Batman's nemesis, especially the psychotic and demonic villain played by Heath Ledger in the 2008 *The Dark Knight*. Ledger depicted the Joker as a shrewd, sardonic psychotic who takes sadomasochistic pleasure in creating mayhem and murder, assisted by a large group of henchmen. Scriptwriters Jonathan and Christopher Nolan provided the Joker with sardonic lines evoking sadomasochism, as in the following exchange between a mobster and the Joker:

The Joker:	[threateningly] You know, I'll settle for his loved ones.
Gentleman at Party:	We're not intimidated by thugs!
The Joker:	[*as he smacks his lips*] You know, you remind me of my father. [*the Joker pulls out his switchblade and brings it to the Gentleman's mouth*]
The Joker:	I hated my father!

66 Torture

Ledger's performance garnered a posthumous Academy Award after the actor's sudden death by accidental drug overdose or suicide in 2008. However, the Joker character depicted by Ledger continues to appeal to those dissatisfied with the status quo and who long to "take down the system". He appeals to anyone that experiences pain and suffering and feels overlooked. This is a profoundly sado-masochistic appeal, with the Joker in the dominant (dom) role and partygoers in the victim's (sub) role.

Nolan's film received an MPAA rating of PG-13 for, ". . . intense sequences of violence and some menace". Nolan, however, limited the amount of graphic carnage to prevent the MPAA from assigning an "R" rating, which would dramatically reduce the potential audience and negatively affect revenue. In several scenes depicting characters being shot, Nolan cut away from the victims, reducing the number of violent images. In one scene, a man slams another man's head down on a pencil tip, but Nolan cuts away from the actual impalement. Later, the Joker slashes a man's face into a grin, but Nolan again cuts away from the actual slashing. In a scene in which a woman dies in a flaming explosion, Nolan cuts away from her to the burning building. When a man is dropped from a height and the audience only hears his legs breaking upon impact is another example of Nolan softening the horror. Much of the film's dialogue, however, expresses violence. The Joker demands that someone reveal Batman's secret identity and promises to kill Gotham citizens one by one until he learns precisely who he is. In the final scene, the Joker wires two people-laden ferries with bombs that can be detonated by each ferry's passengers. He threatens to blow up both ferries if the passengers refuse to blow up each other first. Critic B. Fitzpatrick charges, "No movie I've ever seen has been so emotionally disturbing and spiritually oppressive". Fitzpatrick concludes by labeling Nolan's film a prime example of, ". . . the pornography of violence".[26]

Snuff

In 1975 producer Alan Shackleton revised a 1971 low-budget torture movie called *The Slaughter* by changing its name to *Snuff* (1975). Originally directed by Michael and Roberta Findlay and filmed in Argentina on a budget of $30,000, *The Slaughter* features a Manson-type biker cult committing serial murders. It saw limited release, and Shackleton pulled it from distribution. Four years later he became inspired by reports that a real "snuff" film had been smuggled into the US from South America. He decided to re-release *The Slaughter* under the new name *Snuff* while splicing a simulated snuff scene at the end. The scene involves a script girl (Tina Austin) involved in the wrap-up of *The Slaughter*. The director (Brian Kerry) attempts to seduce her on a bed while the crew secretly rolls cameras. When the girl resists, the director pins her arms and calls for help to restrain her. Then he attacks her with a knife, slicing her shoulder, cutting off a finger and later one of her hands.

He finishes her by stabbing deep in her abdomen, then reaching inside the wound and disemboweling her. Shackleton even gave *Snuff* a new tagline, "The film that could only be made in South America—where life is cheap!" He started rumors that the snuff scene was real, then paid actors to protest against the film's screening at the National Theater in Times Square throughout February 1976. His film ultimately inspired the feminist group Women Against Violence Against Women, which included prominent feminist Susan Brownmiller, to protest against screenings across the country. Shackleton's gambits apparently paid off as the film did very well at the box office in several major cities.[27]

Waterboarding and 9/11 Torture

The 9/11 attacks and the "War on Terror" inspired a firestorm of cinematic violence, gore, and mayhem. At that time, torture became an acknowledged tactic in the US arsenal. President George W. Bush authorized the CIA to capture, detain, and interrogate suspected al-Qaeda members using torture techniques.[28] Secretary of Defense Donald Rumsfeld ordered DOD personnel to, ". . . take the gloves off . . ." when interrogating suspected terrorists. This was carried out despite the fact that the Geneva Convention of 1949 and the Additional Protocols of 1977 banned all forms of torture during internal armed combat including, ". . . outrages upon personal dignity, in particular humiliating and degrading treatment".[29]

In December 2001, American forces found twenty-year-old American John Walker Lindh, a Taliban volunteer in northern Afghanistan, wounded by American forces. Although suffering from a severe leg wound, American guards blindfolded and shackled Lindh, then repeatedly beat and whipped him before stripping him naked, tying him to a gurney, and leaving him in an unheated cement-floor room during the freezing Afghanistan winter. Although Lindh served as a civilian, President George W. Bush referred to him as an "Al Qaeda fighter" and labeled him a "terrorist". His leg wound became severely infected yet he received no medical attention. He is still serving a twenty-year prison sentence.[30]

The Bush-led "war on terror" also practiced a policy of abducting suspected terrorists and transporting them to secret prisons in other countries or to the US prison in Guantanamo Bay, Cuba. Suspects held outside of the US were not governed by American laws according to the Bush government, and could be subjected to extreme interrogation techniques, not only beatings and floggings but also humiliation, sleep deprivation, slapping, and subjection to cold and simulated drowning, known as "waterboarding".[31] Once established, waterboarding became the center of a controversy. Former Minnesota governor, film actor, and professional wrestler Jesse Ventura expressed strong anti-waterboarding views, stating, "It's convenient how everyone who supports waterboarding and torture,

68 Torture

or 'enhanced interrogation techniques' as they like to call it, have [sic] never experienced it themselves. Yet everyone who has, myself included, is firmly against it".[32] Author C.S. Lewis cogently observed, "Answers to leading questions under torture naturally tell us nothing about the beliefs of the accused; but they are good evidence for the beliefs of the accusers".[33]

President Barack Obama ordered the "advanced interrogation techniques" to be disbanded on January 22, 2009. This changed with a new administration. In February 2016, Republication Presidential nominee Donald Trump wrote, "Though the effectiveness of many of these methods may be in dispute, nothing should be taken off the table when American lives are at stake", Trump further wrote, "The enemy is cutting off the heads of Christians and drowning them in cages, and yet we are too politically correct to respond in kind".[34]

Post-9/11 Torture Porn

Socio/political violence of the 1970s, including the Vietnam War, Civil Rights Movement, and Watts riots, also paved the way for violent pop culture, including torture porn. These violent events suddenly seemed almost tame, however, after the terrorist attacks on September 11, 2001. The torture porn genre reappeared, re-energized by the frightened, paranoid public mood. Movies of the classic era were remade for a new generation ripe for vengeful, violent movies featuring torture, mayhem, and murder. *The Texas Chainsaw Massacre* (2003) directed by Marcus Nispel and co-written by Kim Henkel, Tobe Hopper, and Scott Kosar, reprised the 1974 torture classic. Like the original, it features cannibalism, sawed bodies, severed heads, and gallons of blood. The new version immediately achieved stunning success at the box office, earning over $107 million on a production budget of just $9.5 million.[35] Artistically, however, the new version failed to impress critics. *The New York Times* reviewer David Kehn explains, ". . . a long march to the slaughterhouse that seems to take forever to get going and, once it does, goes nowhere that hasn't been visited before by more talented filmmakers".[36] Roger Ebert reacted even more strongly, stating that the new version ". . . is a contemptible film: Vile, ugly and brutal. There is not a shred of a reason to see it".[37]

Saw (2004) opens as Adam Faulkner (Leigh Whannell) wakes up in a dark public restroom, chained inside a bathtub filled with water. He inadvertently pulls the plug, releasing the water. On the other side of the bathroom Surgeon Dr Lawrence Gordon (Cary Elwes), also chained, finds the switch to turn on the lights. Between them, just out of reach, they see a corpse lying in a pool of blood, one hand clutching a tape recorder and the other a revolver. Gordon listens to a tape commanding him to kill Adam before six o'clock or his wife and child will be killed, giving him only seven hours. Adam's tape asks, "Are you going to watch yourself die or do something about it?" Each must saw off one of their feet in order to escape their shackles, seize the handgun in the corpse's hand, and kill the other. Jigsaw, also known as John Kramer (Tobin Bell), a patient of Gordon's, orchestrates

Torture **69**

life-and-death scenarios in which characters must sacrifice something significant, such as a foot, and kill someone else to survive. Jigsaw tests and tortures victims by forcing them to torture and kill others while maiming themselves. It is reminiscent of Nazi porn movies depicting Josef Mengele-like experiments on Nazi prisoners in concentration camps. *Saw*, produced on a miniscule $1.2 million budget, earned an astonishing $104 million.[38]

Mel Gibson's controversial *The Passion of the Christ* (2004) anchored torture porn firmly within a Christianized religious framework. Gibson's film depicts the last twelve hours of the life of Jesus of Nazareth (Jim Caviezel). The scourging scene is certainly the goriest and most painful to view. Two burly Roman torturers secure Jesus's hands around a large stone and begin flagellating him with whips. Their instruments increasingly mark his naked back. Jesus collapses from pain, but he succeeds in struggling up on his feet, at which point the torturers, after a sign from the centurion in charge of the scourging, drop their whips and pick up flagrums, which are designed to rip flesh to shreds. They proceed to tear apart Jesus's back, at one point causing his blood to hit the eye of one of the laughing torturers. The entire scene lasts an excruciating five minutes, leading some reviewers to label it "Christian torture porn".[39] Roger Ebert observed that *The Passion of the Christ*, ". . . is 126 minutes long, and I would guess that at least 100 of those minutes, maybe more, are concerned specifically and graphically with the details of the torture and death of Jesus". He summarized that Gibson's movie, ". . . is the most violent film I have ever seen".[40] Audiences split along religious and ideological lines, with many Evangelical churches promoting Gibson's movie and even arranging for advance screenings for their congregations. Others, like Ebert, expressed disgust and fatigue with Gibson's graphic scenes. However, *The Passion of the Christ* became a huge hit at the box office, raking in over $600 million on a production budget of $30 million.[41]

Eli Roth's *Hostel* (2005) channels fears about environmental degradation, international terrorism, and violent crime. Three young men backpack throughout Europe seeking sex and adventure. While in Amsterdam, Paxton (Jay Hernandez), Josh (Derek Richardson), and Icelander Óli (Eyþór Guðjónsson) meet Alexei (Lubomir Bukovy), a Russian who convinces them go to a Slovak hostel filled with sex-crazed Slovakian women. The backpackers board a train to Slovakia, where they meet a Dutch businessman (Jan Vlasák). They share a room at a hostel with Natalya (Barbara Nedeljáková) and Svetlana (Jana Kadeábková), single, attractive locals who entice Paxton and Josh into a spa, a disco, and soon into their beds. The next morning Oli disappears, and Japanese backpacker Kana (Jennifer Lim) also reports that her friend Yuki (Keiko Seiko) has disappeared. A photo sent from Yuki's phone shows Yuki and Oli beneath large smokestacks at an abandoned factory with the word Sayonara written on it. Unbeknownst to Paxton and Josh, Oli has already been decapitated and Yuki is undergoing extreme physical torture and may be dead. Later that night Paxton and Josh go out with Natasha and Svetlana, drinking to the point of inebriation. Paxton passes out in

70 Torture

the disco's storage room, and Josh awakens hours later handcuffed to a chair in a dungeon-like room filled with power tools and weapons. A Dutch businessman enters wearing a leather apron and gloves and begins to torture Josh. He begins drilling Josh just below his nipples as he explains his unfulfilled dream of becoming a surgeon. Then he cuts Josh's Achilles' tendons and allows him to crawl away before finally murdering him.

Later, Paxton is nearly killed after being lured to the same abandoned factory, where he discovers dozens of prisoners "purchased" from Elite Hunting, a firm that buys and sells human torture victims. He escapes his cell, but not before having his ring and pinky fingers severed by a chainsaw. He runs to a courtyard where he hears a woman screaming. Unable to resist, he returns to the factory and kills an American man in the act of burning Kana's face with a blowtorch. Kana lives, but one lifeless eye dangles from its socket. He and Kana leave the factory, but after she sees her disfigured reflection, she throws herself in front of an oncoming train, committing suicide. Paxton jumps aboard another train, where he sees the Dutch businessman. The businessman disembarks in Austria, followed by Paxton. The businessman heads to a restroom stall at the terminal, once again followed by Paxton, who severs the businessman's ring and pinky fingers, then slices his throat and finally drowns him. In this film the initial torture scenes serve as warm-ups for Paxton's revenge. Like many other torture porn films, the vengeance becomes even more violent than the original atrocities committed, as in most other post-9/11 torture porn movies, Roth's film did extremely well at the box office, earning $80.5 million with a production budget of just $4.8 million.[42]

In 2006, Wes Craven produced a successful remake of 1970s' hit *The Hills Have Eyes* directed by Alexandre Aja. In this version, Aja clearly identifies the film's intended villain. A title card at the beginning explains, "Between 1945 and 1962 the United States conducted 331 atmospheric nuclear tests. Today, the government still denies the genetic effects caused by the radioactive fallout". The first scene features three men testing for radioactivity in a remote part of the New Mexico desert. Suddenly a bloody man appears, begging for help. Pluto (Michael Baily Smith), a mutant disfigured by nuclear testing, stabs one of the men and slams him to the ground. Mutants quickly slaughter the other two technicians, chain their bodies to the back of a car, and quickly drive away. The rest of the film roughly parallels the earlier classic. The next scene features Ethel Carter (Kathleen Quinlan) and her husband, "Big" Bob Carter (Ted Levine), a retired police detective, driving through a remote desert from Cleveland, Ohio, to San Diego, California, on their silver wedding anniversary. They travel with their daughter Brenda (Emilie de Ravin), son Bobby (Dan Byrd), eldest daughter Lynn (Vinessa Shaw), her husband Doug Bukowski (Aaron Stanford), their baby daughter Catherine (Maisie Camilleri Preziosi), and two German Shepherd dogs, Beauty and Beast. As in the 1977 version, the Carter family takes a wrong turn and become trapped on a lonely road. In this version, the gas attendant (Tom Bower) deliberately tells them to take a false "short cut" that turns out to be the trap.

As in the earlier version, Big Bob hikes back to the gas station for help, while Bobby and Doug explore the surroundings. Mutants then attack the trailer, raping Brenda and killing one of the dogs. Papa Jupiter (Billy Drago) captures Big Bob returning from the gas station and, along with his son Lizard (Robert Joy), sets him on fire, drawing attention away from the trailer. Jupiter and Lizard then rape Brenda, kill Ethyl, and abduct baby Catherine. The mutants cook and devour the dead Carters, saving Catherine to serve as the main course in a special dinner.

Craven's version, like the original, drenches viewers in blood and gore as Carters and mutants are beheaded, split open by axe, burned to death, stabbed with a screwdriver, slammed by an iron skillet, blown up by exploding propane, pushed over a cliff, raped, and shot to death. Blood bathes the final sets. The 2006 version bursts with more realistic blood and gore, and successfully simulates human bodies in the process of being cooked and eaten by cannibals. Both versions assume prominent positions in the hierarchy of horror, often ranking among the top twenty horror films of all time.

Post-9/11 torture porn presents bleak, violent visions of human survival. The films revel in blood and gore, along with other forms of sadomasochism. They evoke a violence-saturated society seemingly taken straight out of the Marquis de Sade's repertoire of gore. David Edelstein examined the torture scenes in *Saw, Hostel, The Devil's Rejects*, which are among the most popular of the new torture porn genre. He describes films laden with "freak-show sensationalism" and charges their filmmakers with deliberately "titillating and shocking" audiences. He concludes by asking viewers, "Was it good for you, too?"[43] Torture porn movies and video games display, with bravado, behavior that psychologists would label "pathological" and "deviant". Despite that, legions of fans have made torture porn the fastest growing genre in popular culture.

Michael Kerner's *Torture Porn in the Wake of 9/11* postulates that post-9/11 torture porn places Americans in an untenable dilemma. "On the one hand, we imagine ourselves as agents of righteousness, the torchbearers of freedom and democracy, and on the other hand, we have to acknowledge our implicit or even explicit sanctioning of torture, even if it is designed ostensibly to keep us safe".[44] As revelations from the US's post-9/11 efforts to extract confessions from suspected terrorists surfaced, pop culture continued to reflect the disconnect from idealistic "city on a hill" self-conceptions and the reality of American anti-terrorist intelligence gathering.

Kathryn Bigelow's *Zero Dark Thirty* (2012) represents a hybrid genre somewhere between torture porn and war porn. Bigelow's film, set two years after the terrorist attacks on the World Trade Center and the Pentagon, depicts a post-9/11 military intelligence operation focused on finding and killing Osama bin Laden, the head of al-Qaeda and authorizer of the 9/11 attacks. Bigelow's film features Maya (Jessica Chastain), a young CIA officer fresh from Washington, who arrives at an offshore CIA prison and becomes involved in questioning suspected terrorist Ammar (Reda Kateb). Fellow CIA officer Dan (Jason Clarke) has Ammar bound

72 Torture

and tied to a rope. After Ammar proves recalcitrant under this duress, CIA agents force him down on the ground as Maya hands Dan a bucket and a towel so that Dan can waterboard him.

Internet Torture Porn

Currently, much torture porn resides on the internet in sites like *Real Torture Porn, Sickest Torture Porn, sickestlinks.com, Real Torture Videos, heavy-r.com/free porn/real-torture.html, heavy-r.com/free_porn/extreme-brutal-torture, (TORTURE BANK—BDSM torture tits and pussy pics photos, BDSM BANK FREE BONDAGE TORTURE PORN PICS)*, and "Snuff: Murder and Torture on the Internet" (*theverge.com/ . . . /snuff-murder-torture-internet*). These links often contain related links that are updated daily. In 2012 *The Verge* reported that snuff films were actually appearing on gore sites, also called shock sites, including *BestGore.com, GoreGrish.com*, and *TheYNC.com*, post videos of true-life killings, maiming, torture and abuse devoured by devoted fans involving cam recordings in Syria, Mexico, and the former Soviet Union of drug cartel beheadings, bombings, and private attacks and killings.[45]

Snuff photos and films are generally considered to be urban myths hyped by producers to cash in on whatever audiences exist for real filmed murders. However, the availability of the internet and the ability to photograph and film with mobile phones change that perspective. The series *3 Guys 1 Hammer* focuses on photos of around 20 real victims, kittens and dogs as well as people taken on a cell phone by Dnepropetrovsk Maniacs, a group of Ukraine teenagers that allegedly attacked and murdered nineteen during a one-month period in 2007. The photos depict or show three men attacking a 48-year-old male victim with a screwdriver and a hammer, then cooking and eating a slice of him.[46] *1 Lunatic, 1 Ice Pick* appears to be a real snuff film made by Luka Rocco Magnotta, who posted his murder, dismemberment, and cannibalization of Lin Jun, a Chinese International Student, in May 2012. The video shows a naked victim tied to a bed frame while his captor stabs him in the abdomen with an ice pick. He then slices the victim's throat and begins to slice various other parts of the body. Later he saws the head off with a kitchen knife and has anal sex with what is left of the torso. Using a knife and fork, the captor slices a slab of fatty flesh from the victim's behind and eats it before offering it to a hungry dog. The dog is unable to resist biting into the torso. Once the dog finishes, the captor inserts a bottle neck in the anus and sodomizes the body. In the end, Magnotta lies on a bed holding a severed hand and masturbates. Magnotta, a Canadian, mailed Lin Jun's severed limbs to Canadian elementary schools and federal political party offices. He fled to Germany where he was apprehended in June, 2012, while reading about himself at an internet café. Magnotta was convicted of first-degree murder on December 23, 2014.[47]

Facebook introduced a live-streaming video service in April 2016, inadvertently opening a powerful new venue for snuff films. In June 2016, Antonio Perkins, 28, of Chicago inadvertently broadcast his own murder while streaming a tour of his neighborhood. In July, Philando Castille was shot and killed by a policeman in Minnesota, and his horrified girlfriend streamed the aftermath on Facebook, receiving millions of views. In that same month three men in Norfolk, Virginia, received life-threatening gunshot wounds while being recorded on streaming video.

On January 5, 2017, four young Chicago residents were arrested and charged with felony, aggravated kidnapping, aggravated unlawful restraint, and aggravated battery with a deadly weapon for the horrific kidnapping of a teenager with diminished mental capacity while streaming their attacks on Facebook Live. The streaming video begins with scenes of the bound and gagged 18-year-old victim cowering in a corner when one of his assailants slashes his sweatshirt with a knife. Next, one of the attackers carves off a patch of the victim's scalp with a knife, and the assailants begin violently punching and kicking the screaming victim. When the torturer videotaping the attacks noticed that few Facebook followers were tuned into the streaming torture video, she complained into her microphone, "Y'all not even commenting on my shit!" The four African American attackers screamed, "Fuck Trump!" and "Fuck white people!" at their white victim. The four were charged with hate crimes as well as other felonies committed during the attack.[48]

In February 2017, a two-year-old boy and a man were killed and a pregnant woman wounded in a shooting in Chicago while someone live-streamed it on Facebook. Also in February 2017, the Dominican Republic arrested three males who allegedly shot and killed two radio journalists and injured another radio station staff member during a Facebook Live broadcast earlier in the week. The gunmen fatally shot Louis Manuel Medina as he was reading a radio script, then shot two other radio station employees off-camera.[49]

On Easter Sunday, April 16, 2017, Steve Stephens began filming himself in Cleveland, Ohio, stopping his car, getting out and confronting 74-year-old Robert Godwin Sr who had just finished an Easter meal with family and was holding a shopping bag. "She's the reason this is about to happen to you", Stephens said as he pointed a gun at Godwin's face, who attempted to shield it with the shopping bag. Stephens opened fire, killing Godwin, and posting the video on Facebook. In approximately three hours, Facebook removed the video and deleted Stephens' Facebook page. Their spokesperson explained, "This is a horrific crime, and we do not allow this kind of content on Facebook. We work hard to keep a safe environment on Facebook". The spokesman continued, ". . . and we are in touch with law enforcement in emergencies when there are direct threats to physical safety". In a separate Facebook posting Stephens boasted of killing more than a dozen other people during the Easter period.[50]

Robert Godwin's grizzly murder, and other live-streamed sexual assaults, prompted Facebook CEO Mark Zuckerberg in May 2017, to unveil a special initiative to combat live-streaming violence, primarily by hiring 3,000 additional screeners trained to detect and delete violent videos. Zuckerberg admitted the

74 Torture

ultimate hopelessness of shielding Facebook visitors from every piece of violent content, stating, "No matter how many people we have on the team, we are never going to be able to look at everything". Psychology and social sciences professor Jeanne Croteau assessed Zuckerberg's initiative to shield Facebook users from live-streaming violence, explaining, "Going live is very easy. It requires no verification of age, no pop-up about content, and no warnings about potential consequences for sharing something that is criminal or, at the very least, disturbing. There is no way to even filter whether the video will be appropriate for all ages". Julie Arduini, author of *Surrender Issues* expressed deep concern about Facebook Live, writing, "I can see someone struggling who isn't sure how to cry for help to attempt suicide. Even worse, I can see a desperate person taking their life for all to see. We've already seen a murder. There's pornography".[51]

Live-streaming video created a platform for easily accessible, real snuff and mayhem videos. Should we heed the current fascination with "torture" and "violence" as measured by Google Trends, and should we prepare for a grim and rising tide of real snuff and mayhem videos playing on these live-streaming websites? The rising popularity of torture porn should come as no surprise when one considers the power of torture in our society. The fact that torture currently permeates pop culture in the form of battlefield videos, snuff videos, ultra-violent Hollywood movies, splatter porn, revenge porn, and torture porn reveals a deep appetite for depictions of torture that transgresses traditional social values about the sanctity of life and avoiding pain. Torture in any context lays bare society's dirty secrets: the inequalities, indignities, verbal and physical attacks, maiming, and murders that often lie hidden from public awareness. Ultimately, society's fascination with the genre reflects the sexual power of violence. Sadomasochism appeals both to those suffering from various forms of psychological disorders, including Borderline Personality Disorder, and more dangerous forms of psychosis, as well as to those who enjoy playing the role of victim through masochism.

Punishment is a concept that bears close resemblance to torture. Punishment is, ". . . pain, suffering, or loss that serves as retribution".[52] Torture, on the other hand, is the inflicting of pain, suffering, or loss on a victim. A fine line divides retribution inflicted as punishment and retribution inflicted as torture. School discipline is often featured as subjects of violent pornography. The peaceful dominance normally displayed by teachers and administrators quickly transforms into more salacious roles in porn, while students usually play submissive ones. During the Victorian era "flage" porn, pornography about flagellation (a common punishment for school boys during this era), experienced a spike in popularity. Victorian men frequented a surprisingly large number of "flagellation brothels" to re-experience their childhood punishment, which they later eroticized.[53] Today "Teacher Fucks Student" and "Teacher Fucks Student in Classroom" are favorite porn videos. Likewise, "Principal Fucks Student" and "Principal Blackmails Innocent Teen Student". Churches also foster social and sexual roles, in which nuns, priests, or ministers relate with members of their congregations or students enrolled in their schools or churches. The potential for sexual abuse exists when male and female church officials play dominant roles with children, as revealed by popular porn videos like "Priest Fucks Altar Boys" and "Priest and Altar Boy Porn Gay Videos".

Foreign policy represents still another sadomasochistic human activity as nations test, antagonize, degrade, punish, and sometimes go to war with one another, resulting in tragic loss of life and personal injuries. The same endorphins triggered by torture are triggered by combat. Soldiers assume both sadistic and masochist roles depending upon battlefield conditions, as revealed by "Fucked by Enemy Soldiers" and "Soldiers Brutally Violate Captured Woman". During the ebb and flow of battle, individual combatants may play both aggressor and victim roles, both plotted along a sadomasochistic continuum ranging from sadistic violence to masochistic violence. The torture debate has now transformed into a cultural/political war between advocates of torture, including President Donald Trump and Gina Haspel, Trump's CIA Director who oversaw the CIA's notorious Rendition, Detention, and Interrogation program during the War on Terror. Haspel's appointment which was widely objected to, was confirmed by the Senate in 2018 and marks but one battle in a protracted culture war over the issue of interrogation torture.

Torture porn, including snuff videos, symbolically codifies and reinforces society's deepest fears, prejudices, and transgressions. It symbolically prepares audiences for political, military, and social violence. Perhaps the growing popularity of torture porn foreshadowed political violence against immigrants and other minorities during the Trump administration. Torture porn helps prepare the public for real-life physical and psychological violence. It whets appetites for violence while it justifies a rising level of socio/political violence.

Notes

1. Adam Green, "Why Pop Culture Makes us Think Torture is Normal: But Doesn't Make us Killers," *The New York Times*, May 22, 2005.
2. Tom Pollard, *Hollywood 9/11: Superheroes, Supervillains, and Super Disasters*, Boulder, CO: Paradigm Publications, 2011, p. 156.
3. Agnes Peirron, "House of Horrors," *GrandGuignol.com* accessed April 24, 2019, www.theflea.org/files/uploads/1411575243.pdf
4. Agnès Peirron, "House of Horrors," www.grandguignol.com/history.htm accessed September 1, 2016.
5. See Tom Pollard, *Sex and Violence: The Hollywood Censorship Wars*, Boulder, CO: Paradigm Publications, 2009.
6. Stephen Robb, "How *Psycho* Changed Cinema," *BBC Magazine*, April 1, 2010.
7. Xan Brooks, "Alfred Hitchcock: *Psycho* Was a Joke," *The Guardian*, February 8, 2013.
8. Lezard, Nicholas, "From the Sublime to the Surreal," *The Guardian*, London, February 21, 2009.
9. Jake Coyle, "After *Psycho*, a Shower of Violence in Movies," *The Washington Times*, November 23, 2012.
10. www.boxofficemojo.com/movies/?id=psycho.htm accessed April 25, 2019.

76 Torture

11. Roger Ebert, "Happy Birthday, 'Blood Feast': Digging into the Guts of the Very First Splatter Film," *RogerEbert.com*, July 3, 2013.
12. Roger Ebert, "The Texas Chainsaw Massacre," *Roger Ebert.com*, January 1, 1974.
13. John McCarty, *Splatter Movies: Breaking the Last Taboo of the Screen.* New York City, New York: St. Martin's Press, 1984.
14. Stuart Taylor, Jr. "Hinkley Hails 'Historic' Shooting to Win Love," *The New York Times,* July 9, 1982, www.azquotes.com/author/58839-John_Hinckley...
15. Xan Brooks, "Natural Born Copycats," *The Guardian*, December 19, 2002
16. www.acolumbinesite.com/eric/writing.html
17. "The Flagellation Effect, Can Pain Compensate for Immorality?" *APS: Association for Psychological Science*, January 26, 2011, www.psychologicalscience.org/news/full-frontal-psychology/the-flagellation-effect-can-pain-compensate-for-immorality.html accessed January 7, 2019.
18. Joseph C. Franklin, "How Pain Can Make You Feel Better," *Scientific American*, November 16, 2010.
19. Roger Ebert, "Crash," *Rogerebert.com*, March 21, 1997.
20. Jacob Shelton, "16 Real Life Crimes and Murders Inspired by the Joker," https://www.ranker.com/list/real-crimes-inspired-by-the-joker/jacob-shelton accessed April 25, 2019.
21. Bruno Waterfield and John Bingham, "Joker" Knifeman Kills Children and Worker in Belgian Creche, *The Telegraph*, January 23, 2009, www.telegraph.co.uk › . . . › Europe › Belgium.
22. *Batman: Arhkam Knight* video game 2015.
23. Seb Patrick, "The Joker: The Nature of Batman's Greatest Foe," *Den of Geek*, December 13, 2013. Archived from the original on December 27, 2013 accessed December 26, 2013.
24. Seb Patrick, "The Joker: The Nature of Batman's Greatest Foe," *Den of Geek*, December 13, 2013. Archived from the original on December 27, 2013 accessed December 26, 2013.
25. Mikita Brottman, *Funny Peculiar: Gershon Legman and the Psychopathology of Humor.* London: Routledge, 2013, p. 107.
26. Brian Fitzpatrick, "Dark Knight: The Pornography of Violence," *Human Events*, August 11, 2008.
27. David A. Cook, *Lost Illusions: American Cinema in the Shadow of Watergate and Vietnam.* Berkeley, CA: University of California Press, Ltd., 2000, p. 233.
28. "CIA Tactics: What Is 'Enhanced Interrogation Techniques?'," *BBC.com*, December 10, 2014.
29. "What Does the Law Say about Torture?" *International Committee of the Red Cross*, June 24, 2011 accessed April 25, 2019.
30. Aaron Michael Kerner, *Torture Porn in the Wake of 9/11.* New Brunswick: Rutgers University Press, 2013.
31. "What Is Advanced Interrogation?" *BBC News*, December 10, 2014.
32. www.*azquotes.com* › *Authors* › *Jesse Ventura* accessed April 25, 2019.
33. C.S. Lewis, *The Discarded Image: An Introduction to Medieval and Renaissance Literature.* Cambridge, UK: Cambridge University Press, 1964.
34. David Wright, "Donald Trump Defends Torture: 'Nothing Should Be Taken Off the Table'," *CNN*, February 16, 2016.
35. The Texas Chainsaw Massacre,—Box Office Mojo, 2003, www.boxofficemojo.com/movies/?id=tcm03.htm, accessed April 27, 2019.
36. David Kehr, "Film in Review: The Texas Chainsaw Massacre," *The New York Times*, October 17, 2003.
37. Roger Ebert, "The Texas Chainsaw Massacre," *Roger Ebert.com*, October 17, 2003.
38. The Texas Chainsaw Massacre,—Box Office Mojo, 2003 www.boxofficemojo.com/movies/?id=saw.htm, accessed April 27, 2019.
39. "Christian Torture Porn," *S-USHI, US Intellectual History Blog*, December 12, 2014, s-usih.org/2014/12/christian-torture-porn.html

Torture **77**

40. Roger Ebert, "The Passion of the Christ," www.rogerebert.com/reviews/the-passion-of-the-christ-2004
41. The Texas Chainsaw Massacre—Box Office Mojo, 2003, www.boxofficemojo.com/movies/?id=passionofthechrist.htm, accessed April 27, 2019.
42. Hostel—Box Office Mojo, 2006, www.boxofficemojo.com/movies/?id=hostel.htm, accessed April 27, 2019.
43. David Edelstein, "Now Playing at Your Local Multiplex: Torture Porn," *New York Magazine*, February 6, 2006.
44. Michael Kerner, *Torture Porn in the Wake of 9/11: Horror, Exploitation, and the Cinema of Sensation*. New Brunswick: Rutgers University Press, 2015, p. 25.
45. Leslie Anderson, "Snuff: Murder on the Internet, and the People Who Watch Them," *The Verge*, June 13, 2012.
46. timwbrap, Bestgore.com; The Most Screwed-up Website You Will Ever Visit, May 28, 2012, www.sickchirpse.com/bestgore-com-the-most-screwed-up-website-you accessed April 27, 2019.
47. Alan Woods, "Luka Magnotta Is Convicted of First-Degree Murder," *The Star* (Canada) December 23, 2014.
48. Holly Yan, Sheena Jones, and Steve Almasy, "Chicago Torture Video: Four Charged with Hate Crimes, Kidnapping," *CNN*, January 5, 2017.
49. Kimiyo de Freytas-Tamura, "Dominicans Arrest Three in Killings Streamed Live," *The New York Times*, February 16, 2017.
50. "Police Expand Manhunt for Facebook Video Murder Suspect Steve Stephen," *CBS News*, April 17, 2017. https://www.cbsnews.com/news/police-press-manhunt-for-facebook-video-murder-suspect
51. Jessica Guynn, "Facebook Live Horrifies Users, Who Say Facebook's Still Not Doing Enough," *USA Today*, May 3, 2017.
52. www.merriam-webster.com/dictionary/punishment
53. Tracy Clark-Flory, "'Pleasure Bound': The Victorians' Kinky Side," *Salon*, February 20, 2011.

Bibliography

Anderson, Leslie, "Snuff: Murder on the Internet, and the People Who Watch Them," *The Verge*, June 13, 2012.

Brooks, Xan, "Alfred Hitchcock: *Psycho* Was a Joke," *The Guardian*, February 8, 2013.

Brottman, Mikita, *Funny Peculiar: Gershon Legman and the Psychopathology of Humor*. London: Routledge, 2013, p. 107.

"CIA Tactics: What Is 'Enhanced Interrogation Techniques?'," *BBC News*, December 10, 2014. https://www.bbc.com/news/world-us-canada-11723189

Cook, David A., *Lost Illusions: American Cinema in the Shadow of Watergate and Vietnam*. Berkeley, California: University of California Press, Ltd., 2000, p. 233.

Coyle, Jake, "After *Psycho*, a Shower of Violence in Movies," *The Washington Times*, November 23, 2012.

Ebert, Roger, "Crash," *Rogerebert.com*, March 21, 1997.

Ebert, Roger, "Happy Birthday, 'Blood Feast': Digging into the Guts of the Very First Splatter Film," *RogerEbert.com*, July 3, 2013.

Ebert, Roger, "The Passion of the Christ," www.rogerebert.com/reviews/the-passion-of-the-christ-2004

Ebert, Roger, "The Texas Chainsaw Massacre," *Roger Ebert.com*, January 1, 1974.

Ebert, Roger, "The Texas Chainsaw Massacre," *Roger Ebert.com*, October 17, 2003.

Edelstein, David, "Now Playing at Your Local Multiplex: Torture Porn," *New York Magazine*, February 6, 2006.

78 Torture

Fitzpatrick, B., "Dark Knight: The Pornography of Violence," *Human Events*, August 11, 2008.

"The Flagellation Effect, Can Pain Compensate for Immorality?" *APS: Association for Psychological Science*, January 26, 2011, www.psychologicalscience.org/news/full-frontal-psychology/the-flagellation-effect-can-pain-compensate-for-immorality.html accessed January 7, 2019.

Franklin, Joseph C., "How Pain Can Make You Feel Better," *Scientific American*, November 16, 2010.

Green, Adam, "Why Pop Culture Makes Us Think Torture Is Normal: But Doesn't Make Us Killers," *The New York Times*, May 22, 2005.

Kerner, Michael, *Torture Porn in the Wake of 9/11: Horror, Exploitation, and the Cinema of Sensation*. New Brunswick: Rutgers University Press, 2015, p. 25.

Lezard, Nicholas, "From the Sublime to the Surreal," *The Guardian*, London, February 21, 2009.

McCarty, John, *Splatter Movies: Breaking the Last Taboo of the Screen*. New York: St. Martin's Press, 1984.

Nispel, Marcus, "Film in Review: The Texas Chainsaw Massacre," *The New York Times*, October 17, 2003.

Patrick, Seb, "The Joker: The Nature of Batman's Greatest Foe," *Den of Geek*, December 13, 2013. Archived from the original on December 27, 2013 accessed December 26, 2013.

Peirron, Agnes, "House of Horrors," www.grandguignol.com/history.htm accessed September 1, 2016.

Pollard, Tom, *Hollywood 9/11: Superheroes, Supervillains, and Super Disasters*. Boulder, CO: Paradigm Publications, 2011, p. 156.

Pollard, Tom, *Sex and Violence: The Hollywood Censorship Wars*. Boulder, CO: Paradigm Publications, 2009.

Robb, Stephen, "How *Psycho* Changed Cinema," *BBC Magazine*, April 1, 2010.

"What Does the Law Say about Torture?" *International Committee of the Red Cross*, June 24, 2011.

Wright, David, "Donald Trump Defends Torture: 'Nothing Should Be Taken Off the Table'," *CNN*, February 16, 2016.

5

WAR

The aftermath of 9/11 ushered in a new violent porn genre which appeared featuring increasingly graphic, real-life images of war casualties, shockingly violent combat movies, violent video games, and violence-laden amateur war photos and videos. Pop culture became rife with what was previously described as "superheroes, supervillains, and super disasters".[1] Interest in what critics now label "war porn" ramped up, with the spike beginning in 2012.[2] By 2016 cinematic violence nearly quadrupled from previous decades,[3] stemming in part from the US involvement in Afghanistan, Iraq, Yemen, Syria, Somalia, and Libya. What are the root causes and trajectory of today's "pornographic" fascination with violent combat?

French social theorist Jean Beaudrillard coined the term "war porn", a new pornography genre, in 2004 after viewing the images of torture taken by American occupation troops in Iraq's notorious Abu Ghraib prison. The photographs of naked Iraqi prisoners forced to perform sexual acts on each other, of Pvt Lynndie England holding a naked prisoner by a leash, and of shackled, naked, hooded prisoners forced to stand precariously on stools or in pyramids on fellow prisoners' backs qualified, in his mind, as a new kind of violent pornography. Beaudrillard considered violent combat images and videos pornographic because of the, "excessiveness of a power designating itself as abject and pornographic". He points to an image of a CIA agent making an Arab strip, forcing him into a girdle and net stockings, and then making him sodomize a pig, "all the while taking photographs which he will send to the man's village and all his close relations". He stated that these degrading, violent images and videos, ". . . have become today as virtual as the war itself, and for this reason their specific violence adds to the specific violence of the war".[4]

Beaudrillard's analysis generated broad interest, including that of British journalist James Harkin who concluded, "War porn is designed not to titillate, but

80 War

to humiliate its victims and horrify its audience. Like pornography, its producers heighten their sense of reality by videoing themselves in the act, while its audience does the same by ogling the videos".[5] Critic Matthis Chiroux, in *The Huffington Post*, defines war porn as, ". . . any image or video produced in a combat zone depicting death, violence, gore, brutality, depravity, lewd behavior or any other shocking act that would be perceived unacceptable or even criminal if committed on American soil".[6]

The invasions of Afghanistan and Iraq (2001–2003) resulted in the deployment of more than a quarter of a million American troops plus tens of thousands of allied forces. Troops were issued small helmet and rifle barrel cams that constantly recorded images and videos, including fatalities of US and enemy soldiers. Soon those violent combat images and videos flooded the internet. Thousands of war images, often dubbed with heavy metal or rap music, were uploaded by current or returning US combatants. At the same time, producers of movies, music, and video games ramped up violent content in their depictions of wars in space, in the air, on the ground, and at sea to match the combat currently raging. Real-life violent images quickly inspired pop culture's fascination with warfare.

War porn appears in multiple forms. In 2014, German photographer Christoph Bangert published *War Porn*, a book of war photos that the magazine he worked for declined to publish. Reviewer Monika Griebeler interviewed Bangert about the book, describing a few of the photographs, "A beheaded man's body eaten at by dogs and ditched in a dump. A baby left alone in a basket after a house was stormed. A naked and battered body on a blood-soaked sheet". She asked Bangert, "Do the images of war have to be so brutal?" He replied, "The images have to be as brutal as war itself. A war is nothing sacred, nothing extraordinary. People have been fighting wars throughout human history. That has to be documented just like anything else".[7]

Seattle-based writer David Shields found himself increasingly drawn to graphic combat images printed in *The New York Times*. He spent months going over every front-page war photo from the start of the wars, reviewing more than 1,000 images. From this research Shields published *War is Beautiful: The New York Times Pictorial Guide to the Glamour of Armed Conflict* (2015). In the book's introduction, Shields describes overwhelming feelings of, ". . . rapture, bafflement, and repulsion . . ." regarding the powerful images. He writes about discovering "beauty" as the book's reprinted combat photos began transforming in his mind from "life-like" to "picture-like". He described his project as, ". . . my little war porn addiction".[8]

In 2016, novelist Roy Scranton published a fictional book entitled *War Porn*, the first major work of fiction depicting the rise of war porn media. Critic Michiko Katutani, reviewing the novel in *The New York Times*, explains *War Porn's* division into three separate but interrelated stories, which allows Scranton to, ". . . illuminate the war from different angles, and some stream-of-consciousness-like interludes that suggest links between Iraq and Vietnam and other wars, and the original human sins of violence and hubris".[9] One character, Wilson, deploys to

Baghdad, where he patrols the streets endlessly and feels, ". . . damned to drive the same maze over and over till somebody killed me". Scranton defines war porn as, "Videos, images, and narratives featuring graphic violence, often brought back from combat zones, viewed voyeuristically or for emotional gratification".[10]

Pop culture abounds with sadomasochists like The Joker (Heath Ledger) from *The Dark Knight* who giggles whenever Batman strikes him. *Fight Club*'s Tyler Durden breaks into orgasmic laughter while being bludgeoned by a bar owner. Pearl (Lucy Liu) smiles and licks the blood after a sharp blow to the face and pants excitedly when someone holds a gun to her head. Many pop culture characters, heroes as well as villains, display aspects of combat sadomasochism.

Internet War Porn

War porn images on the internet vary widely and include enemy kill and humiliation shots, as well as people dressed as military having sex with each other or with multiple partners. It also includes images of fierce beasts having sex with young women or young men, cartoon characters identified as military having sex with each other, being raped, or suffering violent attacks. Sexually themed *Star Wars* scenes currently populate the internet, including male Storm Troopers raping female victims. Gun camera footage proliferate on the internet, as well as smart bombs, air bombardment, drone warfare, Hellfire missiles, and "trophy shots". The subjects range from violent to sexual and sometimes a combination of sex and violence. War porn sites are now routinely taken down.

As thousands of American combatants returned from fighting foreign wars, increasing numbers of combat images from those wars became available on many websites. The site (www.gotwarporn.com) became one of the most popular but was later taken down. Combatant-photographed images could be searched for by type of weapons, type of wounds, snuff videos, trophy shots. Helmet and rifle cams captured actual combat scenes later edited for the internet. One bears the label "Intense!!! True Close Ambush from the Taliban", another is called "Sniper Kill Shot", and another announces, "Navy SEALS and 101st Airborne Heavy Firefight in Ramadi, Iraq", while another is labeled, "Close Range Firefight with Taliban Visible". Still another proclaims, "US Soldiers Eliminate Three Taliban Fighters During Ambush". One simply bears the label, "Badass Firefight". One of the first websites to offer war porn was Nowthatsfuckedup.com. Its proprietor, Chris Wilson, explained that combatants in Iraq experienced difficulties using their credit cards in Iraq to access pornography. Accordingly, Wilson offered free access to his sexual porn website to any American combatant in Afghanistan or Iraq who shared graphic combat images, including kill shots, or videos with his viewers. One forum on the site titled "Pictures from Iraq and Afghanistan—Gory" which featured photos of bloody body parts, exploded heads, and intestines spilling out of people, accompanied by running commentary from soldiers celebrating kills and cracking jokes.[11] The US military took umbrage with Wilson's efforts to

82 War

profit from graphic combat images and videos and shut down his website.[12] The website now directs any who attempt to access it to the Polk County, Florida, Sheriff's Office.

Multiple sites advertise "Porn Wars, Porn Videos & Sex Movies" including popular porn Pornhub.com, Redtube.com., and Xvideos.com. They provide free war/sex videos, often featuring sexual abuse of prisoners or simulating sex in military settings. In myriad ways, they combine violent combat and sex, simulating violent sexualized combat situations including raping female prisoners and forcing female captives into "squirt wars". One site advertises "war story with added sex". The internet is also filled with videos having war-themed titles including, "I'm back from war", in a sexual copulation video with naked bodies and no military icons. Another popular video proclaims: "Make Love Not War" and shows naked bodies having sex with each other. Another, titled "Sperm Wars", depicts dueling ejaculating penises. One video is titled "Anal Wars". Another website is titled "Prisoner of War Porn Video".

"Combat sadomasochists" recently arose as a "TV trope". This has evolved into pain addiction, "the pain from combat wounds, both their own and others. When cut, stabbed or shot, they will moan in ecstasy and *lap up the blood*. After harming an opponent, and especially when they take a life, the sensation and expression on their face will be orgasmic".[13] Websites include "All the tropes" and "Playing with TV tropes".

Live Combat

In 2013, public fascination with real combat images and footage resulted in reality-based combat series on *National Geographic*. Meg Gleason of *National Geographic* reports that their series *Eyewitness War*, ". . . takes you right onto the battlefield through footage shot by the men and women on the front lines, themselves. This footage, combined with their interviews about their experiences, tells the story of war from the point of view of the people fighting it". It carries the tagline, "Military engagements narrated and filmed via 1st person helmet cam by the soldiers involved". The series relies on cam footage of the wars in Afghanistan and Iraq. Gleason explains that "Now, more than ever, members of the Armed Forces are recording what they're seeing". These recordings are made possible because of new miniature, affordable, easy-to-use cameras. Gleason explains that

> "They can be attached to anything from a helmet to a tank or machine gun, and record exactly what these soldiers are going through. Using these cameras, we get to experience the chaos of a firefight, witness the destruction of an IED, and feel the panic when a comrade has fallen".[14]

National Geographic supports the series with a website dedicated to the "Fallen Heroes" killed during filming of the combat sequences. They include Ben Chisholm, Charles M. High, IV, Carlos Negron, and Brian Tabata. The youngest two, Charles M. High IV and Brian Tabata, were only 21 when they were killed. The oldest combat fatality, Specialist Carlos J. Negron, was aged 40. Each of these soldiers of the 101st Airborne could wind up on the "Fallen Heroes" website. The civilian photographs of "Fallen Heroes", taken long before they engaged in combat, smile innocently at viewers, evoking both tragedy and irony.

Not to be outdone, in September 2016, the *Discovery Channel* released its own live cam show titled *Taking Fire*, a six-part series featuring solder-shot footage. The new show acquired licensed helmet camera footage from a few soldiers in the 101st Airborne Division for, "their personal, GoPro record of their experiences".[15] Season One launched with "Band of Brothers", in which helmet cams follow an Army assault team for one year in Afghanistan. Rookie soldiers from the 101st Airborne Division deploy to Combat Outpost, Michigan (the name of the outpost). As they climb a ridge, they uncover an ambush that exposes them in the open with no shelter from enemy fire. The enemy, as well as our troops, fire machine guns. A narrator explains that the first minute of any firefight often determines the outcome as one side or the other establishes firepower superiority. This series also includes a section commending "live heroes" including J.J McCool, Kyle "Buddy" Boucher, Kyle Petry, Ken Shriver, Chris Adams, Matthew Shreeve, Blake Trahan, Anthony Ortega, Richard Sandoval, Robert Castellano, and Tom Musgrave. While *Taking Fire* reveals the blood and gore of war, it also valorizes and celebrates wartime bravery. However, the series makes it very clear that the former 101st Rookies quickly became seasoned veterans who will doubtlessly live with PTSD and other combat-related disabilities for the rest of their lives.

Video Games

The popularity of violent video games that feature combat or urban warfare, continues to rise, and fans often become addicted. In 2016, the Entertainment Software Association announced in their annual report that 63% of households include at least one video "gamer". The average age of video gamers is 35 for men and 45 for women, with 59% of regular gamers being males. Men also comprise 60% of those who purchase the games, which feature increasingly high levels of violence.[16] Violence also permeates children's video games. The American Academy of Child and Adolescent Psychiatry discovered that the most popular children's video games include violent, socially questionable content, including standard tropes of murdering humans as well as animals.[17]

Today's video games rely on a combat-like format, allowing players to participate in combat on the battlefield or in the streets. One of the most popular, *Battlefield: Hardline*, invites players to assume the role of cops chasing violent criminals. Players fire pistols, shotguns, and rifles to blast criminals. They engage in nearly continuous firefights producing bloody combat and characters screaming in pain. Some scenes feature execution-style gunshots to the head, and in one, a character being fed to crocodiles. *Bloodborne* tasks players with tracking down and killing subhuman beasts using pistols, scythes, and other weapons, resulting in copious blood being spilled. *Dying Light* features players exterminating zombies by decapitating, electrocuting, and incinerating them, even drenching their avatars in blood. *Hatred* invites participants to assume the role of psychopaths who attempt to kill innocent bystanders and police with guns, flamethrowers, and bombs. Victims scream for mercy before being executed in profanity-laden rants.[18]

Norman Bates (Anthony Perkins) broods beneath fierce raptors, reflecting their threats of violence. Hitchcock based Bates loosely on Ed Gein, notorious Wisconsin serial killer, corpse mutilator, and necrophiliac.

FIGURE 5.1 Alfred Hitchcock, *Psycho*, 1960
Source: Pacific Film Archive

The rising popularity of violent games and videos parallels increasingly popular Hollywood movies containing high levels of graphic violence. A 2014 study reveals that 89.7% of all popular movies depict main characters engaging in violence, and 77% of these violent episodes also depict characters engaging in alcohol, sex, or tobacco. Those percentages remain stable for the past twenty-five years. By contrast, movies depicting smoking tobacco declined from 68% in 1985 to just 21.4% by 2010.[19]

The popularity of war porn images, videos, and movies occurs during a period of heightened foreign combat against ISIS and other terrorist groups. Those wars need to be seen in their historical context since, with only a scant five-year period during the Great Depression, America engaged in armed combat every year since its founding in 1776. With the US fighting perpetual wars, no wonder a growing segment of the public eagerly participates in war porn video games.

Hollywood's War Porn

Writer and former diplomat Peter Van Buren charges that Hollywood creates its own versions of war porn. He notes that combat films rely on a standard formula, from John Wayne in the World War II-era *Sands of Iwo Jima* to today's *American Sniper*, typically conforming to the following template:

> American soldiers are good, the enemy bad. Nearly every war movie is going to have a scene in which Americans label the enemy as "savages", "barbarians", or "bloodthirsty fanatics", typically following a "sneak attack" or a suicide bombing. Our country's goal is to liberate; the enemy's, to conquer.[20]

Hollywood's war films celebrate the courage, tenacity, and combat abilities of Americans while, at the same time, ignoring the military achievements of US adversaries. Van Buren points out pop culture's dominant patriotic strain, explaining, "American soldiers believe in God and Country . . .". However, Van Buren asserts that pop culture depicts "the enemy" as corrupt dictators, religious or political fanatics, ". . . and it goes without saying (though it's said) that his God— whether an emperor, Communism, or Allah—is evil". Because so much popular culture relies on violent scenes and bloody plots, Van Buren labels today's increasingly violence-saturated combat movies "war porn".[21]

Allen Dwan's *Sands of Iwo Jima* (1949) stars John Wayne as Marine Sgt John M. Stryker, an ultra-tough drill instructor charged with transforming raw recruits into seasoned marines. After Stryker's wife leaves him, he pushes the recruits even harder than usual, and some of his fellow marines suspect that he may be taking his frustrations out on his recruits. Wayne's Stryker emerges as a super tough combat instructor and brave commander who serves as role model for his men and who struggles to measure up to his own standards of physical and mental fitness.

86 War

The Japanese forces are stereotyped and one-dimensional. When the entire unit receives orders to join the November 1943 invasion of Tarawa, they are each severely tested in bloody battle. Stryker succeeds in destroying a deadly machine gun nest and eventually leads his men into taking Mt Suribachi in the iconic scene of marines raising the American flag on the summit. However, Stryker never witnesses this achievement because he is shot in the back by a Japanese sniper.

Dwan's film epitomized WWII combat films by glorifying "tough as nails" soldiers, sailors, and marines, pitting them against fanatical, sadistic Japanese fighters in classic combat films. Others include *Guadalcanal Diary* (1943), *The Fighting Seabees* (1944), *30 Seconds Over Tokyo* (1944), *Back to Bataan* (1945), and *Flying Leathernecks* (1951). Filmmakers easily substituted fanatical Nazis for Japanese in Hollywood's depiction of the war against Germany and Italy in films like *Crash Dive* (1943), *Action in the Atlantic* (1943), *Appointment in Berlin* (1943), *The Story of G.I. Joe* (1945), *A Walk in the Sun* (1945), and *Twelve O'Clock High* (1949). These films also conform to Hollywood's standard model, defined by Van Buren, with big doses of propaganda, patriotism, and, of course, violence.

We Were Soldiers (2002)

Randall Wallace's *We Were Soldiers* (2002) follows the exploits of the US Seventh Calvary in the first American battle of the Vietnam War against a far larger force of battle-hardened Viet Cong. Lt Colonel Hal Moore (Mel Gibson), promises his troops that he will be the first to step on the battlefield and the last to step away from it. His troops fight bravely against superior numbers in what the Americans call the Valley of Death. A narrator explains the result of Moore's battles:

> In Saigon, Hal Moore's superiors congratulated him for killing over 1,800 enemy soldiers. Then ordered him to lead the Seventh Cavalry back into the valley of death. He led them and fought beside them for 235 more days. Some had families waiting. For others, their only family would be the men they bled beside. There were no bands, no flags, no Honor Guards to welcome them home. They went to war because their country ordered them to. But in the end, they fought not for their country or their flag, they fought for each other.

Wallace's film received kudos for historical accuracy, and reviewer A.O. Scott comments on the film's "wrenching violence" and describes the action. "Bullets smash faces and rip through bellies inches from the camera, whose lens is occasionally smeared with blood. When the snap of gunfire and the thump of artillery momentarily fall silent, the air is filled with the moans of the wounded".[22] *BBC's* Danny Graydon notes "Gibson is a perfect vessel for the script's dewey-eyed patriotism, and the odd "Braveheart" moment is dutifully recycled in a strong performance".[23] Critic Roger Ebert observed that, "Some will object . . . that the battle scenes consist of Americans with killing waves of faceless, non-white enemies".[24] While some might object to the movie's excessive levels of violence, as Ebert points out, others might relish the film's battlefield carnage.

Rambo (2008)

Sylvester Stallone's *Rambo* (2008) raised the ante for on-screen blood and gore. John Rambo (Sylvester Stallone) and a few fellow mercenaries massacre more people in the final battles with Myanmar troops (239) than those killed in all three other *Rambo* films combined. In this version Rambo personally dispatches 132 thuggish Burmese military in the final scenes.[25] One of the most iconic scenes occurs when Rambo commandeers a 50-caliber machine gun and mows down an entire battalion of Myanmar troops. In the process, he saves hundreds of Christianized Karen people, abused and targeted for extinction by Myanmar military forces. explains to Sarah (Julie Benz), a Christian missionary, his views about war:

> That we're like animals! It's in the blood! It's natural! Peace? That's an accident! It's what is! When you're pushed, killing's as easy as breathing. When the killing stops in one place, it starts in another, but that's okay " . . . cause you're killing for your country. But it ain't your country who asks you, it's a few men up top who want it. Old men start it, young men fight it, nobody wins, everybody in the middle dies . . . and nobody tells the truth!"

In typical action hero fashion, Rambo wields a variety of weapons, including machine guns and his iconic knife. He targets corrupt fighters intent on genocide in the only way he knows they will understand, through violence. With its high body count and copious spilled blood, *Rambo* qualifies as war porn.

300 (2006)

Zack Snyder's *300* (2006), based on a violent graphic novel by Frank Miller, is considered one of the most violent war films of all time. *The Sydney Morning Herald*'s Paul Byrnes observes that Snyder's film "would have Hitler rising from his [grave]". Byrnes notes that Snyder's film "is violent enough to make you shudder and close enough to fascist art to make your skin crawl". The film

> " . . . celebrates all the things the Fuehrer loved—the glorious, operatic spectacle of senseless death, the ruthless weeding out of the weak, the gross caricaturing of the enemy, the indoctrination of the young, even a mountain-climbing ordeal for the hero—and all as it purports to be a movie about freedom".[26]

Snyder's film depicts the historic Battle of Thermopylae, the 480 BC war between Persian king Xerxes's (Rodrigo Santoro) invasion army of 100,000 soldiers against

88 War

Spartan King Leonidas's (Gerard Butler) royal bodyguards of 300 of the best Spartan soldiers assisted by a force of 6,000 drawn from other Greek states. Leonidas selects the Hot Gates of Thermopylae Pass, a narrow mountain pass that the Persians must cross in order to invade Greece, so he can neutralize the Persians' overwhelming numerical superiority. The Greeks construct a wall to delay the Persian onslaught and deploy into their iconic phalanx battle formations, inflicting heavy casualties on the Persians. Xerxes, the Persian king, sends a messenger to King Leonidas:

Messenger: All that God-King Xerxes requires is this: a simple offering of earth and water. A token of Sparta's submission to the will of Xerxes.

King Leonidas: Submission? Well that's a bit of a problem. See, rumor has it the Athenians have already turned you down, and if those philosophers and, uh, boy-lovers have found that kind of nerve, then . . .

Leonidas and his 300 Spartan warriors hold onto the narrow pass against thousands of Persian soldiers, suffering the horrors of battle depicted in gory detail. Critic Roger Ebert observes that this film, ". . . is like a comic book brought to life and pumped with steroids". Ebert notes that unbelievably, "Every single male character, including the hunchback, has the muscles of a finalist for Mr. Universe". Ebert also laments "hundreds, even thousands, of horrible deaths" that occur in this film. "This can get depressing". Finally, he recalls, "In old movies, ancient Greeks were usually sort of noble. Now they have become lager louts. They celebrate a fascist ideal. They assume a bloodthirsty audience, or one suffering from attention deficit (how many disembowelings do you have to see to get the idea?)"[27]

The Hurt Locker (2008)

Kathryn Bigelow's Academy Award-winning *The Hurt Locker* (2008) begins with a quotation from writer Chris Hedges, "The rush of battle is often a potent and lethal addiction, for war is a drug". Bigelow focuses closely on a US Army Explosive Ordinance Unit (EOU) involved in dangerous bomb defusing in 2004. In the opening scene, the leader of the EOU team, Sgt Matt Thompson (Guy Pierce), clothed in a protective suit, is blown apart by an Improvised Explosive Device (IED) after a local merchant with a cell phone sends a special code to the bomb, despite efforts by Thompson's teammates to kill him before he can ignite the explosives. A new leader of the bomb defusing platoon, Sgt William James (Jeremy Renner), successfully defuses a similar IED by using unconventional tactics that anger his teammates. The next day James, wearing a protective suit, defuses a more powerful IED wired to a parked car. The bomb unit continues its ultra-dangerous work of defusing and safely exploding powerful bombs, sometimes while being observed by enemy forces. Events turn chaotic as the city of Baghdad becomes engulfed in enemies attempting to bomb American positions. The activities of the bomb team are reminiscent of real videotaped events captured by soldiers' helmet cams.

Bigelow's film received six Academy Awards, including one for Best Picture and one honoring Bigelow as Best Director. However, many critics identified it as war porn, including historian Marilyn Young, who labeled it, ". . . video game-ish war porn".[28] Iraqi War veteran Jon Davis, who was part of an EOU in Iraq, complained about the film's lack of realism and concluded, "Basically, *The Hurt Locker* is nothing more than war porn".[29] Also, the popular blog "Critical Women" concludes that Bigelow's film is nothing more than, ". . . war porn at the movies".[30]

Argo (2012)

Ben Affleck's *Argo* (2012) received seven Academy Awards, including the Best Picture award. It depicts the role of CIA operatives in rescuing six US Embassy workers from the embassy, hiding them at the residence of the Canadian ambassador to Iran, and spiriting them out of the country by pretending that they were part of the cast and crew of *Argo*, a sci-fi feature film being shot in Iran. Affleck's film earned an astonishing $232 million on a production budget of under $45 million, making it one of the most profitable movies in film history. However, critics decried the film's blatant historical inaccuracies, starting with the depiction of CIA agent Tony Mendez's (Ben Affleck) heroic role in getting six American embassy employees out of Tehran. Affleck's film ignores the leadership role played by Ken Taylor, Canada's ambassador to Iran, the actual hero who performed the deeds attributed to CIA agent Mendez. In fact, prior to *Argo*, the hostage rescue mission was known as the "Canadian Caper".[31]

A further historical inaccuracy in *Argo* lies in its overall depiction of Iranians as aggressive, murderous, fanatical, and completely flat characters, whereas the Americans emerge as complex, sensitive, creative, intelligent, and humanitarian. Critic and former soldier Peter Van Buren labeled Affleck's film, ". . . honorary war porn . . ." because it, ". . . reduces the debacle of years of U.S. meddling in Iran to a high-fiving hostage rescue. All it takes these days to turn a loss into a win is to zoom in tight enough to ignore defeat".[32]

Fury (2014)

David Ayer's *Fury* (2014) depicts the harrowing travels of a US Sherman tank crew during the final days of WWII in Germany. Ayer relied on real American and German tanks lent from private collections, as well as real uniforms. The cast was required to attend a "Boot Camp" that operated 24/7 so that they could appear battle-hardened.[33] Brad Pitt plays Don "Wardaddy" Collier, a gritty tank commander who attempts to assure his crew's survival during battles against Nazis, *Hitlerjugend* teenagers in Nazi uniforms, and powerful 60-ton Tiger and 70-ton Tiger II tanks. The film opens on a devastated battlefield as a lone Nazi soldier rides a horse through a field strewn with grotesque bodies and charred remains of

90 War

tanks and other debris. As he rides beside a seemingly wrecked US tank dubbed "Fury", "Wardaddy" Collier suddenly pops out of the tank and stabs the Nazi repeatedly, then releases the horse and slips back inside the disabled tank to his crew in the midst of emergency repairs so they can return to the base.

Arriving at their base, Collier learns that his tank was the only one to survive the battle. He orders his crew to refuel and prepare for another mission when he is greeted by Norman Ellison (Logan Lehrman), a raw recruit who has never previously served on a tank. Ellison informs him he has been assigned to take over the job of gunner since Collier's previous gunner was killed in action. Collier says, "I started this war killing Germans in Africa, then in Belgium. Now I'm killing Germans in Germany. It will end soon, but before it does a lot more people gotta die". Trini "Gordo" Garcia (Michael Pena) explains:

> In France, we hit the beach right after D-Day and fought through all those fucking hedgerows. We finally broke out into open country and bypassed all these Kraut divisions. We linked up with the Canadians and British and trapped an entire Kraut Army pulling back to Germany. We fucked them up. With planes and artillery. Dead Krauts and horses and busted up tanks and cars for miles. Miles. Your eyes see it but your head can't make no sense of it. We go in there. And for three whole days we shot wounded horses. All day long. Sunup to sundown. Putting down horses. Hot summer days. Ain't smelled nothing like it. The sound of it. Those fucking horses screaming. Black clouds of flies buzzing. Like being in a giant bee hive.

Collier's crew throw Ellison into the tank and order him to kill every Nazi he sees. As they ride through the countryside, they encounter dead bodies, some of them children, with signs around their necks. Collier, who speaks German, translates the signs that say they were killed for refusing to fight for Nazi Germany.

As the tank convoy passes by a densely wooded area, Ellison spots a young boy running between the trees. He hesitates to shoot because of the youth's apparent age, when someone fires an anti-tank shell at the lead tank, causing it to burst into flame. Everyone fires into the woods while the stricken tank commander, screaming in pain and burning to death, shoots himself in the head. The crew searches in the woods and finds three bodies of young boys in *Hitlerjugend* uniforms who were attacking the tank convoy. Collier blames Ellison for the deaths of the companion tank crew, warning him, "Next German you see with a weapon you rake the dog shit outta him, I don't care if it's a baby with a butter knife in one hand and momma's left titty in the other". When Ellison finally hits a Nazi:

Wardaddy:	Norman. It wasn't nothin', right?
Ellison responds:	"Come again, Sergeant?"
Wardaddy says	"Rubbin' out those Heinies. Splashed 'em real good. Wasn't nothin', right?"

| | | War **91** |

Ellison says   [*With an odd look in his eyes*], "Sure, Sergeant. Yeah, it wasn't nothin'. Fact, I kinda liked it".

When *Fury* arrived in theaters to a mixture of praise and complaints. *New York Post's* Kyle Smith wrote: "Brad Pitt should be court-marshalled for 'war porn' *Fury*".[34] Critic Peter Van Buren also labels it war porn, observing that Smith, ". . . mows down ranks of Germans". By focusing almost exclusively on violent combat, Smith's film qualifies as war porn.

American Sniper (2014)

Clint Eastwood's blockbuster combat film *American Sniper*, also filmed in 2014, presents a biopic about the late Chris Kyle, America's most successful wartime sniper. Kyle, a Navy SEAL sniper in the Iraq War, penned the bestselling autobiography on which Eastwood largely based the movie version. Eastwood chose Bradley Cooper to star. In the opening scene Kyle sits on a rooftop looking through the scope of a high-powered rifle, intently watching the path of an American military convoy when he notices a man on another rooftop also watching the convoy while talking on a cell phone. Kyle reports the man to a marine assistant and is informed that the man is reporting troop information and should be shot. Kyle hesitates when his marine backup suggests that the man may simply be speaking to his girlfriend. The man disappears, then suddenly a woman and a boy leave the same building and walk toward the convoy. Kyle notices the woman walking stiffly as if she is carrying something, and suddenly she takes out a loaded grenade launcher from beneath her clothes and places it on the ground. The boy looks at the grenade and Kyle says to himself, "Don't pick it up!" When the boy reaches down to pick up the grenade Kyle warns, "Drop it!" while his fingers start trembling on the trigger. When the boy picks up the grenade and starts running toward the convoy Kyle takes aim and kills him, causing him to drop the grenade. The woman starts wailing but picks up the grenade launcher and starts running toward the convoy, at which point Kyle shoots her, too. The grenade falls harmlessly short of the convoy before exploding. When Kyle returns to his base camp, he is congratulated on his first kill.

Critical reviews of Eastwood's film were mixed depending on the political stance of the reviewer. *Rolling Stone* reviewer Matt Taibbi observed,

> "*Sniper* is a movie whose politics are so ludicrous and idiotic that under normal circumstances it would be beneath criticism. The only thing that forces us to take it seriously is the extraordinary fact that an almost exactly similar worldview consumed the walnut-sized mind of the president who got us into the war in question".[35]

Time's reviewer, Jon Davis, a former marine veteran of the Iraq war, staked out a diametrically opposite approach and heaped praise on Eastwood's film for historical

92 War

accuracy. Davis observes that he was completely captivated by the film's opening scene and felt, ". . . locked in". When it was over Davis observed, "Where this film shines, in my opinion, was in the degree of accuracies it had in its presentation".[36] Liberal *Hang the Bankers* reviewer labeled Eastwood's film "Hollywood war porn propaganda" and claimed, ". . . the masses of Americans have been chomping at the bit to slaughter Muslims".[37] The previously cited Peter Van Buren, former American diplomat assigned to Iraq, observes, "It is fashionable for our soldiers, having a kind of depth the enemy lacks, to express some regrets, a dollop of introspection, before (or after) they kill". In *American Sniper*, Chris Kyle, while back in the US on leave, expresses some doubts about what he refers to as "his work". However, Van Buren continues, "Of course, he then goes back to Iraq for three more tours and over two more hours of screen time to amass his 160 'confirmed kills'".[38]

In his autobiography, Kyle brags about having killed 160 "savages" during four tours of duty in Iraq. "I only wish I had killed more", Kyle wrote in his book, adding. "I loved what I did. . . it was fun. I had the time of my life". He also states, "I don't shoot people with Korans—I'd like to, but I don't". *Variety's* Scott Foundess observed, "Chris Kyle saw the world in clearly demarcated terms of good and evil, and *American Sniper* suggests that such dichromatism may have been key to both his success and survival; on the battlefield, doubt is akin to death". Laura Miller wrote for *Salon,* "In Kyle's version of the Iraq war, the parties consisted of Americans, who are good by virtue of being American, and fanatic Muslims whose 'savage, despicable evil' led them to want to kill Americans simply because they are Christians".[39]

London Has Fallen (2016)

In 2016 *London Has Fallen* appeared. A combat/action/adventure film so larded with graphic violence and destruction that *The Hollywood Reporter's* Todd McCarthy labeled it, ". . . the latest entry in the major world capital's destruction porn subgenre".[40] *The Rolling Stones'* critic Peter Travers began his review of the film, directed by Iranian-born Babak Najafi, with the suggestion that, "There should be a term—maybe even a prison term—for hacks who keep making the same junk movie over and over again. How about sucker punchers?" Travers charges that Najafi's film bears a striking resemblance to a 2013 action/adventure combat movie directed by Antoine Fuqua, *Olympus Has Fallen*, in which North Korean commandoes successfully capture the White House. They also hold the US president, played by Aaron Eckhart, as hostage. After much violence, Secret Service Agent Mike Banning (Gerard Butler) saves President Asher. In his film, Najafi also casts Eckhart as President Benjamin Asher, along with Butler as Special Agent Banning. In fact, Najafi's movie serves as a sequel to *Olympus Has Fallen*.[41]

In Najafi's version of the Olympus formula, a shadowy family of Pakistani arms dealers led by the notorious Aamir Barkawi (Alon Aboutboul) serves as official villains. In the film's first scene, set in Pakistan, Barkawi celebrates his daughter's wedding until an American drone destroys the compound, killing the daughter, maiming Barkawi, and crippling his son. The movie then flashes forward two years to London, where the British Prime Minister has died, and along with most of the world's leaders, President Asher attends a world summit in London in Air Force One with a cautious, wary team of bodyguards headed by Banning. Soon after arriving, President Asher and Banning witness bridges exploding, Westminster Cathedral crumbling, and other London iconic landmarks, including Big Ben, in ruins. Due to astonishingly compromised British security, Islamic militants embark on attacking all officials, especially focusing on President Asher, who survives and, along with Banning, attempts to reach the American Embassy. They eventually encounter a secret enemy base disguised as a British MI5 bastion in which they fight off hordes of Arabic terrorists. At one point, Banning addresses his attackers, "Why don't you boys pack up your shit and head back to Fuckheadistan or wherever it is you're from?"

One of Barkawi's sons informs him that he executed a mole in their organization. Barkawi tells him to be "absolute" about killing the informant, indicating that they must also kill the mole's family to make their point. This sentiment oddly parallel's then-presidential candidate Donald Trump's 2015 statement to an interviewer,

> "The other thing with the terrorists is you have to take out their families, when you get these terrorists, you have to take out their families. They care about their lives, don't kid yourself. When they say they don't care about their lives, you have to take out their families".[42]

Most reviewers gave *London Has Fallen* and its director Najafi good reviews. Matthew Kadish acknowledges that, "*London Has Fallen* actually fixed some of the issues its predecessor had and manages to be a better movie than the first". Like *Olympus Has Fallen*, *London Has Fallen* employs a government traitor who, eager for riches, assists villainous Barkawi. Banning is much more violent in the new version, at one point torturing a prisoner by slowly, relentlessly stabbing him with a knife until he dies, while broadcasting the man's anguished cries to the man's brother. A horrified Asher askes Banning, ". . . was that necessary?" and Banning responds simply, "No". Kadish admits his admiration for *London Has Fallen*,

> "Yes, I guess I'm guilty of liking 'destruction porn', but what can I say? I like what I like. I know this film was criticized for being 'insensitive' at the time of its release due to the various real-life terrorist attacks that occurred back then, but I don't think movies should be judged based on current events".[43]

The British journal *The Independent* called attention to numerous charges of racism and Islamophobia leveled against *London has Fallen*, charging, "Hollywood has fallen into a pit of manure", and labeled the film, ". . . terrorsploitation" and, ". . . fearmongering . . . for Donald Trump Era".[44] Contemporary reviewers expressed sharply divided opinions on *London Has Fallen*, labeling it "destruction porn" and "revenge porn". The MPAA rated *London Has Fallen* "R" for "strong violence and language throughout".

Non-War Combat Films

Gang turf wars and anti-crime efforts assume a combat-like status. War porn-type protagonists currently appear in some of Hollywood's most successful movies. *Kick-Ass* (2010) includes a tagline, "I can't fly, but I can kick your ass!" They exemplify the trend towards vigilante-like characters who slash, shoot, and blast their enemies, a consortium of villainous characters. These films function as disguised war movies. In the original *Kick-Ass*, Dave Lizewski (Aaron Taylor-Johnson), a nerdy and insecure high school student, reinvents himself as Kick-Ass, a crime-fighting superhero. However, when he encounters two street gang members who previously robbed him engaged in another robbery, he fails to stop them and ends up in the hospital, bleeding from multiple stab wounds and injured from being run over by their car. Doctors attach metal sheets to his head and body, inadvertently strengthening him. Also, the attacks resulted in neurological damage, reducing his sensitivity to pain. Armed with these two advantages, Kick-Ass defeats three thugs attacking a lone victim and he becomes famous when witnesses record his deed and post it on the internet.

In *Kick-Ass 2* (2013) Dave teams up with Mindy Macready (Chloe Grace Moretz), another aspiring teenage superhero. She hones her super skills at knife wielding, at one point confronting a gang of thugs led by Alley Hood.

Mindy Macready: If I ever catch you robbing again, shit-burger, I'm going to go to Saudi Arabia on your ass and cut your hand off. Promise me you're done with a life of crime?

Alley Hood: I-I promise.

[*grabs a knife but quickly has his hand severed*]

Mindy Macready: Pants on fire.

Costumed superheroes, in this film, band together to defeat a sadistic gang of supervillains. A superhero, again played by Aaron Taylor-Johnson, confronts Chris D'Amico (Christopher Mintz-Plasse), the son of a notorious crime boss, who transforms into a supervillain named The Motherfucker. Kick-Ass joins Justice Forever, a group of superheroes including Colonel Stars and Stripes (Jim Carrey) that battle with The Motherfucker. After The Motherfucker and his henchmen brutally murder ten New York policemen, they attempt to launch a nuclear missile aimed at Manhattan, but Kick-Ass and Justice Forever fend off the attacks, leaving The Motherfucker maimed and crippled. Mindy Macready, also known as Hit-Girl, summarizes the film's message, "You don't have to be a bad-ass to be a superhero . . . You just have to be brave".

Kick-Ass 2 began to seem too violence-saturated after the massacre at Sandy Hook Elementary School in 2012 which occurred just as filming ended for Kick-Ass 2. Jim Carrey abruptly refused to participate in promotions or publicity for the film. He tweeted, "I did Kickass a month b4 Sandy Hook and now in all good conscience I cannot support that level of violence, My apologies to others involved [sic] with the film. I am not ashamed of it but recent events have caused a change in my heart".[45]

Reality and Technology

War porn now appears in all genres of pop culture, including the internet, movies, television, video games, comic books, novels, and graphic novels, sometimes embellished by images shot by helmet cams or neighborhood crime watch cams, recording violence from both victims' and soldiers' perspectives. Actual war photos and videos now provide greater realism than previously achieved by Hollywood studios. Helmet-cam combat footage with soundtracks and musical backgrounds currently inspire a growing number of pop culture creators who desire to depict war's most violent, gory, brutal, and evil sides. These blood-soaked movies, videos, and images titillate because they transgress from the norms of a peaceful, healthy, prosperous world. Combat, with its strong elements of brutality, mayhem, and murder, attracts precisely because it flouts peaceful, feminized worlds with violent-laden hells of rage and retribution.

In response, Hollywood redoubles its previous use of technology with 3-D and more realistic (and expensive) computer-generated images (CGIs), and, as the popularity of individual-produced videos steadily increases, producers of Hollywood movies rely more heavily on CGI, hand-held shots, simulated surveillance cam or helmet-cam points of view, 3-D, and other special effects. Technology helps provide an aura of amateurism, authenticity, and realism. Technology also enables amateurs to direct videos and create meaningful cultural content. YouTube hosts a growing number of interactive videos in which participants actively shape the plot. Other applications like SnapApp allow video producers to insert questions, calculations, results, and personality assessments directly into their video experience, thereby customizing their productions.

War porn's increasing popularity and ease of production presage more combat violence in popular culture. Technology currently drives corporate creators of war porn films and video games closer to individual, Go Pro cam porn reality. Amateurs now create and shape war porn narratives with little experience or expense. Currently, user-created combat and crime fantasies dominate the internet and appear destined to play ever larger roles in future popular culture. In a violence-addicted society engaged in nearly constant warfare and burdened by high-violence crimes, including mass murder, demand for war porn will certainly remain strong.

96 War

Notes

1. See Tom Pollard, *Hollywood 9/11: Superheroes, Supervillains, and Super Disasters*. Boulder, CO: Paradigm Publications, 2011.
2. "According to *Google Trends*," https://trends.google.com/trends/explore?q=war%20 pornography retrieved April 29, 2019.
3. "According to *Google Trends*," https://trends.google.com/trends/explore?q=movie%20 violence retrieved April 29, 2019.
4. Jean Baudrillard, "War Porn," *Libération* translated by Paul A. Taylor, *International Journal of Baudrillard Studies*, vol. 2, no. 1, January 2005.
5. Peter Warren Singer, "War Porn: What Is It and What Does It Say about Us?" *Frontline*, April 29, 2009.
6. Matthis Chiroux, "Is Our Military Addicted to 'War Porn'?" *The Huffington Post*, March 16, 2012.
7. Monika Griebeler, "'War Porn' Book Describes What Few Care to See," *DW*, June 17, 2014.
8. David Shields, *War Is Beautiful: The New York Times Pictorial Guide to the Glamour of Armed Travel.* New York: PowerHouse Books, 2015, www.salon.com/.../ my_little_war_porn_addiction_david_shields_o...
9. Michiko Katutani, "Review: *War Porn* Widens the Field of Vision about the Costs in Iraq," *The New York Times*, August 8, 2016.
10. Roy Scranton, *War Porn.* New York: Soho Press, 2016, dustjacket.
11. Shukail Malik, "The War in Iraq and Visual Culture," *Journal of Visual Culture*, vol. 5, no. 1, 2006.
12. Mathis Chiroux, "Is Our Military Addicted to 'War Porn'?" *The Huffington Post*, March 16, 2012.
13. tvtropes.org/pmwiki/pmwiki.php/Main/CombatSadomasochist retrieved April 29, 2019.
14. Meg Gibson, "First-Person Soldier Footage Brings Combat to Life in New Series *Eyewitness War*," *National Geographic*, July 1, 2013.
15. Andy Dehnart, "Discovery's Must Watch Taking Fire Takes Us into Combat in Afghanistan," *Discovery Channel*, September 13, 2016.
16. Allegra Frank, "Take a Look at the Average American Gamer in New Survey Findings," *Polygon*, April 29, 2016.
17. "Video Games and Children: Playing with Violence," *American Academy of Child and Adolescent Psychiatry*, no. 91, June 2015 retrieved April 29, 2019. https://www.aacap.org/.../Children-and-Video-Games-Playing-with-Violence-091.aspx
18. Jeff Haynes, "10 Most Violent Video Games of 2015 (and What to Play Instead)," *Common Sense Media*, October 26, 2015. https://www.commonsensemedia.org/blog/10-most-violent-video-games-of-2015-and-what-to...
19. Annenberg Public Policy Institute University of Pennsylvania, "Movie Violence Associated with Sex, Violence, Alcohol and Tobacco Abuse," www.annenbergpublicpolicycenter.org/movie-violence-associated-with... retrieved April 29, 2019.
20. TomGram: Peter Van Buren, Watching the Same Movie About American War for 75 Years," *TomDispatch*, February 20, 2015.
21. Peter van Buren, "America Loves Its War Porn: *American Sniper* and the Hollywood Propaganda Machine," *TomDispatch.com*, February 21, 2015.
22. Anthony O. Scott, "Early Vietnam, Mission Murky," *The New York Times*, March 1, 2002.
23. Danny Grayson, "We Were Soldiers, Press Views," *BBC News*, March 12, 2002.
24. Roger Ebert, "We Were Soldiers," *Rogerebert.com*, March 1, 2002.
25. Garth Franklin, "New Rambo Has Biggest Body Count," *Dark Horizons*, January 24, 2008
26. Paul Byrnes, "300," *The Sydney Morning Herald,* April 6, 2007.
27. Roger Ebert, "300," *Rogerebert.com*, August 4, 2008.

28. Marilyn Young, "The Hurt Locker: Video Game-ish War Porn," *Splice Today*, splicetoday. com/moving-pictures/the-hurt-locker-video-game-ish-war-porn

29. Jon Davis, "What Do Iraq and Afghanistan Veterans Think of the Movie 'The Hurt Locker'?" www.quora.com/What-do-Iraq-and-Afghanistan-veterans-think-of-the-mo...

30. Prairie Miller, "The Hurt Locker: War Porn at the Movies," *Critical Women on Film*, criticalwomen.blogspot.com/2009/12/screening-room.html

31. Steven Chase and Kirk Makin, "History Must Reflect 'Argo' Was Mainly a Canadian Mission," *The Globe and Mail*, February 24, 2013.

32. Peter Van Buren, "Hollywood's Tired War Porn," *The American Conservative*, February 19, 2015.

33. Steve 'Frosty' Weintraub, "30 Things to Know about David Ayer's *Fury* from Our Set Visit," *Collider*, July 1, 2014.

34. Kyle Smith, "Brad Pitt Should Be Court-Marshalled for 'War Porn' *Fury*," *New York Post*, October 16, 2014.

35. Matt Taibbi, "American Sniper Is Almost Too Dumb to Criticize, Almost," *Rolling Stone*, January 21, 2015.

36. Jon Davis, "A Former Marine's Review of American Sniper," *Time*, February 9, 2015.

37. "American Sniper: Hollywood War Porn Propaganda," Hang the Bankers, January 28, 2015 https://hangthebankers.com/american-sniper-hollywood-war-porn... retrieved April 29, 2019.

38. Peter Van Buren, "America Loves Its War Porn: *American Sniper* and the Hollywood Propaganda Machine," *Tomdispatch.com*, February 21, 2015.

39. Lindy West, "The Real *American Sniper* Was a Hate-Filled Murderer: Why Are Simplistic Patriots Treating him as a Hero?" *The Guardian*, January 6, 2015.

40. Todd McCarthy, "*London Has Fallen* Film Review," *The Hollywood Reporter*, March 2, 2016.

41. Peter Travers, "London Has Fallen. Gerard Butler Must Save the President in This Islamophobic Sequel to Olympus Has Fallen," *Rolling Stone*, March 4, 2016, www. rollingstone.com/movies/reviews/white-house-down-20130627

42. Tom Loblanco, "Donald Trump on Terrorists: 'Take Out Their Families," *CNN*, December 3, 2015.

43. Matthew Kadish, "London Has Fallen," *Letterboxd*, July 22, 2016, https://letterboxd. com/matthewkadish/film/london-has-fallen/ accessed February 1, 2016.

44. Adam Sherwin, "London Has Fallen Movie Condemned as Racist 'Terrorsploitation' for Donald Trump Era," *The Independent*, March 3, 2016.

45. Mike Ryan, "Jim Carrey Was Probably Right," *The Huffington Post*, August 14, 2013.

Bibliography

Baudrillard, Jean, "War Porn," *Libération* translated by Paul A. Taylor, *International Journal of Baudrillard Studies*, vol. 2, no. 1, January 2005.

Chiroux, Matthis, "Is Our Military Addicted to 'War Porn'?" *The Huffington Post*, March 16, 2012.

Dehnart, Andy, "Discovery's Must Watch Taking Fire Takes Us into Combat in Afghanistan," *Discovery Channel*, September 13, 2016.

Ebert, Roger, "*300*," *Rogerebert.com*, August 4, 2008.

Ebert, Roger, "We Were Soldiers," *Rogerebert.com*, March 1, 2002.

Frank, Allegra, "Take a Look at the Average American Gamer in New Survey Findings," *Polygon*, April 29, 2016.

Gibson, Meg, "First-Person Soldier Footage Brings Combat to Life in New Series *Eyewitness War*," *National Geographic*, July 1, 2013.

Griebeler, Monika, "'War Porn' Book Describes What Few Care to See," *DW*, June 17, 2014.

98 War

Haynes, Jeff, "10 Most Violent Video Games of 2015 (and What to Play Instead)," *Common Sense Media*, October 26, 2015.

Katutani, Michiko, "Review: *War Porn* Widens the Field of Vision about the Costs in Iraq," *The New York Times*, August 8, 2016.

Malik, Shukail, "The War in Iraq and Visual Culture," *Journal of Visual Culture*, vol. 5, no. 1, 2006.

Pollard, Tom, *Hollywood 9/11: Superheroes, Supervillains, and Super Disasters*. Boulder, CO: Paradigm Publications, 2011.

Scott, Anthony O., "Early Vietnam, Mission Murky," *The New York Times*, March 1, 2002.

Scranton, Roy, *War Porn*. New York: Soho Press, 2016.

Singer, P. W., "War Porn: What Is It and What Does It Say about Us?" *Frontline*, April 29, 2009.

Van Buren, Peter, "America Loves Its War Porn: *American Sniper* and the Hollywood Propaganda Machine," *TomDispatch.com*, February 21, 2015.

Van Buren, Peter, "Watching the Same Movie about American War for 75 Years," *TomDispatch*, February 20, 2015.

"Video Games and Children: Playing with Violence," *American Academy of Child and Adolescent Psychiatry*, no. 91, June 2015. https://www.aacap.org/AACAP/Families_and_Youth/Facts_for_Families/ retrieved April 29, 2019.

Young, Marilyn, "The Hurt Locker: Video Game-ish War Porn," *Splice Today*, splicetoday.com/moving-pictures/the-hurt-locker-video-game-ish-war-porn

6

FASCISM

Fascism: Goose-stepping Nazi SS soldiers rounding up Jews, BDSMQ, Poles, Gypsies, and disabled peoples, Holocaust horrors, Hitler rants, and concentration camps. The Nazi regime of Germany invaded Poland, Czechoslovakia, France, Holland, Norway. Firebombs and missiles rained down on Britain as U-boats torpedoed Atlantic ships. Italy under Benito Mussolini pioneered the use of concentration camps and genocide and launched invasions of Ethiopia and Greece. Benito Mussolini and Adolf Hitler reigned over the rise of twentieth-century fascism in Europe.

Although fascism suffered seemingly ignominious defeats at the end of WWII, it still inspires adherents and cannot be ignored. Many decades after the nightmares of WWII, fascism appears again on the world stage as nationalist political movements threaten minorities and democratic values in Europe, Asia, and in the US. Hungary and Poland are already governed by rightist "populists" and Slovakia, Macedonia, Croatia, Serbia, and Greece harbor strong rightist sentiments. In 2018 Germany's far-right party, Alternative for Germany, garnered 12.6% of the vote, the first time since the rise of Adolf Hitler that such a rightist party has won seats in the German parliament.[1]

Despite the increasing frequency of its usage, the word fascism remains nebulous to most. Benito Mussolini, fascism's founder, defined it in 1919 as, "Everything in the state . . ." indicating that the government is supreme, the country is all-encompassing, and all within it must conform to the ruling body, often a dictator, so, ". . . nothing outside the state". It also means, ". . . everything for the state . . ." and ". . . nothing against the state". Fascists never tolerate anyone questioning their government. "Those that do not see things our way, you are wrong. If you do not agree with the government, you cannot be allowed to live and taint the minds of the rest of the good citizens". It results in, ". . . the erosion and

100 Fascism

abandonment of individualism". World domination becomes the goal, often left unstated, of any fascist nation.[2] Mussolini and other fascists embraced "Corporatism", the theory and practice of organizing all citizens into "corporations", non-voluntary associations that provide stability and guidance and remain subordinate to the nation state. All citizens owed their allegiance to the supreme leader. Twentieth-century leaders like Benito Mussolini (Italy), Adolf Hitler (Germany), and Francisco Franco (Spain) amassed immense power and eventually dictated every aspect of their respective societies.

Mussolini's Italy (1922–1943) inspired Adolf Hitler's National Socialist German Workers Party (NAZI), which governed Germany from 1933 to 1945. Spain under General Francisco Franco (1939–1975) also embraced a fascist ideology. Fascist-inspired governments of the 1920s included Mustafa Kemal Ataturk's Republic of Turkey, established in 1923, and today's President Erdogan, also authoritarian, continues the fascist tradition. Other countries with significant fascist parties or movements include Syria, Bulgaria, Armenia, Romania, Venezuela, Bolivia, France, Denmark, Greece, Ukraine, the Netherlands, Hungary, and the US.[3] Neo-right movements, today labeled "alt-right", continue gaining power and influence in Europe and the US. Greece's Golden Dawn movement adapts fascist populism and political violence. In France, Marine Le Pen's National Front moved to within striking distance of the French Presidency. Dutch alt-right Geert Wilders's Party for Freedom threatens to transform the Netherlands into a fascist state, while Italian activist Beepe Grillo's Five Star Movement blends Silvio Berlusconi-style authoritarianism with contemporary alt-right anti-immigration policies. In the US, a renaissance of fascist-oriented rhetoric appeared after Donald Trump's election as the 45th President of the United States.

Fascist Porn

Of all pornography's subgenres, none transgress traditional social/cultural values and beliefs more than "fascist porn", and none is more violent. Michael Newall notes that although pornography in general transgresses and breaks social norms, some forms transgress more than others, including depictions of sexual violence (featured in fascist porn), bestiality (occasionally found in fascist porn), sex between members of different social classes (Stalag porn), and sex with strangers (a prominent feature of fascist porn). To Newall, transgressive, norm-breaking pornography intentionally evokes disgust, humor, and awe. All pornography unintentionally transgresses cherished values, and fascist porn actively and intentionally violates socio/political norms and values for effect.[4] To illustrate deliberately transgressive porn, Newell selected the Marquis de Sade's long suppressed novel *120 Days of Sodom* (1785) because of its provocative or "transgressive" content. Newell claims that de Sade, a powerful, compelling writer, deliberately crafted his novel to shock readers into questioning society's most sacred norms and values. One of the most sexually violent of any literary work, de Sade's novel chronicles the 600 "passions", including "simple passions", which include non-penetrative sexual activities and progresses to "complex passions", "criminal passions", and "murderous passions". These progress from fondling victims before exposing oneself to voyeurism, and on to chaining a starving victim to a wall with abundant food just out of reach, then leaving a large knife for her to cut off one of her hands to avoid death by starvation. Murderous passions include pouring molten lead down a victim's throat and mortally wounding another victim with a knife.[5] They exemplify patriarchal sexual domination and unbridled violence.

Fascist movements always possess transgressive panache and attraction. Writer/activist Susan Sontag (1933–2004) observed, "The tastes for the monumental and for mass obeisance to the hero are common to both fascist and communist art, reflecting the view of all totalitarian regimes that art has the function of 'immortalizing' its leaders and doctrines". Sontag argued, "Extreme right-wing movements, however puritanical and repressive the realities they usher in, have an erotic surface". Nazism maintains primacy over other right-wing movements in terms of pornography because of its greater sadomasochistic appeal. "Nazism fascinates in a way other iconography staked out by the pop sensibility (from Mao Tse-tung to Marilyn Monroe) does not". Susan Sontag remarked that although Nazis of all stripes inspire makers of pop culture, the SS proved the most inspirational to pornographers. Sontag's fascination with the SS arises "Because the SS seems to be the most perfect incarnation of fascism in its overt assertion of the righteousness of violence, the right to have total power over others and to treat them as absolutely inferior".[6] Although Nazi Germany maintained an outwardly strict, conservative demeanor, once in power, Hitler and the Third Reich, both intentionally and inadvertently, encouraged sexuality, corruption, and violence. Salacious sexual and violent policies, both secret and public, provided an undercurrent of erotically charged violence, explaining the enduring popularity of Nazi, neo-Nazi, and alt-right pornography. The brutality of the Nazi regime, which effectively transformed Germany into a nation of dominative masters attacking and eventually annihilating all minorities, added to the sadomasochistic appeal of the German Reich. Sontag concludes that Nazi Germany created the ultimate sadomasochistic state, observing "Never before in history was the relation of masters and slaves realized with so consciously artistic a design".[7]

The ancient authoritarian states of Sparta and Athens foreshadowed aspects of Nazism. Sparta, a regimented, militarized, paternalistic society, epitomizes fascist fascination with paternalistic militaristic authoritarianism. Spartan males favored pederasty, a homoerotic practice favoring "man/boy" relationships between teenage boys and adult men. Sparta, which functioned as a military dictatorship, epitomizes fascistic paternalism.

Sodomy, either heterosexual or homosexual, has long been associated with sadomasochistic, militaristic societies. Interest in Greek pederasty fluoresced during WWI when a German homoerotic intellectual movement arose and later became covertly embraced by the Nazi Party. Its spokesman, German philosopher

102 Fascism

Hans Blüher, claimed that pederasty and male bonding proved stronger than traditional bonds inside heterosexual families and institutions. Blüher advocated the "male-male Eros" that operated inside the "male community", i.e. the German military. Hitler avidly devoured Blüher's books.[8] A contemporary example of mixed public support, and disapproval, of pederasty occurred in 2017. Alt-right provocateur Milo Yiannopoulos witnessed his position in journalism as well as a lucrative book contract dissolve after he defended pederasty at length during an interview, in which he expressed approval for boys as young as 13 and "sexually mature" to form sexual relationships with gay adult men, then joked that his own experiences of molestation as a young boy had taught him how to properly perform fellatio.[9]

At the turn of the twentieth century Adolf Brand, writer and publisher, espoused a "Butch" homoeroticism that influenced the coming Nazi movement while advocating an ultra-masculine, militaristic culture based on ancient Greek pederasty. In 1902 Brand organized the "Community of the Elite", consisting of males who, ". . . thirst for a revival of Greek times and Hellenic standards of beauty . . .". It became one of the forerunners of the Nazi movement.[10]

By contrast to the "Butch" element, German "Femmes" advocated a gay rights agenda that sought tolerance of gays by decriminalizing homosexuality. Karl Heinrich Ulrichs and Magnus Hirschfeld, prominent Femmes, advocated repeal of Paragraph 175 of the German Criminal Code that criminalized male sodomy.[11]

During the Weimar Republic (1918–1933), Germany grew openly tolerant of homosexuality, as contemporary societies also became more tolerant. The science of "transsexuality" was founded in Berlin at the Institute of Sexual Science where the first male-to-female surgery was performed. The words "homosexual" and "transvestite" were German innovations. German magazines offered gay- and lesbian-friendly services to the gay subculture, including health care professionals trained in "sexual disturbances", detective agencies offering to investigate gay lover blackmail threats, as well as gay-friendly dressmakers and restaurants. Male prostitution thrived in Berlin bars, nightclubs, and cabarets populated by gay men, lesbians, and transsexuals, and Berlin itself embodied an openness to BDSMQ sexuality.[12] After Hitler assumed power he transformed Germany into what historian Richard Grunberger describes as an "all-male collective" that valorized masculine virtues like strength, courage, cruelty, and violence. Fascist practices of demonizing minorities, coupled with absolute state power, encouraged many forms of violence. Nazi Germany organized itself around a supreme, authoritarian, male leader and a cult of masculinity that some charge provided a "homosexually tinged ethos" pervading the Reich from start to finish. It became apparent in Nazi-era German films, for example the Air Force film *D3 88* in which a squadron leader and a chief maintenance engineer symbolically act out their respective roles for training purposes as father and mother, with the female "parent" attempting to wrest concessions from the male "parent" for their children.[13]

Fascism **103**

Third Reich Corruption and Sexuality

After seizing power on January 30, 1933, the Nazi government began leaking sensational acts of corruption during the Weimar Republic (1919–1933) that it had just replaced. The Barmat scandal of 1924 proved the most salacious. Julius Barmat, with assistance from his brother Henry, both Ukrianian Jews, amassed a fortune by arranging for mass quantities of Dutch food to be imported into Germany, bypassing the British blockade designed to starve Germany during WWI. The Barmat company became rich on that trade, but in 1924, after Julius made a series of unwise investments in currency, the company went bankrupt. The emerging Nazi Party exploited the Barmat scandal as an example of Weimar corruption during the 1932 election.[14]

Economic corruption often appears in conjunction with moral and ethical corruption. Rank corruption ravaged the Third Reich in every sphere during the twelve years of its reign. Conservative Lutheran values gave way to a dramatic loosening of traditional family structure. Concerns about falling birthrates justified mass prostitution, marital infidelity, secret pornography, and homosexuality. Nazi Germany developed a myopia about anti-Semitism, warmongering, and the loosening of social restraints on sexual relationships. Patrick Buisson labeled it "erotic shock . . . or exploring new territories of pleasure".[15]

Even as Nazi leaders indicted Weimar rivals as corrupt, their own corruption, hidden at first from the German people, quickly surpassed the transgressions of their predecessors. Both military and civilian leaders began amassing huge fortunes and seizing palaces and estates. Hermann Göring served as Prime Minister of Prussia, Economic Overlord of the Reich, Commissioner of the Four-Year-Plan, Minister of the Air, Marshal of the Air Force, Speaker of the Reichstag, and National Hunt Master. These powerful positions, in addition to substantial book royalties, boosted his annual income to over 1,250,000 Deutsche Marks, or over 3 million US dollars at that time. In addition, Göring supplemented his legitimate income with huge sums raised by bribery and other forms of corruption. As Prussian Prime Minister, Göring refrainded from prosecuting a large German tobacco firm and subsequently received 3,000,000 Deutsche Marks. Göring's case was not atypical as rampant corruption erupted in all echelons of the Third Reich. Richard Grunberger observes that "Corruption was in fact the central organizing principle of the Third Reich".[16] However, most of the German population remained unaware of corruption's ubiquitous and pernicious reach. Professor Raymond Fisman of Boston University found "systemic corruption" occurs in a society when sufficient economic and political corruption exists. "Once systemic corruption takes hold", he explained, "it can quickly infect an entire system, encouraging or even forcing bad behavior".[17]

104 Fascism

Homoeroticism

The Third Reich evinced a powerful, subliminally homoerotic subculture, even though once in power Adolf Hitler distanced himself from gay people. Ernst Röhm, an early confidant of Adolf Hitler and co-founder of the Sturmabteilung ("assault battalion" or Nazi Party militia), came out socially as gay. In 1919, Röhm recognized Hitler as a unique leader and urged Hitler to develop his political potential. The two maintained a fifteen-year friendship. During that time, Röhm rose to Chief of Staff of the SA, Hitler's paramilitary militia and transformed it from a handful of hardened goons and embittered ex-soldiers into a massive fighting force of 2.5 million troops. He began advocating for inclusion of the regular army, the Wehrmacht, into the SA. After his election in 1933, Hitler came under pressure to eliminate Röhm from power before Röhm managed to absorb the regular army into his SA. At that time, Röhm demanded that the SA be counted as equal with the Nazi Party, and he had secretly ridiculed Hitler. Hitler quietly allowed Röhm's arch rivals, Hermann Göring and Heinrich Himmler, to murder Röhm and many of his closest followers on June 30–July 2, 1934, in a massacre known as "The Night of the Long Knives", and in Germany as the *Röhm Putsch*. To solidify his grip on power, Hitler simultaneously ordered the assassination of the left-wing Strasserist faction of the Nazi Party (NSDAP), along with its figurehead, Gregor Strasser. In addition, he liquidated conservative anti-Nazis (including former Chancellor Kurt von Schleicher and Gustav Ritter von Kahr, who had suppressed Adolf Hitler's Beer Hall *Putsch* in 1923).[18] By these actions Hitler crystallized his grip on power and created an image of himself as a superman whose name would survive long after his death.

After the Night of the Long Knives, Hitler began rigorous enforcement of Paragraph 175 of the German Penal Code that criminalized anal intercourse. On June 28, 1935, near the one-year anniversary of The Night of the Long Knives, Hitler revised Paragraph 175, retitled Paragraph 175a, that now banned not only sodomy but ten newly prohibited sexual "acts" between members of the same gender, including kisses, embraces, and all homosexual fantasies. He ordered gay bars to close throughout Germany and instructed Himmler to round up thousands of homosexuals and incarcerate them in Germany's concentration camps, housed in special barracks. Once in the camps, gays were forced to wear pink triangles, identifying them as gay, and were subject to beatings, to being stripped naked and made to stay outside on cold winter nights, to being raped, and to other abuse by guards and other inmates.[19] Paragraph 175 remained German law until 1994. Gay concentration camp prisoners faced daunting survival odds. L.D. Classen von Neudegg, a rare concentration camp survivor, relayed the following story in his book about gay prisoners:

> Three men had tried to escape one night. They were captured, and when they returned they had the word "homo" scrawled across their clothing. They were placed on a block and whipped. Then they were forced to beat a drum and cheer, "Hurrah! We're back! Hurrah!" Then they were hanged.[20]

In 1937 Heinrich Himmler, Nazi Germany's second in command, decided to rid Germany of all gays. He set out to discover the identity of all gays by soliciting citizens to turn any and all gays' names over to the police. He ordered the judiciary to try and convict all practicing gay men on sodomy charges. He urged the courts to mete out a hefty fine for any violations. Then, "Following completion of the punishment imposed by the court, they will be sent, by my order, to a concentration camp, and they will be shot in the concentration camp, while attempting to escape. I will make that known by order to the unit to which the person so infected belonged".[21] Although many gay prisoners were shot "trying to escape", others were tortured to death by guards. Himmler allegedly offered gays the services of camp prostitutes who were ordered to make special efforts to transform them into heterosexuals by providing healing "heterosexual sex" for them.[22] Austrian concentration camp survivor Hans Neumann (AKA Heinz Heger) asserts that Himmler required all gay male prisoners to visit camp bordellos once a week.[23]

Although outwardly socially conservative, secret sexual practices in Nazi Germany flourished. Himmler's establishment of over 500 secret brothels inside concentration camps throughout Europe presents a striking example of Nazi sexuality. These Nazi brothels, called *Largerbordell*, catered to SS officers and soldiers. Nazis coerced captive women to become sex workers in concentration camps, including Auschwitz, Dachau, Buchenwald, and Sachsenhausen.[24] Over 34,000 prisoners were forced into prostitution in Nazi brothels.[25] Jewish women escaped work in some brothels because of Nazi anti-Semitism. In addition, no Jewish or Soviet prisoners could use the SS brothels' services. Concentration camp prostitutes, mostly in their early twenties, were provided more food than other prisoners and were promised release after six months of service, a promise never kept. Camp prostitutes were required to have sex with selected male prisoners or SS soldiers and officers every evening from eight until ten, and every Sunday afternoon. SS guards strictly regulated the use of brothels, spying on their sexual activities through peep holes. German prisoners could only patronize German prostitutes. Captured Slavic women, forced into sexual slavery by the SS, were allegedly reserved for Slavic prisoners only.[26]

In 1935, Nazi Germany launched the secretive *Lebensborn* program designed to allow Aryan women to conceive children by Aryan SS officers. To offset a steep decline in German births, SS chief Heinrich Himmler ordered construction of dozens of birth clinics across the country and later in Nazi-held countries across Europe in which SS-impregnated women received assistance in giving birth and, if they desired, for having their illegitimate offspring placed in foster homes or orphanages. It afforded male SS officers, most of whom were married, extramarital sexual liaisons to increase the Aryan population. Himmler, addressing a large conference of SS officers in 1937, explained,

> "The people which has many children has the candidature for world power and world domination. A people of good race which has too few children

106 Fascism

has a one-way ticket to the grave, for insignificance in fifty or a hundred years, for burial in two hundred and fifty years . . . ".[27]

During WWII, over 8,000 Lebensborn children were born in Germany and over 12,000 in Norway. The program's objective, to foster the birth of thousands of Aryan children who would become useful German citizens, was realized, but most of these children were never told about their true parentage, and many only discovered their origin later in life. After the war, the program became known as "Nazi breeding farms".[28]

The Nazi movement attracted a significant number of LGBTQ members, who found themselves attracted to the movement's militant, macho image. Later, they were rounded up, along with thousands of gay civilians, and placed in concentration camps. Lively and Abrams claim that two diametrically opposed movements existed within the German LGBTQ community, a violently macho "Butch" faction that revered the homoeroticism of ancient Greece and a "Femme" faction that valorized sensitive, effeminate gays.[29] Heinrich Himmler, himself widely suspected of bisexuality, headed both the Gestapo and the SS. As *Reichsführer*, second in command next to Hitler, Himmler outwardly attacked everything non-German, including Jews, gays, Gypsies, Jehovah's Witnesses, and the disabled.

Soon after seizing power in 1933, Hitler established the Reich Ministry of Public Enlightenment and Propaganda under Joseph Goebbels, charged with assuring that Nazi visions of racism, anti-Semitism, and anti-Communism prevailed in art, literature, cinema, and news media. Goebbels espoused the racist philosophy of the Nazi party, officially promoting racial hatred, which applied to all non-Aryans. At the same time, Goebbels conducted a secret, taboo affair with an "inferior" Slav, Czech movie star Lída Baarová. They met when Baarová was only twenty. He courted her avidly. In 1938, he informed her that he had revealed their relationship to his wife Magda, who demanded a meeting of the three of them so that they could discuss terms. Magda secretly asked Hitler to allow her to divorce Goebbels, but Hitler refused and threatened to remove Goebbels from his office. Hitler himself earlier became attracted to Baarová and invited her to attend intimate parties hosted by him. Upon learning of her affair with Goebbels, he banned her from Berlin and banned the screening of her films. Fearful of further antagonizing Hitler, Goebbels reluctantly broke off all relations with Baarová.[30]

Long after WWII ended, researchers discovered that Nazis clandestinely produced pornographic movies for viewing by senior Nazi officials. Copies of two of these films, *Desire in the Woods* and *The Trapper*, appeared in 2004. They feature attractive German women having sex with German men, including a three-way liaison. These films were eventually traded to North African locals during WWII, who were eager to exchange them for insect repellant and other commodities. The films produced by this clandestine pornographic film industry are called *Sachsenwald* films. The revelations of their existence only added to the growing reputation of the Nazi Party as hyper-sexual and hypercritical.[31]

Norman Ohler charges Nazis with another secret transgressive behavior: massive drug use. In his book *Blitzed, Drugs in Nazi Germany*, Ohler reveals what has now been confirmed, "The Third Reich was on drugs", including methamphetamines and cocaine. Methamphetamines became widespread in Nazi Germany as a panacea for, ". . . everything from depression to hay fever". During the war millions of methamphetamine pills were given to the German military. "Hopped up soldiers would sprint tirelessly through the Ardennes", at the beginning of the war. A general bragged his troops had stayed awake for seventeen straight days. This heightened physical performance proved crucial during the *Blitzkrieg* into Norway and Poland, but the inevitable downer occurred during Operation Barbarossa, Hitler's ill-starred invasion of the USSR. Hitler's physician prescribed oxycodone and cocaine, a mixture described as a "classic speedball".[32]

Because of Nazi authoritarianism, brutality, and corruption, Hitler's Third Reich inevitably became pornographic. Hitler's megalomaniacal assertion of the *Führerprinzip* ("Leader principle"), which demands absolute obedience of subordinates to their superiors, led to one of history's most authoritarian regimes. To Hitler, German society formed a steep pyramid of power, with himself, always infallible, at the pinnacle.[33] Meanwhile, prominent Reich leaders like Hermann Göring conducted clandestine affairs, sometimes with forbidden non-Aryan women, while tens of thousands of prisoners served as sex slaves. The Nazi movement embodied latent sadomasochism by empowering a tiny elite with absolute power.

Post-War Nazi Sadomasochism

Nazi drug use, brutality, racism, and sadomasochism did not end with WWII. After the war, Nazis in hiding began to appear. In 1961, former Nazi corporal Paul Schäfer turned charismatic Evangelical minister, accused of child abuse, emigrated to Chile, bringing along a large number of his supporters. With their assistance, he purchased a large swath of land north of Santiago and founded Colonia Dignidad (Dignity Colony). However, the immigrants to Colonia Dignidad, and local forest inhabitants, soon learned that their dignity mattered little to Schäfer. In his secretive cult, Schäfer enacted a sexualized Gestapo fantasy featuring himself with young boys. He abused not only young boys but all his other workers, beating them and subjecting them to electroshock torture and drugs. Emulating WWII Nazi slave labor camps, Schäfer forced his semi-enslaved employees to work sixteen-hour days for low wages and ordered that married couples live apart and turn over their children to him for probable sexual abuse.

In 1973, General Augusto Pinochet seized power in Chili, relying on his friend Schäfer to subject Pinochet's enemies to torture and eventual murder in Colonia Dignidad. Three hundred Pinochet enemies were imprisoned in an underground potato bunker there, and 100 were murdered and buried. Schäfer, safe in his private fiefdom of pederasty and worker abuse, accepted Pinochet's request, vastly increasing his revenue. Schäfer's Colony became a frequent vacation getaway for General

108 Fascism

Pinochet and his followers, along with other Nazis, including the notorious Auschwitz torturer Dr Josef Mengele and Nazi fugitive Walter Rauff, inventor of the portable gas chamber. Eventually horrific tales of abuse circulated as stories leaked from Colonia Dignidad, and in 1997, the Chilean government began investigating Schäfer for child abuse, tax fraud, illegal weapons, forced labor, torture, and the disappearance of prisoners. Schäfer fled to Argentina, but he was captured in 2005 and finally incarcerated in a modern Chilean prison in 2010, five years into a 20-year sentence. He was 88.[34]

Hollywood Nazis

Following WWII, Hollywood revisited the Nazi transgressive behaviors. Nazi prisoners of war camps, or Stalags, served as the settings for many Hollywood films and television series. Billy Wilder's *Stalag 17* (1953), based on a successful Broadway play, ushered in Hollywood's take on Nazi prison camps. Wilder's film stars William Holden as Sergeant J.J Sefton, an unlikable American prisoner who freely gambles and trades with his German captors, earning both the enmity and envy of his fellow prisoners. The all-male cast limited the sexuality of Wilder's film, although his conniving star character, Sefton, trades some contraband goods for some fun in the Russian women's barracks. Wilder's film avoids any mention of the sexuality in Nazi camps. It later inspired television's hit series *Hogan's Heroes* (1965–1971).

As sexually explicit information leaked about Nazi sexuality, erotic depictions of sexually transgressive Nazis began appearing in popular culture. Israeli writer K. Tzetnik, a survivor of Auschwitz, published *The House of Dolls* in 1955, a sexually graphic novella about women prisoners forced into prostitution by Nazis. Tzetnik's account was likely derived from his own memories as a concentration camp survivor. The success of this novella inspired a flurry of other Israeli "Stalag novels", including *Stalag 13* and *I was Colonel Schultz's Private Bitch*. Their plots featured sadistic imprisonment, mainly of Allied soldiers, and emphasized erotic sexual brutalization by female SS guards. In the end the prisoners eventually escape and, out of revenge, rape and murder their tormentors.[35] However, after the arrest and trial of Adolf Eichmann in 1960, Israel banned Nazi-themed novels and films, lest Israel would be branded as hypercritical for prosecuting Eichmann while avidly devouring Nazi porn novels.

In 1969 the first Nazi exploitation film appeared in the US titled *Love Camp 7*. Directed by Lee Frost and produced by Bob Cresse and Wes Bishop, it stars Maria Lease and Kathy Williams as two American military officers who infiltrate an SS "love camp" designed to pleasure German military officers with female Jewish sex slaves. Officially, Nazis did not employ Jewish women in camp bordellos. *Love Camp 7* also departs significantly from Israeli Stalag novels by depicting female sex slaves abused by male SS officers and guards. Also, in Frost's film, no swastika-wearing dominatrices appear.

During the late 1960s and 1970s, Nazi chic began appearing in pop music. John Lennon advocated strongly that Hitler's face grace the cover of the Beatles' *Lonely Hearts Club Band* album, but EMI Studios, the album's producer, refused.[36] Lennon, avowedly not a racist or fascist, along with David Bowie, a contemporary rocker, became infatuated with Nazism and other forms of fascism during the early 1970s. Bowie explained in a 1974 *Playboy* interview that he became fascinated with Hitler because the *Führer* was ". . . one of the first rock stars. Look at some of the films and see how he moved. I think he was quite as good as Jagger . . .". Bowie admired, ". . . this thing that governed and controlled the show for those twelve years. The world will never see his [Hitler's] like again. He staged a country". In 1974 Bowie was detained by custom officials on the Russian/Polish border for possessing a large cache of Nazi literature.[37]

Followers of the punk rock movement of the late 1960s through the 1970s and 1980s also embraced Nazi chic. They desired to distance themselves as far from what they deemed a malignant, corrupt mainstream culture, and Nazi gestures, symbols, and clothing helped accomplish that goal. Johnny Rotten and the Sex Pistols modeled t-shirts emblazoned with swastikas, upside-down crosses, with the word "DESTROY". In December 1976, Rotten appeared on the *Today Show* wearing the swastika t-shirt, and the band wore them in the music video *Pretty Vacant* (1977).[38] Other punk rockers, like Siouxsie Sioux of Siouxsie and the Banshees, and Sid Vicious also appeared in this period wearing swastika armbands and black leather.[39]

Ilsa: She Wolf of the SS (1975)

World War II-era fascism today provides violent pornographers with infinitely variable sadomasochistic scenarios. Critic Lynn Rapport reminds us that, starting in the 1970s, violent pornographers appropriated and exploited Nazi iconography by linking Nazi political power and violence with sex. Rapport calls it "Holocaust pornography".[40]

In 1970 a powerful, highly sexualized dramatic persona reappeared in pop culture: the dominatrix. The image of domineering, aggressive, sadistic women, often wearing Nazi uniforms and usually topless, exploded in popular culture with the arrival of *Ilsa: She Wolf of the SS* (1975), a Canadian production directed by Don Edmonds. It was the first of many Nazi-themed horror/porn features of the late 1970s, and it is easily the most memorable. Edmonds's film loosely follows the pattern of the earlier Israeli Stalag literature through graphic depictions of sadomasochistic torture. It opens in a WWII Nazi concentration camp where bloody, lifeless, naked bodies of a young man and a young woman twist upside down, hanging by ropes. Sex-obsessed Commandant Ilsa (Dyanne Tome) reverses the usual prostitution film by making male prisoners prostitute themselves to the beautiful Commandante Ilsa. She lines up naked female prisoners, dividing them between those destined as concentration camp prostitutes and those who will be

110 Fascism

subjected to various forms of torture designed to test their endurance. Either way, there will be no escape. She also lines up naked male prisoners for inspection, selecting for sexual trysts. In one scene, a sexual partner ejaculates too soon, and Ilsa cries "Not yet, no, please! You should have waited". She casually has him arrested. He protests, "But you promised I didn't have to go back to camp!" Two female guards escort him to an operating table, where Ilsa castrates him, exclaiming, "My little man, I kept my promise—you will never leave the camp again!"

Ilsa addresses some newly arriving female prisoners, "We are doctors. We are here to help you". The "help" she provides includes abundant sexual abuse and progressively harsher torture as she orders the prisoners whipped, shocked, frozen, boiled, beaten until bloody, and tormented by her and her female Nazi guards. The film shows prisoners being shocked beyond endurance by an electric wand thrust into their vaginas and burned by a flame-wielding Ilsa. She taunts the hardiest one, who is close to exhaustion, "You think that you can hold out, but you are wrong!" as she shocks her body with a diabolical-looking machine. The female prisoners become unwilling participants in a Mengele-like medical experiment to determine how much pain they can endure before expiring. A visiting Nazi general exclaims, "You use no anesthetics?"

To further Nazi research into the limits of human endurance, Ilsa slowly and increasingly wounds her female prisoners, then has them infected with virulent diseases to help develop new biological warfare agents. Finally, they become infected with maggots. One day while inspecting a line of naked male prisoners she taunts them, "You call yourselves men? I see no manhood between your legs". Wolfe (Gregory Knoph), a tall blond American, replies "Size is not everything". She gives him a trial run and is very satisfied as he had mastered the skill of postponing orgasms.

When the camp receives a visit from General Wolfgang Roehm (Richard Kennedy), Ilsa plans an elaborate dinner for her guest. The centerpiece of the feast consists of a naked female prisoner standing on a block of ice, her head in a slightly slack noose. As the dinner progresses the ice melts and the prisoner is hanged. General Roehm presents Ilsa with the *Reichsführer* Cross for "Service to the Reich", and when Ilsa offers to sleep with him he lays down on the floor and begs her to urinate on him instead. (This is the "golden shower" act widely publicized during the 2016 Presidential Elections). After the last guests depart, the prisoners stage a revolt, echoing ones depicted in the Israeli Stalag novels of the 1950s. Wolfe ties Ilsa's hands to a bed, then rapes her. At that point German army troops occupy the camp. A blond officer executes her by shooting her in the head, then telephones a report to his superior, "General, your orders have been carried out. Camp 9 ceases to exist". Because of its potent blend of sex and violence, *Ilsa* became the model for other fascist porn movies of the 1980s and 1980s.

Ilsa represents a fictionalization of actual Nazi concentration camps where brutal experiments were designed to test the limits of human endurance, although none were headed by female officers. SS doctors conducted horrific experiments

Fascism **111**

on prisoners in Sachsenhausen, Dachau, Natzweiler, Buchenwald, and Neuengamme. In Auschwitz, the notorious Dr Josef Mengele experimented on twins and gypsies. He subjected his victims to increasingly intolerable torture, including forcing tubes through their orifices until they collapsed from pain and exposing them to increasingly higher temperatures to determine the maximum amount of heat humans can endure before being burned to death. Mengele's subjects never survived his experiments, earning him the nickname "The Angel of Death".[41] While real Nazi medical experiments horrified the public when revealed, *Ilsa* and other films of Nazi medical experiments attracted wide audiences.

Despite excoriation by critics, *Ilsa, She Wolf of the SS* became a financial success, inspiring three sequels, including *Ilsa, Harem Keeper of the Oil Sheiks* (1976), *Ilsa, the Wicked Warden* (1977), and *Ilsa, the Tigress of Siberia* (1977). Today Ilsa seems embedded in pop culture, the theme of many amateur gonzo porn videos. Another popular Stalag film was *The Beast in Heat* (*SS Hell Camp*) (1977). It follows a similar plot and depicts a senior SS officer, Dr Kratsch (Macha Magall) who creates a half-man/half-beast hybrid creature and uses it to rape female captives. Kratsch employs a variety of other torture techniques, seemingly inspired by one of Europe's "torture museums" that feature exhibits from Inquisition-era torture devices.

Bitch of Buchenwald

Ilsa's perennial popularity suggests that she touches a sensitive nerve, the excitement that may be generated by a violent sexual woman who combines sex with torture and death. *Ilsa* was loosely based on Ilse Koch, the "Bitch of Buchenwald". Ilse worked as a concentration camp guard who reportedly engaged in numerous affairs with SS officers and even prisoners. In 1936, she added Karl Koch to her list of conquests. In 1936 she married him and he later became the Commandant of Buchenwald concentration camp. After their marriage, Ilse Koch routinely examined naked male prisoners and selected some based on attractive tattoos. Then she would have them executed and their skin made into an ornament. She reportedly possessed a collection of lampshades, desk pads and other goods fashioned from human skin and adorned with tattooed pictures and allegedly ordered lampshades to assist one of her lovers, SS Dr Erich Wagner, who was writing a dissertation on tattooing and criminality. Buchenwald's Jewish inmates recall the Commandant's wife often dressed in horse-riding attire, riding around the camp while keeping a watch out for prisoners with beautiful tattoos. After tapping a victim with her riding cane, the SS guards would remove him to the camp hospital, and he was never seen again. One inmate recalled a vivid memory of Ilse and a prisoner named Jean who was bare-chested.

> "It was a hot day. Some prisoners were working without a shirt. Mrs. Koch arrived on a horse. There was a comrade . . . and he was known throughout camp for his excellent tattoos from head to toe. On his chest he had an exceptionally well-tattooed sailboat with four masts. Even today I can see it before

112 Fascism

my eyes very clearly. Mrs. Koch rode over . . . She took his number down. Jean was called to the gate at evening formation. We didn't see him anymore".[42]

In 1940, Ilse Koch allegedly persuaded her husband to construct a private sports arena in Buchenwald at the cost of over 250,000 Reichsmarks, which Colonel Koch allegedly stole from Jewish prisoners.[43] Toward the end of the war Nazi Germany executed Karl Koch for embezzling camp funds to please Ilse, but she herself went unpunished. Merely killing Jews for their tattooed skins did not constitute a crime in Nazi Germany. But after the war, at the Dachau Trials, Ilse Koch received a life sentence even though it was never proved that she had had lampshades and other decorative items made out of human skin. In 1967, at age 60, Koch committed suicide by hanging herself in prison.

Although Ilse Koch was the most infamous Nazi female to be convicted of war crimes, another monstrous Nazi was Maria Mandl, a female SS guard who started at Ravensbrück and was later reassigned to Auschwitz. She achieved infamy by abusing Jewish prisoners and was promoted to *SS-Lagerführerin* (Commandant of the women's camp responsible only to the Commandant). She became known for keeping Jews as pets, then abruptly sending them off to the gas chamber when she grew tired of them. She was reputedly personally responsible for the deaths of 500,000 prisoners at Auschwitz.[44]

The *Ilsa* films and other Stalag movies transformed real-life criminals like Ilse Koch and Maria Mandl into sexual dominatrices who torture and rape helpless male prisoners. The iron-hard Nazi women in these films pose a threat to paternalism, which cannot be sustained in Nazi porn. Eventually, strong males reassert male dominance by staging a rebellion and rape and kill their dominatrices, thereby restoring the "natural" (paternalistic) sexual order.

Dr Samuel J. Betchen observes that "The dominatrix profession originated as a specialization within brothels, before evolving into its own unique craft". He notes that real and fictional dominatrix characters provide their "submissives" (prisoners) with complex emotional stimuli. Betchen speculates that ". . . the dominatrix has had more of an impact than most care to believe".[45] Other Nazi-porn movies include *SS Experiment Love Camp* (1976) set at Nazi Camp 5 in the final days of WWII. In this film, several female prisoners arrive at a concentration camp to serve as sex slaves for camp officers and as human guinea pigs for horrific Mengele-like medical experiments.

Last Orgy of the Third Reich (Italian, 1977)

Last Orgy of the Third Reich (Italian, 1977) depicts hyper-sexualized Nazis engaging in a violent orgy. Directed by Cesare Canevari, this film focuses on an abusive BDSMQ relationship between Kommandant Conrad von Starke (Andriano Micantoni) and prisoner Lise Cohen (Daniela Poggi). When a shipment of female prisoners arrives at the camp, some are immediately sent to the gas chamber, some are burned alive, and others are stripped naked and gang-raped by SS guards. The

Fascism **113**

guards eagerly viewed pornographic films depicting rape, mother-daughter incest, bondage, and coprophagia. After raping the newly arrived female prisoners, the officers sodomize them with bats and inflict other sexual humiliations on them. Kommandant von Starke and his SS Officer lover Alma (Maristella Greco) secretly view their activities, becoming sexually stimulated. Later von Starke and his guards decide to order a few of the prisoners to be cooked for dinner. When one of the female prisoners passes out from shock, they douse her with brandy and set her alight, afterwards consuming her body.

Meanwhile, von Starke becomes intrigued by Lise's stoicism in the face of the guards' extreme brutality. He redoubles his effort to break her body and spirit, dangling her naked over a quicklime pit and lowering her into a box teaming with rats. Finally, von Starke becomes attracted to her indomitable spirit and professes his love for her. She seems favorable to his advances and testifies on his behalf after the Red Army liberates the camp, saving him from certain execution. Following the war, the two meet secretly in a remote location to have sex, at which point she pulls out a pistol and kills him. The ending, as in the other Stalag films, attempts to set the world to rights with additional violence, but von Starke's death hardly addresses the massive abuses depicted in this film. It only adds to the film's violent content.

Salon Kitty and *Fräulein Devil*

Salon Kitty (1976) and *Fräulein Devil* (1977) are based on the true story of a Nazi brothel in Berlin that doubled as a clandestine espionage base. It was named *Salon Kitty* after Katharina Zammit, also known as Kitty Schmidt. During WWII, the SS, desperate to stem intelligence leaks of vital war information, demanded that Schmidt allow them to spy and record all visits to her popular bordello with hidden microphones and cameras. Over 10,000 men visited Salon Kitty each year. Any grumbling about Hitler were considered treasonous and merited arrest and incarceration in concentration campus. At one point the SS recorded Mussolini's son-in-law, Count Galeazo Ciano, who served as Foreign Minister in Mussolini's fascist government, ridiculing Hitler and implying that his father-in-law regarded the *Führer* as an arrogant buffoon.[46] In 1943, after Mussolini fell from power, Count Ciano fled to Germany, where the Nazi government secretly turned him over to Mussolini to have him arrested, tried, and executed, which occurred in 1944.[47] *Salon Kitty* and *Fräulein Devil* expanded Nazi porn's scope from concentration camp brothel films to urban brothels. Together, both subgenres contribute to the impression of a sex-obsessed Nazi Germany.

The Night Porter (Italian 1974)

Lilian Cavani's widely screened *The Night Porter* (Italian 1974) depicts the 1957 chance encounter of Holocaust survivor Lucia (Charlotte Rampling) and Max (Dirk Borgarde), the Nazi officer who inflicted sado/masochistic torture upon

114 Fascism

her thirteen years earlier during WWII, in a hotel in Vienna. Inexorably, they find themselves drawn toward each other and renew their earlier BDSM relationship. The plot seems thin but provides ample opportunity for sexy sadomasochism. Although it attracted a wide fan base, Cavani's film failed to impress critics. Roger Ebert wrote, *"The Night Porter* is as nasty as it is lubricious, a despicable attempt to titillate us by exploiting memories of persecution and suffering".[48] *The New York Times'* Norma Sayer observed " If you don't love pain, you won't find 'The Night Porter' erotic—and by now, even pain buffs may be satiated with Nazi decadence".[49]

Salò, or the 120 Days of Sodom (1975)

Although 1970s' fascist porn films featured sadomasochism, none acquired the controversial reception and critical acclaim more so than Pier Paolo Pasolini's film *Salò, or the 120 Days of Sodom* (1975), loosely based on the Marquis de Sade's novel *120 Days of Sodom* (1875). Instead of de Sade's original characters, Pasolini uses Italian fascist characters. He set his film in the period shortly after the fall of Italian dictator Benito Mussolini while Italy still functioned as a fascist nation. Four prominent libertines (believers in unbridled erotic and violent pleasure) including a Duke, a Bishop, a Magistrate, and the President hire four teenage boys to serve as guards and four young male "studs", also referred to as "cock mongers" and "fuckers" to assist them in creating a four-month violent, sexual orgy. They forcibly kidnap numerous teenage boys and girls and whisk them off to a palace near the Italian city of Salò. There they add four middle-aged "collaborators", former prostitutes and madams, to recite salacious stories to the four men and assembled staff and victims. During the coming four months the libertines engage in increasingly violent sexuality with their victims, ultimately torturing and murdering all but one of the captives, who enjoyed her experiences and becomes a libertine herself.

Salò justifiably received a "fascist porn" label because it depicts fascism and its controversial, violently transgressive nature and because of its setting. The Republic of Salò, was a holdout of fascist Italy, complete with sadomasochistic characters. *American Cinematheque* warns potential viewers, "Be prepared, Salò is not for the weak of heart". It, "depicts with cold precision the sexual and psychological atrocities visited on sixteen young men and women, held hostage by a group of depraved nobles at the end of WWII".[50] Pasolini never saw his film screened because on November 1, 1975, an unknown person or persons assassinated the iconic filmmaker on the streets of Rome. He was last seen alive by an Italian rent boy who confessed to the Rome police that Pasolini offered, "Come ride with me, and I'll give you a present".[51] He may have been murdered for his gayness, Communist leanings, or for this controversial final movie. His unsolved killing only adds to the allure of one of the most shockingly transgressive films ever released in a mainstream theater.

Pasolini's film faced censorship in most countries for decades, including in the US, where it earned a reputation for being the "most banned". In 1994, nearly twenty years after release, the owners of an LGBTQ bookstore in Cincinnati, Ohio, were arrested and charged with "pandering" for hosting a public screening of the film. The case caught the attention of scholars and filmmakers, including director Martin Scorsese and actor Alec Baldwin, who signed a legal brief extolling the film's artistic merits. The Ohio Supreme Court eventually dismissed the case against the owners because the police had violated their Fourth Amendment rights.[52]

In July 2003, Chicago's Gene Siskel Film Center booked *Salò* for a one-week screening. *Chicago Tribune* critic John Petrakis cautioned viewers, "Though it is clearly intended as an attack on power, intolerance and even consumerism, it isn't always simple to remind yourself that you are witnessing an extended metaphor as violent acts unfold on screen".[53]

Transgressive Movement

The release of Salò occurred during an artistic movement that many now refer to as "transgressive". During 1984–5, New York artist/author/filmmaker Nick Zedd became a spokesperson for a loose-knit group of filmmakers and artists employing black humor and shock to intensify their work. It became known as the Cinema of Transgression because of its controversial, sexual/violent nature. Zedd maintained, "If it's not transgressive, it's not underground. It has to be threatening the status quo by doing something surprising, not just imitating what's been done before".[54] Zedd's film titles suggest their violent, transgressive content, including *They Eat Scum* (1975), *Thrust in Me* (1984), *School of Shame* (1984), *Go to Hell* (1986), and *Whoregasm* (1988).

The 1970s and 1980s witnessed the Skinhead Movement, first appearing in Great Britain around 1969, then spreading to the US by the early 1980s. Skinheads, also called neo-Nazis, embrace the Nazi symbols of swastikas, black boots, and leather jackets, and most famously, they shave their heads or part of their heads. In 1986, Romantic Violence, also known as CASH (Chicago Area Skinheads), became one of the first true racist skinhead gangs in the US, soon followed by the Confederate Hammerskins in Dallas. Former California Klan leader Tom Metzger formed the Aryan Youth Movement in 1988, a skinhead division of his white supremacist group White Aryan Resistance (WAR). That same year, members of the Confederate Hammerskins patrolled Robert E. Lee Park in Dallas, beating and harassing all non-whites who appeared there. Police broke up an attempt by armed Hammerskins to destroy Jewish businesses on November 9, 1988, the 50th anniversary of *Kristallnacht*, the Nazi pogrom also known as the "Night of Broken Glass". The gang was suspected of dozens of crimes in the 1990s, including the vandalism of a Dallas synagogue. In succeeding years, skinheads marched through downtown Birmingham, Alabama, where they murdered a homeless African

116 Fascism

American man. Other 1990s' skinhead crimes include killing a Denver policeman, killing a mother and child, and murdering two anti-racist activists near Las Vegas. In 1999, Hammerskin Nation organized its first annual Hammerfest, the group's hate rock concert, attracting hundreds of participants from around the country.

In 2007, a group of Taiwanese university students established the National Socialism Association, a neo-Nazi political movement advocating national strength, unity, and strict curtailment of immigration. Their website features a bold swastika. One of the movement's founders stated that the group's membership is open to those, ". . . who do not dislike Hitler". Taipei official Emile Sheng cautioned, "People here don't really understand what Nazism is. They're not really racist or anti-Jewish. They don't even know what it means".[55] In recent years, many Asians acquired a taste for Nazi chic. In 2014, the all-female Korean band *Pritz* created a stir when it appeared wearing Nazi-inspired costumes. *Pritz's* costumes featured sleek, heavy black dresses, high collars, and red armbands with black crossing the center of a white circle—reminiscent of swastikas. *Pritz's* creators claimed that the costumes were similar to Nazi uniforms by coincidence. In fact, many Koreans have a tradition of Nazi chic that goes back to 2000, when *Time* wrote about the country's Nazi-themed bars like The Fifth Reich. The bar entrance bears a likeness to Adolf Hitler, and a larger picture of the *Führer* stands behind the bar. Barmaids dressed in Nazi-style uniforms and wore swastikas on their arms. *Time* labeled it "Nazi chic, Korean-style".[56]

Following the election of President Barack Obama in 2008, membership in skinhead and other white racist organizations in the US spiked dramatically, and in 2012 police arrested members of the Outlaws motorcycle club and the neo-Nazi 1st SS Kavallerie Brigade Motorcycle Division for planning to blow up buildings and assassinate rivals. Also in 2012, Wade Michael Page, member of the Northern Hammerskins and white supremacist band member, emptied a 9 mm automatic pistol into a Sikh temple in Oak Creek, Wisconsin, killing six members and wounding three others, including a police officer.[57]

Fascist porn, especially Nazi Germany's powerful influence on pornography, grew in recent years from a fringe art form into a mainstream venue. The former trickle of Nazi and other fascist porn and fascist violence, fueled by the internet, transformed into a flood. Today fascism's legacy of violence and subjugation appears minimized or completely forgotten as consumers of popular culture indulge in Nazi chic and other forms of what enthusiasts now label "alt-right" culture. Their followers seek to shock adults and "the establishment" with the ultimate cultural *faux pas*—reverence for fascism. Elements of fascist porn appear in the mainstream in the US and other countries. Citizens United vs Federal Election Commission, the monumental 2010 US Supreme Court case that equates business corporations with individuals as far as rights of "free speech" are concerned opened vast corporate coffers and abolished previous limits on campaign financing. The landmark ruling allowed billionaires David and Charles Koch to pledge $900 million to influence the 2016 election. *Alternet's* Thom Hartman observed in February 2015 that the court's decision quickly led to a rise in fascism and promise, ". . . democracy's dispiriting demise". Hartman charged that, ". . . the oligarchs are plotting their final takeover by using their economic dominance to capture governmental power".[58]

In 2016 Presidential candidate Donald Trump promised the creation of a special police force to round up and deport roughly 11 million illegal immigrants while vowing to ban immigration from many countries and to ban Muslims entirely. He also promised to reinstitute torture in American prisons and impose criminal penalties on pregnant women who had abortions. He will long be remembered for his campaign's incessant and jarring calls regarding his opponent Hillary Clinton to, "Lock her up!" In keeping with the "sadomasochistic trope", Trump and surrogates enact and speak from dominant or "dom" perspectives, threatening exclusion, incarceration, torture, and even death to a growing number of "subs".

Today some wonder if Donald Trump will become a new Hitler. Of course, both leaders began their careers very differently. Hitler started as a failed artist and decorated WWI corporal, while Trump began as a millionaire real-estate developer who became a billionaire developer and reality television star. Both employed bombast and verbal abuse. Like Hitler, Trump threatens opponents with violence. While Hitler used the then-new technology of radio to spread his ideology, Trump tweets short blurbs and employs radio, television, and internet media. Jane Caplan, who studies fascism, wrote in January 2017 that she had begun witnessing disturbing parallels between President Trump and Hitler and Mussolini:

> Against my own better judgment, I have been spotting Mussolini in this gesture or turn of phrase, Hitler in that one. I have been watching the manipulated interactions of speaker with audience, the hyperbolic political emotions, the narcissistic masculinity, the unbridled threats, the conversion of facile fantasies and malignant bigotries into eternal verities, the vast, empty promises, the breath-taking lies.

Caplan acknowledges that "The U.S. has proved vulnerable to the threat of a type of movement that groups itself on the edge of the body politic and does not guarantee to play by the rules of the political or—potentially—the constitutional game". The threat today, as in the 1930s, comes from fascism, which is expressed not only by, ". . . mass rallies and extreme violence . . ." but also by, ". . . inserting violence, demagoguery, and contempt for the rule of law into the heart of popular politics". For Caplan, our only hope is through countering fascism with strong pro-diversity, pro-democratic values, expressing, ". . . respect for what is alien", and, ". . . tolerance for what is unpalatable . . .".[59]

Internet Fascist Porn

Currently, an internet search for "Fascist Porn Videos" yields 1,650,000 results, and internet searches for Nazism spiked after the election of Trump. Trump embodies authoritarianism, along with contemporary leaders like Hungary's Viktor Orban,

118 Fascism

France's Marine Le Pen, Austria's Sebastian Kurz, Russia's Vladimir Putin, and North Korea's Kim Jong-un. These leaders are also self-styled "nationalists", a term applied to Hitler and Mussolini.

On the internet, Nazi porn remains popular, with strong, unabating interest.[60] Commercial sites include Nazi Porn Videos www.pornhub.com/video/search?search=nazi, Ape Tube free Nazi porn www.apetube.com/search/Nazi, and Large Porn Tube Nazi videos www.largeporntube.com/search/?q=nazi. One site advertises, "Welcome to the Nazi concentration camp", adding "welcome ladies". www.xvideos.com/ . . . the_nazi . . . nazi_concentrati". Another site advertises "Nazi Porn Videos and Sex Movies www.redtube.com/?search=nazi".

Although fascist porn was once created by males and produced for predominately male audiences, females increasingly find themselves producing and starring in their own Nazi porn, often with them in the role of dominatrix. Nazi Germany continues to serve the most popular culture setting for fascist porn videos because of the sadomasochistic nature of Nazi Germany, which combined unbridled exercise of power with a clandestine obsession with sexual violence. Nazi Germany's violence-fueled sadomasochism continues to allure and attract audiences from all ages and social classes, which now includes a growing number of females.

Notes

1. "German Far-right AfD Surpasses Social Democrats to Become 2nd Strongest Party—Poll," *RT Newsletter*, February 20, 2018 www.rt.com/news/419286-afd-surpass-social... retrieved April 29, 2019.
2. www.urbandictionary.com/define.php?term=fascism retrieved April 29, 2019.
3. www.reference.com › Government & Politics › Types of Government retrieved April 29, 2019.
4. Michael Newall, "The Aesthetics of Transgressive Pornography," in Jerrod Livingston and Hans Maes, eds., *Aesthetics and Pornography*, Oxford: England, in press.
5. *Ibid.*
6. Susan Sontag, "Fascinating Fascism," *The New York Review of Books*, February 6, 1975.
7. *Ibid.*
8. Hans Blüher, "Die Rolle der Erotik in der Männlichengesellschaft," *Jena: E. Diederichs*, vol. 1, 1921, pp. 6–7.
9. Beatrice Verhoeven, "Ann Coulter on Milo 'Meltdown:' Pederasty Acceptable Only for Refugees and Illegals," *The Wrap*, February 20, 2017.
10. Harry Oosterhaus and Hubert Kennedy, eds., *Homosexuality and Male Bonding in Pre-Nazi Germany*. New York: Harrington Park Press, 1991.
11. Lively, Scott, and Abrams, Kevin, *The Pink Swastika: Homosexuality in the Nazi Party. Founders Publishing. Corporation*, Danville: Illinois, 1995, p. 7.ISBN 978-0-9647609-0-5.
12. Catherine Howe, "Berlin Was a Liberal Hotbed of Homosexuality and a Mecca for Cross Dressers and Transsexuals Where the First Male-to-Female Surgery Was Performed: Until the Nazis Came to Power, New Book Reveals," *Daily Mail*, November 25, 2014.
13. Richard Grunberger, *The 12-Year Reich*. New York: Ballantine Books, 1971, p. 425.
14. C. Paul Vincent, *The Politics of Hunger*. Akron, OH: Ohio University Press, 1985.
15. frenchpubagency.com, "1940–1945, the Erotic Years: Vichy, or, the Misfortunes of Virtue," *frenchpubagency.com*, 2012 accessed December 11, 2012.

Fascism **119**

16. Richard Grunberger, *The 12-Year Reich*. New York: Ballantine Books, 1971, p. 425.
17. Amanda Taub, "How 'Islands of Honesty' Can Crush Corruption," *The New York Times*, December 11, 2016.
18. Richard Evans, *The Third Reich in Power*. New York: Penguin Group, 2005. ISBN 978-0-14-303790-3.
19. James Steakley, "Homosexuals and the Holocaust: Homosexuals and the Third Reich," *The Body Politic*, no. 11, January/February 1974. People with a History: An Online Guide to Lesbian, Gay, Bisexual and Trans History.
20. Johan Hari, "The Strange, Strange Story of the Gay Fascists," *The Huffington Post*, May 25, 2011.
21. Ben S. Austin, "Homosexuals and the Holocaust," *Jewish Virtual Library*, www.jewishvirtuallibrary.org/jsource/Holocaust/homo.html retrieved April 23, 2018.
22. Richard Plant, *The Pink Triangle: The Nazi War against Homosexuals*. New York: Holt, 1988, p. 303.
23. Heinz Heger, *The Men With the Pink Triangle: The True Life-and-Death Story of Homosexuals in the Nazi Death Camps*. New York: Alyson Books, 1994, p. 137.
24. Auschwitz, Dachau, Buchenwald, and Sachsenhausen, "Nazi Sex Slaves: New Exhibition Documents Forced Prostitution in Concentration Camps," *Spiegel International*, January 15, 2007. https://www.spiegel.de/international/nazi-sex-slaves-new-exhibition-documents-forced...
25. Nanda Habermann, Hester Baer, and Elizabeth Roberts Baer, *The Blessed Abyss, Inmate #6582 in Ravensbrück Concentration Camp for Women*. Detroit: Wayne State University Press, pp. 33–34.
26. David Graham, "New Book Reveals Horror of Nazi Camp Brothels," *Reuters Lifestyle*, August 17, 2009.
27. "Nazi Leader Heinrich Himmler on the 'Question of Homosexuality'," *United States Holocaust Museum*, www.ushmm.org/.../homosexuals.../... accessed August 24, 2016.
28. David Crossland, "Nazi Program to Breed Master Race: Lebensborn Children Break Silence," *Spiegel Online International*, November 7, 2007.
29. Scott Lively and Kevin Abrams, *The Pink Swastika: Homosexuality in the Nazi Party*, Danville, Illinois, 1995.
30. Paul Roland, *Nazi Women: The Attraction of Evil*. London, England: Arcturus Publishing, 2014, pp. 140–142.
31. www.filmmakermagazine.com/blo.../nazi-porn.php
32. David Segal, "High on Hitler and Meth: Book Says Nazis Were Fueled by Drugs," *The New York Times*, December 9, 2016.
33. Ian Kershaw. *The Nazi Dictatorship: Problems and Perspectives of Interpretation*. London and New York: Routledge, 1993 [1985], pp. 170, 172, 181. ISBN 978-0-34055-047-2.
34. Villa Baviera, "Slavery! Sex Abuse! Suffering! Inside Chili's Sinister Nazi Torture Cult . . . That Is Now a German-Themed Tourist Resort," *The Sun*, August 2, 2016.
35. "Documentary Looks at Nazi Porn in Israel," *UPI*, September 6, 2007. https://www.upi.com/.../2007/.../Documentary-looks-at-Nazi-porn-in-Israel/50001189...
36. IMDB, "Adolf Hitler," www.imdb.com/title/tt0070760/
37. Joseph Pearce, *Race with the Devil: My Journey from Racial Hatred to Rational Love*, Charlotte, NC: Saint Benedict Press, 2013.
38. Jon Bennett, "What Happened When the Sex Pistols Appeared on the Bill Grundy Show," *Classic Rock*, December 2, 2016.
39. Vivian Goldman, "Never Mind the Swastikas: The Secret History of the UK's 'Punky Jews'," *The Guardian*, February 27, 2014.
40. Lynn Rapaport, "Holocaust Pornography: Profaning the Sacred in Ilsa, She-Wolf of the SS," *Journal of Jewish Studies*, vol. 22, no. 1, Fall 2003.
41. "Medical Experiments of the Holocaust and Nazi Medicine," *A People's History of the Holocaust & Nazi Medicine*, remember.org/educate/medexp

120 Fascism

42. Mark Jacobson, "Skin," *New York Magazine*, September 5, 2010.
43. Louisa Aguilar, "The Most Evil Women in History Ilse Koch" *YouTube*, October 6, 2016.
44. Paul Roland, *Nazi Women: The Attraction of Evil*. London, England: Arcturus Publishing, 2014, p. 222.
45. Samuel J. Betchen, "Sexually Dominant Women and the Men Who Desire Them, Part 1," *Psychology Today*, October 20, 2014.
46. Paul Roland, *Nazi Women: The Attraction of Evil*. London, England: Arcturus Publishing, 2014.
47. "Mussolini's Daughter's Affair with Communist Revealed in Love Letters," *The Telegraph*, April 17, 2009 accessed January 20, 2010.
48. Roger Ebert, "The Night Porter," *Rogerebert.com*, February 10, 1975.
49. Nora Sayre, "The Night Porter: Portrait of Abuse, Stars Bogarde," *The New York Times*, October 2, 1974.
50. "Salo" http://www.americancinemathequecalendar.com/content/the-decameron-salò-or-the-120-days-of-sodom.. retrieved April 29, 2019.
51. Ed Vulliamy, "Who Really Killed Pier Paolo Pasolini?" *The Observer*, August 23, 2014.
52. "Salo: or the 120 Days of Sodom (1975)-trivia-IMDB" https://www.imdb.com/title/tt0073650/trivia retrieved April 29, 2019.
53. John Petraakis, "Pasolini's Last Film a Look at Controversy, Depravity," *Chicago Tribune*, July 25, 2003.
54. Mike Everleth, "1985: The Cinema of Transgression Manifesto Is Published", *Underground Film Journal*, November 23, 2018.
55. "Taiwan Students Launch Neo-Nazi Movement," *Associated Press*, March 14, 2007. https://www.foxnews.com/story/taiwan-students-launch-neo-nazi-movement Retrieved April 29, 2019.
56. Donald Macintyre, "They Dressed Well," *Time*, June 5, 2000.
57. "Racist Skinheads: Understanding the Threat," *Southern Poverty Law Center*, June 25, 2012, www.splcenter.org/.../racist-skinheads-understand . . . accessed September 1, 2016.
58. Thom Hartman, "Fascism Is Rising in America: The Koch Brothers and Democracy's Dispiriting Demise," *Salon*, February 8, 2015.
59. Jane Caplan, "Is the World Turning Fascist and Does It Matter?" *Newsweek*, January 13, 2017.
60. www.google.com/trends/explore?q=nazi%20porn retrieved April 29, 2019.

Bibliography

An Aesthetics of Transgressive Pornography, https://kar.kent.ac.uk/id/eprint/31635
Blüher, Hans, "Die rolle der erotik in der männlichengesellschaft," *Jena: E. Diederichs*, vol. 1, 1921, pp. 6–7.
Evans, Richard, *The Third Reich in Power*. New York: Penguin Group, 2005. ISBN 978-0-14-303790-3.
frenchpubagency.com, "1940–1945, the Erotic Years: Vichy, or, the Misfortunes of Virtue," *frenchpubagency.com*, 2012 accessed December 11, 2012.
Grunberger, Richard, *The 12-Year Reich*. New York: Ballantine Books, 1971, p. 425.
Hari, Johan, "The Strange, Strange Story of the Gay Fascists," *The Huffington Post*, May 25, 2011.
Howe, Catherine, "Berlin Was a Liberal Hotbed of Homosexuality and a Mecca for Cross Dressers and Transsexuals Where the First Male-to-Female Surgery Was Performed: Until the Nazis Came to Power, New Book Reveals," *Daily Mail*, November 25, 2014.
Lively, Scott; Abrams, Kevin (1995). *The Pink Swastika: Homosexuality in the Nazi Party*. Founders Publishing. Danville, Illinois ISBN 978-0-9647609-0-5.

Newall, Michael, "The Aesthetics of Transgressive Pornography," in *Aesthetics and Pornography*, edited by Jerrod Livingston and Hans Maes. Oxford: England, in press.

Oosterhaus, Harry, and Hubert Kennedy, eds., *Homosexuality and Male Bonding in Pre-Nazi Germany*. New York: Harrington Park Press, 1991.

Sontag, Susan, "Fascinating Fascism," *The New York Review of Books*, February 6, 1975.

Steakley, James, "Homosexuals and the Holocaust: Homosexuals and the Third Reich," *The Body Politic* no. 11, January/February 1974.

Taub, Amanda, "How 'Islands of Honesty' Can Crush Corruption," *The New York Times*, December 11, 2016.

Verhoeven, Beatrice, "Ann Coulter on Milo 'Meltdown:' Pederasty Acceptable Only for Refugees and Illegals," *The Wrap*, February 20, 2017.

Vincent, C. Paul, *The Politics of Hunger*. Athens, OH: Ohio University Press, 1985.

7

SADOMASOCHISM AND REVOLT

The dynamic relationship between "dominants" and "submissives" finds expression in popular culture at all levels. Popular culture, from Hollywood movies, studio pornography, and written materials including newspaper editorials, embraces the "dom" versus "sub" dynamic. Technology now allows individuals to produce low-cost films and videos by creating and starring in their personal pornography. Violent pornography is a close companion to personal sadomasochism. Sadomasochism, according to psychologist D. Langdridge, includes common features like the consensual exchange of power through dominance and submission, the inclusion of pain or intense stimulation, elements of role-taking or role play, and various levels of bondage.[1] These activities occur on the personal level. However, some suggest sadomasochism encompasses much more than personal choices regarding sexuality and relationships.

Psychologist and author Lynn Chancer theorized that sadomasochism functions on a societal level as well as individual in her influential book *Sadomasochism in Everyday Life: The Dynamics of Power and Powerless* (first published 1992). In her pioneering study, Chancer states, ". . . rather than sadomasochism being the property of individuals, our culture is deeply oriented in a sadomasochistic direction . . .", because we are daily bombarded, ". . . with experiences of domination and subordination". These images appear far more often than, ". . . sensations and inklings of freedom and reciprocity". She notes that dynamic relationships between workers and capitalists become strained as all sides advocate advantageous policies and laws which become "literally a life-and-death situation: the worker requires the job for his or her subsistence or the subsistence of his or her family; the capitalist requires the worker's labor". Chancer finds sadomasochism influential in institutions far beyond the interpersonal realm, permeating schools, churches, courts, the workplace, and, in fact, every social institution. Examples abound,

Sadomasochism and Revolt **123**

including authoritarian teachers and school administrators, pushy law enforcement officers, controlling judges, and ministers.[2] The current sexual harassment crisis engulfing the Catholic Church presents a cogent example of sadomasochism. Even hotel and casino workers experience sexual harassment on a regular basis. Last year 58% of hotel workers and 77% of casino workers reported being sexually harassed by a guest. One hotel worker described a scene she witnessed in a room in which she had been invited by the guest: "he was masturbating, and I was crying". The worker "felt dirty".[3]

Social sadomasochism manifests itself in complex ways, with individuals playing multiple and often widely disparate roles, a practice often called "role reversal". An abusive husband, for example, who is dominant and sadistic toward his wife and family, may simultaneously enact a subordinate, even a masochist role with his supervisor at work. Likewise, women who play subordinate, masochistic roles with their domineering husbands may assume more sadistic roles while disciplining children. Workers experiencing economic powerlessness may exhibit racist, homophobic, misogynistic, and/or anti-semitic behavior to compensate for their weak, powerless social positions.[4]

Clinician and author Michael J. Formica concluded a decade ago that sadomasochism permeates and shapes everyday relationships. "In every relationship, there is a minimizer and a maximizer. The minimizer tends to be more subdued within the context of the relationship, while the maximizer tends to be more evocative". Furthermore:

> In a relationship driven by power and control, rather than compassion and cooperation, one partner becomes "parentalized" and the other "infantilized". Most often, the maximizer, being more emotional, tends to become infantilized and submissive for fear of angering or disappointing their partner. The minimizer, being more contained, tends to gather the power in the relationship, whether by intention or default, and, in this way, becomes parentalized.

"As the submissive/infantilized partner withdraws emotionally and physically in a misguided effort not to 'rock the boat', the dominant/parentalized partner becomes anxious and begins to 'ramp up' the activity in the relationship, becoming more attentive, more needy. . . more infantile". Eventually, the relationship stabilizes. "When the underlying dynamic shifts to one of compassion, cooperation and communication from one of push and pull, the cycle ceases, or at least recedes into the background, and the stage for an authentic relationship is then set". Formica also discovered that relationship partners conforming to either dominant or submissive roles may shift roles playfully and swap being dominant or submissive for the opposite role.[5]

In *Degradation Rituals: Our Sadomasochistic Society* (2014), Lisiunia A. Romanienko also calls attention to deep social roots of sadomasochism, much of it hidden

124 Sadomasochism and Revolt

within social institutions. She finds sadomasochism in exploitative power relations, observing,

> "The willingness of ever-increasing numbers of individuals to engage in sexual exploitations of power and control through the design of, or submission or contestation of conventional bodily control of men over women, women over other women, or men over other men is resulting in increasing popularity of sadomasochistic practices that, to date, have remained elusive to objective scholarly inquiry beyond the lagging field of psychoanalysis".

Sadomasochism subtly defines the family, education, military, judicial, legislative, business, and private institutions and organizations.

> "While many researchers have examined sexual behavior in a historical context, few have established sexual behavior in light of power relations in our increasingly cruel, sadomasochistic culture. In both realms power is often conceived as one causing upheaval and instability with chaos reigning in both political systems and private action in response to those arrangements".

Romanienko concludes that American society itself is permeated by "social sadomasochism", noting recent anti-feminist legislation, ". . . that criminalizes tampons, legalizes rape, coerces women into mandatory invasive vaginal ultrasound procedures, and moves reproductive health care decisions from the intimate sphere to that of the state . . .".[6] This scenario ". . . provides preliminary evidence for an explicit causal connection between cognitive and cultural dimensions of degradation and cruel authority in the contemporary war on women and the reassertion and reclamation of control in women's daily sensual lives".[7]

Clinical psychologists Margi Kaplinsky and Shulamet Geller obtained surprising insights from their practice about the sources of sadomasochism.

> "We came to believe that sadomasochistic relations mark not only extreme cases of suffering and abuse but are also prevalent in daily life. This cuts through all levels of personal organization—to such an extent that one might generalize and argue that sadomasochistic games characterize the whole of human existence".

They observed that complaints about deprivation, experiences of inconsolable, persistent pain, bitterness, conscious envy, victimization, self-blaming, and accusation are among the widespread phenomena that might be observed. "The concept of sadomasochism refers to the fact that what ostensibly reveals itself as suffering involves a complexity of feelings and relations".[8]

To psychologists and psychiatrists, sadomasochism involves giving and/or receiving pleasure from giving and/or receiving pain. More extreme cases manifest as "Sexual Sadism Disorder", a condition of, ". . . recurrent and intense sexual arousal from the physical or psychological suffering of another person, as manifested by fantasies, urges, or behaviors".[9] During the 1970s and 1980s, according to Megan Yost, feminist authors often presented sadomasochism (SM) as, ". . . a form of sexual aggression in which one partner inflicts pain on an unwilling partner who is powerless in the relationship". Yost concludes that advocates of, ". . . this feminist perspective promoted the belief . . . that SM was a violent, non-feminist activity that disempowered women and should be condemned".[10] Feminists at that time believed that SM replicated patriarchal relationships and encouraged both violence against women and unequal power relationships, and that SM validated and promoted patriarchy.[11] Today, no consensus exists about the alleged harms of pornography. After more than a decade of lobbying from BDSMQ advocacy groups the American Psychiatric Association finally agreed in 2013 to drop sadism and masochism from their DSM list of psychiatric disorders.[12]

Submissive Revolt

The roots of today's contentious social movements originated during the early twentieth century as pioneering labor organizers, strike leaders, and community organizers arose to protest widespread economic abuses of women and an unrelenting campaign of sexual violence against women. Today pioneer Rose Schneiderman receives belated recognition as, ". . . an unsung forerunner of the #MeToo movement" who organized women to fight for laws to protect them from sexual harassment and assault by higher-ranking men in their work spaces. She ascended the ranks of labor unions in the aftermath of New York's disastrous Triangle Shirtwaist factory strike in 1909 and is currently recognized as a forerunner to the #MeToo movement.[13] Interest in her speeches and biography is currently spiking.[14]

African American women long faced a daunting set of atrocities, including rape and other forms of sexual abuse at the hands of white men. A bitter struggle against white gang rapes and sexual abuse of African American women by southern white males began in earnest after brutal gang rapes of African American mother Recy Taylor (1944), and Gertrude Perkins (1949), and justice committees formed for them by Rosa Parks helped inspire a wider civil rights movement. Following the Brown v. Board of Education of Topeka (1954) Supreme Court decision ending "separate but equal" Jim Crow laws and practices, southern white males redoubled their efforts to sexually abuse African American females, who launched brave resistance efforts that ultimately resulted in the trial and surprising convictions and life sentences of four young white males for brutally raping Jesse Jean Owens in Tallahassee, Florida in 1959. This case was soon followed by several other convictions of white rapists of African American women, and a "long transition" began to unfold confronting white sexual violence against African American females.[15]

Jesse Jean Owens' rape case, like the Recy Taylor and Gertrude Perkins cases in the 1940s, helped raise awareness about the unofficial campaign of sexual violence against African American women. A turning point arrived in the mid-1970s as feminists increasingly challenged American culture, including the criminal justice system for its refusal to protect women's rights to sexual consent. Journalist Sasha Cohen observes that by the 1970s an anti-sexual harassment campaign became, ". . . the natural extension of the grassroots anti-rape and anti-battering movements, which grew out of consciousness-raising sessions in which women shared personal stories and realized they were not alone in their experiences".

The term "sexual harassment" first appeared in 1975, coined by a group of women at Cornell University in support of former university employee Carmita Wood, who filed a claim for unemployment benefits in 1975 after resigning from her job due to unwanted touching by her supervisor. Initially, Cornell refused Wood's request for a transfer, then denied her benefits citing that she quit for, ". . . personal reasons". Wood, working with activists at the university's Human Affairs Office, formed a group called Working Women United. At a "Speak Out" event hosted by the group, secretaries, mailroom clerks, filmmakers, factory workers and waitresses shared their stories, revealing that the problem extended far beyond the university setting.[16]

"Rape-Revenge" Movies

Pop culture eventually responded to rising sentiment against sexual violence by creating a class of (often feminine) heroes who act decisively to right ancient wrongs and unleash violent punishment against aggressors. Anti-rape campaigns

FIGURE 7.1 Quentin Tarantino, *Kill Bill vol 2*, 2004

Source: Pacific Film Archive

Sadomasochism and Revolt **127**

of the 1940s, 1950s, and 1960s inspired a new pop culture movement, which scholars named "rape-revenge" thrillers. These films first appeared in anti-rape B-level cinemas in the 1970s and 1980s and continue to the present era with films like *Kill Bill vols. 1* (2003) *and 2* (2004), and *The Girl With the Dragon Tattoo* (2011). They feature young, innocent women subjected to vicious sexual attacks by sadistic males. Their female heroes survive by transforming into violent sadists that incorporate the methods and brutality of their attackers, rendering them more masculine.

Elle Driver (Darryl Hannah), the one-eyed assassin, finds herself stalked by The Bride (Uma Thurman), one of her former assassin colleagues who turned on her on Bill's (David Carradine) orders. The Bride systematically destroys her would-be assassins including Bill.

Noah Berlatsky points out that critics, once hostile to the rape-revenge genre, now validate it as, if not feminist, at least feminist-friendly. Berlatsky argues that the rape-revenge genre, ". . . revels not just in images of violence in general, but in images of sexualized violence, particularly against women". Audiences enjoy rape-revenge films due to righteous indignation against villainous males. He concludes, ". . . rape-revenge fits feminism into male genre narratives that Hollywood can embrace".[17]

Technology

Over the past decade, technology has transformed videography by the miniaturization of video cameras and recorders. Anyone possessing a smart phone and internet access can create, perform, and post (broadcast) their own "movies", empowering millions to become media creators. Clay Shirkey noted in 2008 that the twentieth century, with the spread of radio and television, represented "The Broadcast Century". At that time, ". . . the normal pattern for media was that it was created by a small group of professionals and then delivered to a large group of consumers". However, in the twenty-first century, ". . . people like to consume media, of course, but they also like to produce it . . . and they like to share it . . .". Self-producing broadcast exponentially increases an individual's influence, leading Shirkey to label the current epoch as "The Communication Century".[18]

Revenge Porn

The explosion of Revenge Porn, personally produced and posted intimate photos and videos without consent of the subject, constitutes a prime example of an egregious aspect of contemporary communications. The unauthorized publishing of another's intimate photos and videos is now criminalized by 41 US states at the time of this publication. Revenge porn victims and their advocates launched successful campaigns for states to criminalize these acts of online aggression, and in July 2016, California Congresswoman Jackie Spier (D) introduced a bill in the House of Representatives to make revenge porn a federal crime. Although

128 Sadomasochism and Revolt

Congresswoman Spier's bill garnered initial media support, to date it remains only a potential. Anti-revenge porn activism is another side of the anti-sexual violence campaigns in alignment with the #MeToo movement.

Recently a disturbing manifestation of sophisticated AI technology used for nefarious purposes began surfacing as celebrities as well as private individuals have had their faces superimposed on raucous pornography videos, typically in a hard-core scene, a practice known as "deepfake porn". In 2018 actress Scarlett Johansson revealed she was an innocent victim of deepfake Porn. Johansson complained, "Nothing can stop someone from cutting and pasting my image or anyone else's onto a different body and making it look as eerily realistic as desired", she said. "The fact is that trying to protect yourself from the Internet and its depravity is basically a lost cause . . . ".[19]

War Porn

Like revenge porn, other pop culture genres like movies, graphic novels, anime, and video pornography may transgress readers' and viewers' personal values. A new genre emerged during the post-9/11 era now labeled war porn, featuring extreme violence, gore, and other graphic images that appeal to a wide variety of viewers. Graphically violent movies like *Rambo* (2008), *We Were Soldiers* (2002), *Fury* (2014), and *American Sniper* (2014) conform to war Porn, or pornographically violent images, scenes, and characters.

By 2004, combat-footage stills and videos of the conflicts in Iraq and Afghanistan showing graphic violence and death began flooding the internet. Violent photos and video clips, once an underground phenomenon, leaked photos and videos of prisoner abuse in Iraq's Abu Ghraib. These soldier-photographed graphic war videos and photos whetted an appetite for ultra-violent images. Today, thousands of Americans turn to the web to enjoy a dose of war porn.[20] Google Trends reveals that internet searches for "war porn" continually increase and periodically spike, with most searches coming from Missouri, Kentucky, Pennsylvania, Washington, and Ohio.[21]

Authoritarianism and Fascism

In the past few years, the ideas, terminology, and motivations of those professing to believe in "fascism" and "libertarianism" enjoyed renewed popularity, including the ideals of Italian fascism. Author Jay Griffiths, in a recent essay, describes the contemporary nature of an alleged return to the ideals of Italian fascism. Fascism, both its contemporary manifestations and its historical roots, ". . . is hostile to egalitarianism and loathes liberalism. It champions 'might is right', a Darwinian survival of the nastiest, and detests vulnerability: the sight of weakness brings out the jackboot in the fascist mind, which then blames the victim for encouraging the kick". Fascism promotes and relishes violence, cherishes audacity and bravado

Sadomasochism and Revolt **129**

while promoting, ". . . charismatic leaders, demagogues and 'strong men', and seeks to flood or control the media". Although purporting to support common people, ". . . it creates the rule of the elite, a cult of violent chauvinism, and a nationalism that serves racism".[22] Recent examples of Fascist Pornography on the internet reveal today's violent alt-right videos, memes, and speeches designed to transform democratic institutions into authoritarian ones primarily serving elites.

Authoritarianism, or insistence on obedience and submission to authority, represents another defining feature of sadomasochism, and of pornography in general. Psychologists report significant increases in diagnoses for "Authoritarian Personality Disorder" or "Authoritarian Personality Syndrome". They theorize that a significant segment of the population, representing millions of Americans, possesses a personality disorder linked to authoritarianism. Philosopher and sociologist Theodore Adorno wrote *The Authoritarian Personality* in 1950 to learn how fascists captured Italy and Germany during the 1920s and 1930s. Adorno isolated nine "F Factors" or indications of fascist markings as follows:

> Blind allegiance to conventional beliefs about right and wrong; Respect for submission to acknowledged authority; Belief in aggression toward those who do not subscribe to conventional thinking, or who are different; A negative view of people in general—i.e., the belief that people would all lie, cheat or steal if given the opportunity; A need for strong leadership which displays uncompromising power; A belief in simple answers and polemics—i.e., the media controls us all; Resistance to creative, dangerous ideas; A black and white worldview; A tendency to project one's own feelings of inadequacy, rage, and fear onto a scapegoated group; A preoccupation with violence and sex, along with rigidity, aggression, and socio/political conformity.[23]

Authoritarianism, of course, often appears in politics. John Dean, Former White House Counsel to President Richard Nixon, discovered in 2005 that mainstream Republicans conform to what Dean labeled "political authoritarianism". In *Conservatives Without Conscience* (2005), Dean divided Republicans into two groups: those that self-identified as "Leaders" and others that self-identified as "Followers". Dean found that Leaders often exhibit authoritarianism through dominating, self-aggrandizing, manipulating, cheating, and lying. They exhibit high degrees of prejudice against minorities, immigrants, women, and BDSMQ (bondage, discipline, sadism, masochism, queer). GOP "Followers" exhibit submissiveness, conventionality, acceptance of authority, and possess little to moderate education. Dean concludes that GOP "Followers", like "Leaders", hold minorities, women, and BDSMQ in contempt.[24]

Authoritarianism lies at the foundation of families, businesses, and other social organizations. Psychoanalytic anthropologist William Manson recently noted a return to the formerly widespread practice in which children become subjected to chastisement and "correction" via strict parenting and schooling, or "spare the rod and spoil the child". Manson observes that individuals who submit to

130 Sadomasochism and Revolt

authoritarianism in childrearing practices may ultimately wish to achieve "commanding status". They suppress, ". . . emotional 'weakness' through a psychological 'identification-with-the-aggressor', such persons may then vindictively *displace* their rage onto newly available, vulnerable 'subordinates'".[25] Author Amy Chua notes, "Authoritarian parents are the ultimate authority. They have complete control over their children. Children are not allowed to question the parents". Defying parents results in consequences, ". . . like the kids being lectured, insulted, shamed or punished".[26]

Authoritarians fear and distrust free speech and free press while advocating repressive, xenophobic policies. They stress harsh punishments to dissuade others from engaging in banned behavior. *The New York Times* columnist Amanda Taub reported that during the 2016 election in South Carolina, exit polls discovered that 75 % of Republican voters supported banning Muslims from the US, while 33% of Trump voters advocated banning gays and lesbians from the country. In addition, 20% of Republican voters regretted that Abraham Lincoln had signed the Emancipation Proclamation that freed the slaves. Although advocates of hypernationalism, social sadomasochism, and restricted human rights exist in every era, current trends suggest growing support for authoritarianism and, ultimately, fascism. Taub notes that support for then-Presidential candidate Trump rose in every geographical region and among many socioeconomic groups. Trump supporters, of whatever demographic, strongly embraced nationalism, xenophobia, and racism conforming to the standard definition of authoritarianism.[27]

#MeToo Movement

Women suffer far more violence than men and frequently lack "agency" to act effectively. However, women benefit by shifting ideology and rapidly transforming technology expanding the reach and power of protesting sexual violence. In 2007 African American activist Tarana Burke created Just Be Inc., a non-profit organization that helps victims of sexual harassment and assault. She called it "Me Too", an anti-sexual violence grassroots organization, because, "Black women are magic and we rock, mostly because we are resilient. We have a long history of taking what we have to make what we need. That's how this movement was born".[28]

On May 15, 2012, Congresswoman Gwen Moore (D Wisconsin), the first African American elected to Congress from Wisconsin, updated 1960s' activist H. Rap Brown's observations about violence being, ". . . as American as apple pie" from her own experience, "Violence against women is as American as apple pie. I know, not only as a legislator, but . . . as an adult". While Brown emphasized the ubiquity and acceptance of violence in American life, Moore specifically denounced male sexual violence against females.[29]

Revolt against misogyny results in rape-revenge movies, television, and videos. In 2011, David Fincher released a Hollywood version of the 2009 Swedish film *The Girl with the Dragon Tattoo*, starring Lisbeth Salander (Rooney Mara), who opens the film as a teenage ward of the state. After her newly appointed guardian forces her to perform oral sex and later rapes her, she plans to entrap him. His next attack comes as he handcuffs her to his bed and anally rapes her, leaving her bloodied and bruised. Lisbeth's revenge entails hacking her assailant's cell phone and creating a miniature surveillance system to track his movements. Then, she tasers him, knocks him unconscious, and handcuffs him to his bed. She strips him naked and forces him to watch a video of his rape while ramming a metal dildo into his anus. Then she tattoos "I AM A RAPIST PIG" across his stomach. Mara found her role, ". . . disturbing, difficult, and emotional . . . . It was a really hard week", she explained. "We shot all of the scenes, when I get raped and the revenge scene. We shot them all back-to-back".[30]

Sadomasochism and Activism

Personal sadomasochism, as commonly practiced in the BDSMQ community, as well as in the general population, ultimately undermines and upends social sadomasochism. Sadomasochistic role-reversal activities involving women subvert restrictive female gender roles and provide personal autonomy from wider authoritarianism. "Reversal rituals" allow females, often for the first time, to experience "agency" in exercising "unusual control" over their bodies, space, and time. They are also able to extend this temporary autonomy and control, ". . . over the temporarily submissive male and his body".[31] Personal sadomasochism practices, when accompanied by gender role reversals, may distance participants from traditional dominant/subservient (sadistic versus masochistic) socio/political dichotomies, enabling rebellion from subservient populations.

Amazon lists dozens of recent books on gender role reversal, including: *Alternate Reality: Gender Role Reversal Story, In a Female Dominant Future: Spanked by the New Girlfriend, An Experiment: A Tale of Gender Role Reversal, Role Reversal: First Time Feminization, The Revolution—Gender Role Reversal: When Women Rule the World.* They represent recent social movements expressed in popular culture.

Women's Porn

The ability to record and create video and audio files and post on the internet in "The Communication Century" inspired the creation of new porn genres created by and focused on women, freed from traditional, expensive, male-dominated professional porn studios. Whereas traditional pornography depicts females as passive victims of male aggression, newly created "women's porn" sites.[32] In 2015 British photographer Amanda de Cadenet joined with Marie Claire to survey women in Britain regarding pornography consumption. They learned that one in three women surveyed admitted viewing pornographic videos at least once per week. This figure belies official porn consumption data from Pew and other polls in which 8% of women surveyed

132 Sadomasochism and Revolt

admit to consuming porn. The majority of those surveyed by de Cadenet and Claire revealed that they viewed pornography alone for their own enjoyment.[33]

Critics also note a rise in women's pornography, with traditional sadomasochism refocused on female interests, i.e. "girls on girls" porn. Jennifer Moorman surveyed 40 female creators of "extreme porn" regarding their attitudes toward depictions of violence against women. She observed that female pornographers adopt a variety of rationale for their productions. One group features the upending of older patterns of male versus female abuse in favor of female avengers redressing the balance of power between genders, while another group depicts rough sex but includes conventions like the use of safe words to opt out of unwanted acts. Moorman concludes:

> The women who make extreme porn contribute to changing perceptions about femininity, a woman's point of view, and the roles of women as cultural producers. Their agency is doubtless constrained by the patriarchal structure of the adult video industry, but their work presents a meaningful challenge to the repressive structure of government regulation.[34]

Sadomasochism and Revolt

In 2007, filmmaker Rory Kennedy, daughter of Robert F. Kennedy, released *Ghosts of Abu Ghraib*, a documentary film that strongly suggests that responsibility for sadistic photos and torture of prisoners in the historic prison goes to the highest levels of American government. Kennedy interviewed prisoners and prison guards and recorded the following description from a prisoner, "The most painful thing for the inmates there, were the cries of the people being tortured. One day, they brought sheets to cover the cell . . . They began torturing one of them, and we could hear what was happening. We listened as his soul cracked. The sound of his voice really twisted our minds and made our hearts stop".

Nancy Buirsky's documentary *The Rape of Recy Taylor* (2017) introduced the 1944 Alabama gang rape case to contemporary viewers often unaware of the tragic history of white sexual abuse of African American women. They view shocking images of Taylor's brutal rape and of her father hiding in a tree with a shotgun to protect his family after Recy accused whites of raping her. Another popular documentary, *The Rape of Gwendolyn Perkins* (2017), depicts the notorious 1949 police gang rape of a young African American woman in Montgomery, Alabama.

Men, of course, also endure sadomasochistic brutality. In 1991 a video captured on a Sony Handycam of LA police officers savagely beating a helpless African American man named Rodney King went viral and inspired widespread rioting in much of Los Angeles and other American cities. King's beating was recalled nearly three decades later after videos of unarmed African American Oscar Grant also went viral during an era of increased social media. Journalist Otis R. Taylor, Jr. observes, ". . . videos of his killing exposed police brutality in a fashion that was unencumbered by traditional pipelines and guidelines".[35]

During his presidency, President Trump consistently attacked the #MeToo movement. At an October 2018 rally, he stated, "It is a very, very scary time for young men in America, where you can be guilty of something you may not be guilty of . . . . This is a very, very—this is a very difficult time". This comes after seventeen women accused candidate Trump of sexual harassment, which he denied while promising to sue each of them after his election. In fact, on this occasion, he asserted "Women are doing great!" After two years in office he has failed to sue any of his accusers.[36]

In the fall of 2018, the #MeToo movement paused after one year as some reflected on gains and losses. In an NPR-Isos poll, 69% felt that the movement had made some sexual harassers feel vulnerable and "accountable". However, 40% also believed that the movement had "gone too far", citing, ". . . a rush to judgment, the prospect of unproven accusations ruining peoples' careers or reputations, and a bandwagon effect that may prompt some to claim sexual misconduct for behavior that doesn't quite rise to that level". Defenders and detractors divided along party lines, with 85% of Democrats willing to believe whistleblowers, while only 67% of Republicans afforded them any credibility. In addition, 77% of Republicans believe false accusations are common, compared with only 37%t of Democrats, but nearly twice the number of Republican women worry that "their man" might be falsely accused of sexual harassment.[37]

Consent

A first step in addressing the legitimacy and legality of sadomasochism, including social sadomasochism, is to establish legal boundaries for submissive consent. The BDSMQ community has established a series of conventions designed to protect Subs from unwanted harm, including "contracts" between doms and subs and the use of "safe words" to terminate sadomasochism once deemed as uncomfortable or harmful by the partner. These conventions are displayed in the *50 Shades of Grey* novel and movie series and are designed to protect both doms and subs from the consequences of sadomasochism. Unwanted sexual aggression weakens the patina of civility and social mores facilitating human interaction and cooperation. Will today's rapidly evolving social movements succeed in curbing society's sadomasochistic tendencies? Many envision a safe society in which doms seek consensual relationships with willing subs, instead of forced or coerced criminal encounters. Given sexual harassment's deep psychological and social roots, and the long history of paternalism and authoritarianism, a society schooled in expressing sadomasochism through consensual, non-threatening means appears promising. Pornography provides glimpses of such a society.

134 Sadomasochism and Revolt

Australian Criminologist Terry Goldsworthy notes that proof of violent sexual crimes ultimately centers around whether victims participated voluntarily in sadomasochistic actions as Submissives or were forced to endure unwanted sexual violence. Goldsworthy observes, ". . . in Australian jurisdictions, consent is generally held to include free and voluntary agreement given by the complainant". In the United Kingdom, consent to participate in violent sadomasochism means "agreement by choice", implying that the consenting individual has the freedom and capacity to agree to participate in sadomasochist activities.[38]

Behavioral Scientist Alexandra Rutherford advocates that victims of sexual abuse be provided forums and outlets to discuss abuse issues and courses of action to be taken. She observes, "We need to create forums where all kinds of women from all sectors of society can talk about sexual victimization in all of its complexity and be taken seriously as narrators of their own experiences, whatever terms they choose to use".[39]

Eliminating sexual violence once and for all would be "almost unimaginable", according to Brian McNair. "Even removing all porn from the face of the earth tomorrow would neither reduce nor end sex crime, which has existed in all societies at all times in human history". Instead of our, ". . . circular and repetitive debate about the particular harms of pornography", he concludes, we should embark on, ". . . an ambitious and determined global effort to continue building on the progressive changes in sexual politics and culture seen since the 1980s".[40] Today massive social movements continue to grow in which formerly submissive groups demand respect and retribution for past offenses.

Notes

1. Darren Langdridge, "Speaking the Unspeakable: S/M and the Eroticisation of Pain," in Darren Langdridge and Meg Barker, eds., *Safe, Sane and Consensual: Contemporary Perspectives on Sadomasochism*. New York: Palgrave Macmillan, 2007, pp. 91–103.
2. Lynn Chancer, *Sadomasochism in Everyday Life: The Dynamics of Power and Powerlessness*. New Brunswick, NJ: Rutgers University Press, 2006, 34.
3. Dave Jamieson, "He Was Masturbating and I Was Crying," *The Huffington Post*, November 20, 2017.
4. Lynn Chancer, *Sadomasochism in Everyday Life: The Dynamics of Power and Powerlessness*. New Brunswick, NJ: Rutgers University Press, 2006, 92.
5. Michael J. Formica, "Sadomasochism in Everyday Relationships," *Psychology Today*, January 13, 2008.
6. Eric W. Hickey, ed., *Sex Crimes and Paraphilia*. Upper Saddle River, NJ: Pearson Education, 2006, pp. 197–199. ISBN 9780131703506.
7. Lisiunia A. Romanienko, *Degradation Rituals: Our Sadomasochistic Society*. New York: Palgrave MacMillan, 2014, p. 141.
8. Margi Kaplinsky and Shulamet Geller, "The Sadomasochism of Everyday Life," *Psychoanalytic Inquiry*, vol. 35, 2015, pp. 245–256.
9. Diagnostic and Statistical Manual (DSM-5) of the American Psychiatric Association, p. 696.
10. Megan R. Yost, "Development and Validation of the Attitudes about Sadomasochist Scale," *Journal of Sex Research*, vol. 47, no. 1, 2010.

Sadomasochism and Revolt **135**

11. Ruth R. Linden, Darlene R. Pagano, Diana E H. Russell, and S. L. Star, eds., *Against Sadomasochism: A Radical Feminist Analysis.* San Francisco: Frog in the Well, 1982.
12. Weinberg Bezreh and Timothy Edgar, *American Journal of Sexual Education*, p. 39; and P.J. Kleinplatz and C. Moser, eds., *Sadomasochism: Powerful Pleasures.* New York: Routledge, 2011.
13. Peter Dreier, "The #MeToo Movement's Roots in Women Worker Rights Movements," *Yes! Magazine*, October 8, 2018.
14. *Ibid.*
15. Danielle L. McGuire, *The Dark at the End of the Street: Black Women, Rape, and Resistance: A New History of the Civil Rights Movement from Rosa Parks to the Rise of Black Power.* New York: Random House, 2011, p. 190.
16. Danielle L. McGuire, *The Dark at the End of the Street: Black Women, Rape, and Resistance: A New History of the Civil Rights Movement from Rosa Parks to the Rise of Black Power.* New York: Random House, 2011, p. 190.
17. Noah Berlatsky, "The Rape-Revenge Genre's Gender Revelations," *The Establishment*, December 29, 2015.
18. Clay Shirkey, *Here Comes Everybody: The Power of Organizing without Organizations.* New York: Penguin Books, 2008.
19. Drew Harwell, "Fake Porn Videos are Being Weaponized to Harass and Humiliate Women," *The Washington Post*, December 30, 2018.
20. The Week Staff, "Is It Wrong to Watch War Porn?" *The Week*, May 5, 2010.
21. https://trends.google.com/trends/explore?q=war%20porn&geo=US retrieved April 30, 2019.
22. Jay Griffith, "Fire, Hatred, and Speed: The Glamour, Bullying, and Violence of the Libertarian Alt-Right," *Aeon*, February 8, 2017.
23. Theodore Adorno, *The Authoritarian Personality.* New York: Harper and Row, 1950.
24. whale.to/b/authoritarian_personality_traits.html accessed November 17, 2017.
25. William Manson, "Authoritarian Sadism Unbound," *Counterpunch*, May 9, 2014.
26. Authoritarian, "Strict Parenting versus Permissive: Which Is Better?" www.raisesmartkid.com/all-ages/1-articles/47-authoritarian-strict-parenting-vs-permissive-which-is-better accessed November 15, 2017.
27. Amanda Taub, "The Rise of American Authoritarianism," *Vox*, March 1, 2016.
28. Alanna Vagianos, "Tarana Burke Tells Black Women Me Too Is Your Movement Too," *Huffpost*, September 10, 2018.
29. Patricia Murphy, "Rep. Gwen Moore on Her Own Sexual Assault," *The Daily Beast*, March 29, 2012.
30. Margi Kaplinski and Shulamet Geller, "The Sadomasochism of Everyday Life," *Psychoanalytic Inquiry* vol. 35, no. 3, 2015.
31. Romanienko, *Degradation Rituals: Our Sadomasochistic Society.* New York: Palgrave Macmillan, 2014, p. 133.
32. Jill Hamilton, "The 19 Best Porn Sites for Women," *Cosmopolitan*, April 26, 2018.
33. Erica Tempesta, "Revealed: One in Three Women Admit They Watch Porn at Least Once a Week: And Most Say They Use Their Cell Phones to View the X-Rated Footage," *Daily Mail*, October 20, 2015.
34. Jennifer Moorman, "The Hardest of Hardcore: Locating Feminist Possibilities in Women's Extreme Pornography," *Signs: Journal of Women in Culture and Society*, April 1, 2017.
35. Otis R. Taylor, Jr., "Videos Shed Lasting Light on Brutality," *San Francisco Chronicle*, December 30, 2018. https://www.upi.com/.../2007/09/06/Documentary-looks-at-Nazi-porn-in-Israel/50001189125300
36. Betsy Klein, Allie Malloy, and Kate Sullivan, "Trump Mocks the #MeToo Movement," *Again CNN*, October 11, 2018.
37. Tovia Smith, "On #MeToo, Americans More Divided by Party Than Gender," *NPR*, October 31, 2018.
38. Terry Goldsworthy, "Yes Means Yes, Moving to a Different Model of Consent for Sexual Interactions," *The Conversation*, January 29, 2018.

136 Sadomasochism and Revolt

39. Alexandra Rutherford, "What the Origins of the '1 in 5' Statistic Teaches Us about Sexual Assault Policy," *Behavioral Scientist*, September 17, 2018, http://behavioralscientist.org/what-the-origins-of-the-1-in-5-statistic-teaches-us-about-sexual-assault-policy/ accessed December 26, 2018.
40. Brian McNair, "Rethinking the Effects Paradigm in Porn Studies," *Porn Studies*, vol. 1, no. 1, 2014, FF.

Bibliography

Adorno, Theodore, *The Authoritarian Personality*. New York: Harper and Row, 1950.

American Psychiatric Association, *Diagnostic and Statistical Manual of Mental Disorders* (5th ed.). Arlington, VA: American Psychiatric Publishing, 2013, p. 696.

Authoritarian, "Strict Parenting versus Permissive: Which Is Better?" www.raisesmartkid.com/all-ages/1-articles/47-authoritarian-strict-parenting-vs-permissive-which-is-better accessed November 15, 2017.

Berlatsky, Noah, "The Rape-Revenge Genre's Gender Revelations," *The Establishment*, December 29, 2015.

Betsy, Klein, Allie Malloy, and Kate Sullivan, "Trump Mocks the #MeToo Movement," *Again CNN*, October 11, 2018.

Bezreh, Tanya, Thomas S. Weinberg, and Tim Edgar, *American Journal of Sexual Education*, p. 39; and Peggy J. Kleinplatz and Charles Mposer, eds, *Sadomasochism: Powerful Pleasures*. New York: Routledge, 2011.

Chancer, Lynn, *Sadomasochism in Everyday Life: The Dynamics of Power and Powerless*. New Brunswick, NJ: Rutgers University Press, 2006, p. 34.

Dreier, Peter, "The #MeToo Movement's Roots in Women Worker Rights Movements," *Yes! Magazine*, October 8, 2018.

Formica, Michael J., "Sadomasochism in Everyday Relationships," *Psychology Today*, January 13, 2008.

Goldsworthy, Terry, "Yes Means Yes, Moving to a Different Model of Consent for Sexual Interactions," *The Conversation*, January 29, 2018.

Griffith, Jay, "Fire, Hatred, and Speed: The Glamour, Bullying, and Violence of the Libertarian Alt-Right," *Aeon*, February 8, 2017.

Hamilton, Jill, "The 19 Best Porn Sites for Women," *Cosmopolitan*, April 26, 2018.

Harwell, Drew, "Fake Porn Videos Are Being Weaponized to Harass and Humiliate Women," *The Washington Post*, December 30, 2018.

Hickey, Eric W., ed., *Sex Crimes and Paraphilia*. Upper Saddle River, NJ: Pearson Education, 2006, pp. 197–199. ISBN 9780131703506.

Jamieson, Dave, "He Was Masturbating and I Was Crying," *The Huffington Post*, November 20, 2017.

Kaplinsky, Margi, and Shulamet Geller, "The Sadomasochism of Everyday Life," *Psychoanalytic Inquiry*, vol. 35, 2015, pp. 245–256.

Langdridge, D., "Speaking the Unspeakable: S/M and the Eroticisation of Pain," in *Safe, Sane and Consensual: Contemporary Perspectives on Sadomasochism*, edited by D. Langdridge and M. Barker. New York: Palgrave Macmillan, 2007, pp. 91–103.

Linden, Robin Ruth, Darlene R. Pagano, Diana E. H. Russell, and S. L. Star, eds., *Against Sadomasochism: A Radical Feminist Analysis*. San Francisco: Frog in the Well, 1982.

Manson, William, "Authoritarian Sadism Unbound," *Counterpunch*, May 9, 2014.

McGuire, Danielle L., *The Dark at the End of the Street: Black Women, Rape, and Resistance: A New History of the Civil Rights Movement from Rosa Parks to the Rise of Black Power*. New York: Random House, 2011, p. 190.

McNair, Brian, "Rethinking the Effects Paradigm in Porn Studies," *Porn Studies*, vol. 1, no. 1, 2014.

Moorman, Jennifer, "The Hardest of Hardcore: Locating Feminist Possibilities in Women's Extreme Pornography," *Signs: Journal of Women in Culture and Society*, April 1, 2017.

Romanienko, Lisiunia A., *Degradation Rituals: Our Sadomasochistic Society*. New York: Palgrave MacMillan, 2014, p. 141.

Rutherford, Alexandra, "What the Origins of the '1 in 5' Statistic Teaches Us about Sexual Assault Policy," *Behavioral Scientist*, September 17, 2018, http://behavioralscientist.org/what-the-origins-of-the-1-in-5-statistic-teaches-us-about-sexual-assault-policy/ accessed December 26, 2018.

Shirkey, Clay, *Here Comes Everybody: The Power of Organizing without Organizations*. New York: Penguin Books, 2008.

Smith, Tovia, "On #MeToo, Americans More Divided by Party Than Gender," *NPR*, October 31, 2018.

Taylor, Otis R., Jr., "Videos Shed Lasting Light on Brutality," *San Francisco Chronicle*, December 30, 2018.

Tempesta, Erica, "Revealed: One in Three Women Admit They Watch Porn at Least Once a Week: And Most Say They Use Their Cell Phones to View the X-Rated Footage," *Daily Mail*, October 20, 2015.

Vagianos, Alanna, "Tarana Burke Tells Black Women Me Too Is Your Movement Too," *Huffpost*, September 10, 2018.

The Week Staff, "Is It Wrong to Watch War Porn?" *The Week*, May 5, 2010.

Yost, Megan R., "Development and Validation of the Attitudes about Sadomasochist Scale," *Journal of Sex Research*, vol. 47, no. 1, 2010.

INDEX

Note: Page numbers in *italic* indicate a figure on the corresponding page.

9/11 55, 67–68, 70–71, 79, 128

activism 2, 46, 100–101, 116, 126–127, 130–131
Adorno, Theodore 129
Affleck, Ben *see Argo*
aggression vii, 4–5, 8–9, 19–20; and fascism 109; porn consumption and 9; and revolt 124, 127, 129, 131, 133; and torture 61; and war 89
Aja, Alexandre *see Hills Have Eyes, The*
al-Qaeda 67, 71
American Sniper 85, 91–92, 128
Anderson, Paul Thomas *see Boogie Nights*
antifascism 4
anti-Semitism 103, 105–106, 123
Argo 89
authoritarianism 5, 100–102, 107, 117, 123, 128–130, 133
Ayer, David *see Fury*

Baldwin, Alec 115
Barton Fink 58
Basic Instinct 27
BBC 45, 57, 86
BDSMQ vii, 12, 28, 99, 102, 112; authoritarianism and 129; consent and 133; personal sadomasochism and 131; revolt and 125
Behind the Green Door 26
Bergman, Ingmar *see Virgin Spring, The*

Bigelow, Kathryn *see Hurt Locker, The*; *Zero Dark Thirty*
Binet, Alfred 56
black comedy 57–58, 61
Black Lives Matter vii, 28
Black Throat 26–27
bloodletting 59
Bloom, Sandra L. 32–33
Blüher, Hans 102
Boogie Nights 27–28
Brand, Adolf 102
Brennan, Thomas 47–48
brothels 74, 105, 112; *see also* Salon Kitty
Brown, H. Rap 2

Canevari, Cesare *see Last Orgy of the Third Reich*
Cannes Film Festival 26
Cavani, Lilian *see Night Porter, The*
censorship 11–12, 34, 56, 59, 115; origins of 23–27
Clockwork Orange, A 57–58, *58*
clowns 37, 65–66
Coen brothers *see Barton Fink*
combat 3, 79–83, 85–86, 91–92; combat footage 95, 128; live combat 82–83; non-war combat films 93–94; and revenge 47; and torture 67, 73, 75
consent 45–50, 125, 127, 133–134
copyright *see under* laws

Index **139**

Crash 62–64, *63*
Crash Dive 86
Craven, Wes *see Hills Have Eyes, The*; *Last House on the Left, The*
Cronenberg, David *see Crash*

Dark, Gregory *see Black Throat*
Debbie Does Dallas 26
de Lorde, André 56
Denby, David 24, 26
de Sade, the Marquis 5–7, 11, 71, 100, 114
dominant roles vii, 10–11, 28, 51; and fascism 117; and revolt 122–123, 131; and torture 61, 66, 75; and war 85
doms *see* dominant roles
Dr. Strangelove 58
Dwan, Allen *see Sands of Iwo Jima*

Eastwood, Clint *see American Sniper*
Ebert, Roger 27–28, 37, 41, 114; on torture in film 60, 63, 68; on war porn 86–88
Edelstein, David 55, 71
Edmonds, Don *see Ilsa: She Wolf of the SS*
elections: of Barak Obama 116; of Claire McCaskill 49; of Donald Trump vii, 13, 110, 117, 130, 133; of Eric Greitens 48; and the Nazi Party 103–104
extreme porn *see* gonzo porn

fascism 6, 87–88, 99–100, 128–130; fascist porn 100–102; Hollywood Nazis 108–111; and homoeroticism 104–107; and internet porn 117–118; and sadomasochism 107–108; and sexuality 103; and the transgressive movement 115–117; *see also Fräulein Devil*; *Ilse: She Wolf of the SS*; Koch, Ilse; *Last Orgy of the Third Reich*; *Night Porter, The*; *Salon Kitty*; *Salò, or the 120 Days of Sodom*
Fargo 58
feminism 2, 6, 9, 21–23; and revenge 41–42, 48–49, 51; and revolt 124–125, 127; and torture 67
Ferrara, Abel *see MS.45*
Fifty Shades of Grey 28
Fincher, David *see Girl with the Dragon Tattoo, The*
Franco, Francisco 100
Fräulein Devil 113
Fury 89–91, 128

gang rape 36, 42, 125, 132
Gein, Ed 84
Gillis, Jamie *see On the Prowl*

Girl with the Dragon Tattoo, The 126–127, 130
Giroux, Henry A. 3
gonzo porn 21–23, 111, 131–132
Göring, Hermann 103–104, 107
Graydon, Danny 86

Harold and Maude 58
Haspel, Gina 75
healthcare 4
Hedges, Chris 2, 88
Hills Have Eyes, The 60–61, 70–71
Himmler, Heinrich 104–106
Hirschfeld, Magnus 102
Hitchcock, Alfred *see Psycho*
Hitler, Adolf 87, 99–107, 109, 113, 116–118
Hitlerjugend 89–90
Hollywood: censors and 56–57; Hollywood violence 11–12, 74; and rape-revenge 127; and war porn 85–86, 92–95; and Nazis 108–109
Hollywood Reporter, The 92
homoeroticism 101–102, 104–107
Huffington Post, The 20, 80
humour noir 58
Hurt Locker, The 88–89

Ilsa: She Wolf of the SS 109–112
internet porn 1, 13, 18–22; in combat films 94; and Donald Trump 117; and fascism 116, 118; and revenge 45–48; and revolt 127–129, 131; and war 80–82, 94; and torture 55, 72–75
Islamophobia 93
I Spit on Your Grave 36–37, 41–42, 51

James, E.L. *see Fifty Shades of Grey*

Kerner, Michael 71
kidnapping 36, 43, 73, 114
Kill Bill 28, 39–42, *41*, 51, 126, *126*
King, Martin Luther 4
King, Rodney 132
Koch, Ilse 111–112
Koch, Karl 111
Koch brothers 116–117
Koepp, David *see Stir of Echoes*
Kubrick, Stanley *see Clockwork Orange, A*; *Dr. Strangelove*

Last House on the Left, The 35–36, 51
Last Orgy of the Third Reich 112–113
Lawrence, D.H. 11
Lawrence, Jennifer 46

140 Index

laws 11, 23, 45, 104; anti-revenge porn 46–48; copyright 48–49; *see also* censorship
Levin, Simone Lieban 9
live-streaming 72–74
London Has Fallen 92–93

Mandl, Maria 112
Marchès, Léo 56
March for Our Lives vii
Martin, Mike 41
Martinez, Nathan 62
Maurey, Max 56
#MeToo movement vii, 13, 28, 125, 127, 130–133; and revenge 49, 51
Miller Test 11
misogyny 41–42, 46, 123, 130
Mitchell brothers 26
Morel, Pierre *see Taken*
Motion Picture Producers and Distributors of America (MPPDA) 56
MS. 45 37–38
Mussolini, Benito 99–100, 113–114, 117–118

Najafi, Babak *see London Has Fallen*
Natural Born Killers 61–62
Nazi Party 101–106
Night Porter, The 113–114
non-suicidal self-injury (NSSI) 62

Obama, Barack 13, 68, 116
On the Prowl 21
Ovid 11

Pasolini, Pier Paolo *see Salò, or the 120 Days of Sodom*
patriarchy 9, 39, 101, 124–125, 132
pop culture vii–viii, 2–4, 7–8, 11–13, 21, 28; and fascism 101, 108–109, 111, 116, 118; and revolt 122, 126, 128, 131; and torture 55, 58, 62, 64, 68, 71, 74; and violence 8; and war 79–81, 85, 95
pornography: defined 18–19; fascist porn 100–102, 110, 114, 116–118; racist porn 9–11; revenge porn 8, 41–42, 45–51, 74, 93, 127–128; soft porn 18, 23, 27–28, 59; torture porn 8, 42, 55, 61, 68–75; and violence 20–21; war porn 8, 71, 79–82, 85–95, 128; *see also* censorship; gonzo porn; porn stars; women's porn
porn stars 9, 19–20, 23

Porter, Marsha 41
Psycho 25–26, *25*, 57–59, 84, *84*
Pulp Fiction 58

racism 4, 13, 22, 93; and fascism 106–107, 109, 115–116; racist porn 9–11; and revolt 123, 129–130
Rambo 87, 128
rape-revenge 2, 8, 34–35, 37–39, 41–42, 51; movies 126–127, 130; on television 44–45
reality 12, 19, 22, 42, 71, 80, 82; reality porn 19; and technology 95
revenge *see* rape-revenge; revenge porn
revenge porn 8, 41–42, 45–51, 74, 93, 127–128
revolt vii, 110, 122–125; and authoritarianism 128–130; and consent 133–134; and the #MeToo movement 130–131; and rape-revenge movies 126–127; and revenge porn 127–128; and sadomasochism 131–133; submissive 125–126; and technology 127; and war porn 128; and women's porn 131–132
Röhm, Ernst 104
role reversal 123, 131
Romanienko, Lisiunia A. 123–124

Sacher-Masoch, Leopold von 7–8
sadomasochism viii, 1, 4–9, 11, 13, 20–22, 27; and activism 131; and authoritarianism 128–130; and clowns 65–66; and consent 133–134; and fascism 101, 107–109, 114, 117–118, 128–130; and the #MeToo movement 130–131; and revenge 41, 43, 126–128; and revolt 122–126, 132–133; and technology 127; and torture 61, 71, 74–75; and war 81–82, 128; and women's porn 131–132; *see also* BDSMQ
Salò, or the 120 Days of Sodom 6–7, 114–115
Salon Kitty (brothel) 113
Salon Kitty (film) 113
Sands of Iwo Jima 85–86
Schmidt, Kitty *see* Zammit, Katharina
Scorsese, Martin *see Taxi*
Scott, A.O. 86
Scott, Ridley *see Thelma and Louise*
self-torture 62–64
sexting 50
Shakespeare, William 11
smart phones 13, 19, 22, 50, 127

Index   141

Snow, Aurora 9–10
snuff 66–67, 72, 74–75, 81
Snyder, Zack *see 300*
Sontag, Susan 101
Stalag 100, 108–113
Stallone, Sylvester *see Rambo*
Stir of Echoes 39
Stone, Oliver *see Natural Born Killers*
submissive roles vii, 7, 11–12, 19, 21; and
    fascism 112, 117; and revenge 51; and
    revolt 122–123, 125–126, 129, 131,
    133–134; and torture 61, 66, 74
subs *see* submissive roles
superheroes 41, 51, 64, 94
supervillains 64, 79, 94

Taken 42–44
Tarantino, Quentin *see Kill Bill; Pulp
    Fiction*
Taxi 61
technology 20, 22, 28, 117; reality and 95;
    and revolt 122, 127–128, 130
television 12, 19; and fascism 108, 117;
    rape-revenge on 44–45; and revolt 127,
    130; and torture 55, 62; and war 95
terror 3, 15; and torture 56, 60, 62; violence
    as 12; and war 85, 93; *see also* 9/11
Thelma and Louise 38–39
Third Reich 101, 103–104, 107; *see also
    Last Orgy of the Third Reich*; Nazi Party
    300 87–88
#Time's Up movement 13, 28
torture 7, 13, 55–61; and fascism 105,
    107–114, 117; movie-inspired
    torture 61–62; and 9/11 67–68; and
    revenge 41–43; and revolt 132; and
    sadomasochistic clowns 65–66; self-
    torture 62–64; snuff 66–67; torture porn
    8, 42, 55, 61, 68–75; and war 79, 93
transgressive movement 115–117

Trump, Donald vii, 13, 19; and fascism
    100, 117; and revolt 130, 132–133; and
    torture 68, 73, 75; and war 93

Ulrich, Karl Heinrich 102

Van Buren, Peter 85–86, 89, 92
Verhoeven, Paul *see Basic Instinct*
video games 55, 71, 79–80, 83–85, 89, 95
violence vii, 18–19, 22, 26–28; and
    censorship 11; culture of 2–5; and
    fascism 100–102, 109–110, 113,
    115–118; and Hollywood 11–12; and
    patriarchy 9; and pop culture 8; porn
    and 20–21; and porn consumption
    9; and racist porn 9–11; and revenge
    33–34, 36, 42, 44, 49–51; and revolt
    125–130, 132–134; and sadomasochism
    5–8; sex and 1–2; as terror 12; and
    torture 55–59, 61, 66–68, 71, 73–74; and
    the 2016 election 13; and war 79–81,
    83–87, 92–95
Virgin Spring, The 34–36, *35*

Wallace, Randall *see We Were Soldiers*
war 3–4, 75, 79–81; and live combat
    82–83; and video games 83–85; war
    porn 8, 71, 79–82, 85–95, 128; *see also*
    fascism
War Horse, The 47–48
waterboarding 13, 67–68, 72
Weimar Republic 102–103
We Were Soldiers 86–87, 128
women's porn 131–132

Yiannopoulos, Milo 102

Zammit, Katharina 113
Zarchi, Meir *see I Spit on Your Grave*
Zero Dark Thirty 71–72